Return to Nature?

Return to Nature?

An Ecological Counterhistory

Fred Dallmayr

UNIVERSITY PRESS OF KENTUCKY

Scholarly publisher for the Commonwealth,
serving Bellarmine University, Berea College, Centre College of Kentucky, Eastern
Kentucky University, The Filson Historical Society, Georgetown College,
Kentucky Historical Society, Kentucky State University, Morehead State University,
Murray State University, Northern Kentucky University, Transylvania University,
University of Kentucky, University of Louisville, and Western Kentucky University.
All rights reserved.

Editorial and Sales Offices: The University Press of Kentucky
663 South Limestone Street, Lexington, Kentucky 40508-4008
www.kentuckypress.com

The Library of Congress has cataloged the hardcover edition as follows:

Dallmayr, Fred R. (Fred Reinhard), 1928-
  Return to nature? : an ecological counterhistory / Fred Dallmayr.
    p. cm.
  Includes bibliographical references (p.   ) and index.
  ISBN 978-0-8131-3433-8 (hardcover : alk. paper)
  ISBN 978-0-8131-3434-5 (ebook) 1. Philosophy of nature. I. Title.
  BD581.D243 2011
  113—dc23   2011021824

ISBN 978-0-8131-6634-6 (pbk. : alk. paper)

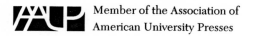

In memory of Thomas Berry (1914–2009),
ecological thinker and activist

and

Raimon Panikkar (1918–2010),
sage, ecosophist, and mentor

May their work serve as a beacon of light
for ecologically endangered and spiritually starved humanity

There is no such thing as a "human community" without the earth and the soil and the air and the water and all the living forms. . . . The large community is the sacred community.

—Thomas Berry

Whatever prompts people to live in harmony with each other and with nature is good, whereas whatever brings discord is bad.

—Spinoza

The foundation for purpose and the striving to realize it is found in nature.

—Dewey

This flesh of my body is shared by the world . . .
. . . they are in a relation of transgression or overlapping.

—Merleau-Ponty

It is true that we are consanguineous with nature. But as humans, we must make ourselves worthy of such a relationship.

—Tu Weiming

Contents

Preface

In December 2009 a large international conference on climate change was held in Copenhagen, Denmark. Among many people around the world, plans for that conference triggered strong hopes, especially the expectation that the lopsided and exploitative relation between humanity and nature would be corrected or at least ameliorated. As we know in retrospect, these hopes were not fulfilled—although the demand for corrective measures is steadily gaining in urgency. As a prelude to the Copenhagen conference, another smaller meeting was held in Aarhus, Denmark, dealing with the issues of climate change, ecology, and human culture. As a forum designed not to produce policy proposals but to stimulate intellectual discussion, the Aarhus meeting catered to academics from a great variety of disciplines—among whom I was fortunate to be included. Participation in that meeting prompted me to focus in a sustained way on the humanity-nature issue—something I had not done before despite the fact that the issue had always been a strong undercurrent in all my writings.

As it seems to me, nature in modern times has tended to be marginalized, colonized, and abused. In the dominant strand of modern Western thought, nature survived only as an exile or resident alien. This is in stark contrast to the situation in premodern and classical times when "nature" often served as a synonym for the comprehensive matrix encompassing all beings. In the course of modernization, this original unity was progressively differentiated and parceled out into separate domains or compartments, into the *disjecta membra,* or dispersed fragments of wholeness. What is becoming increasingly evident in our time is that this dispersal also involves the steady fragmentation and dismemberment of human life. Hence, the widely felt need for a change of course—a change that can be captured in such mottos as "back to nature" or "letting nature back in" (from its exile). To be sure, such mottos cannot or should not be misconstrued as counseling a lapse into crude "naturalism" neglectful of ethical and spiritual aspirations. Still more important, watchwords of this kind cannot sanction a nostalgic "return" or retreat: a retreat into a holistic "primordialism" antithetical to legitimate differentiation and to the demands of individual freedom. As it seems to me, modernization is the unfolding of potentials for good and ill; but the "ill" cannot be cured by a simple cancellation of evolving potentialities.

The present book stands in a sequence of recent writings in which I have tried to articulate a perspective of "relationism," or differentiated holism from various angles. In my books *In Search of the Good Life* (2007) and *The Promise of Democracy* (2010), the interhuman and intersocietal relation was in the foreground. In the text *Integral Pluralism* (2010), the intercultural relation was expanded to embrace also the human-divine or secular-spiritual connection. The book presented here rounds out the nexus of relationships by exploring the issue of how to bring nature back into modern and contemporary awareness, not just as a topic of esoteric philosophical discussion, but as a leaven of human reorientation and renewal—intimating a forgotten "pathway to Eden."

As always, I am greatly indebted to many friends and colleagues. The book is dedicated to the memory of two intellectual guides and mentors: Thomas Berry, who, ahead of almost everybody else, issued the clarion call for "metanoia" and a "return to nature," and Raimon Panikkar, whose work stressed the triune "cosmotheandric" relation and whose idea of "ecosophy"—combining ecopiety and ecophilosophy—was a steady inspiration as I was writing this book. Among other like-minded colleagues and friends I should single out Hwa Yol Jung, Calvin Schrag, William Connolly, and Tu Weiming. As I should also mention, my relation to nature has been cultivated and deepened over the years by the group of cats sharing our house. They have been steady companions of my family, especially my wife, Ilse—without whom nothing would ever have been written.

South Bend, Indiana
September 2010

Introduction

Letting Nature Back In

One of the urgent issues in our time—perhaps the most urgent—is human survival in the world, in the midst of a nature whose resources are relentlessly exploited and perhaps eventually depleted. During the last hundred years, the issue has been steadily gaining momentum, largely due to the processes of globalization and global industrialization and the incredible advances in technology and engineering. However, the roots of the problem reach much further back, at least as far back as the onset of Western modernity and its attendant separation of "man" and nature. This separation was introduced and thematized by numerous philosopher-scientists, like Galileo and Francis Bacon, but it was articulated most powerfully and cogently in the philosophy of René Descartes (1596–1650), with its stark dualism or opposition between human thought or reason, on the one hand, and external matter or nature, on the other. For Descartes, it was necessary to distinguish sharply between two "substances"—the *res cogitans* (thinking substance) and the *res extensa* (extended matter)—with a tenuous bridge only provided by divine providence. This division gave rise to a reciprocal expulsion or alienation: mind or reason was purged of any "naturalistic" premises, while nature itself was demoted from a partner or ally to a detached target of analysis and manipulation. From this time forward, nature was increasingly treated as a mere resource, utensil, or instrument for human and social benefit. In due course this alienation was extended to fellow human beings, who came to be seen as strangers, competitors, and even enemies. In a completely upside-down and misleading manner, this general condition of hostility was described (following Thomas Hobbes) as the "state of nature."[1]

1

More recently, the long-standing attack on nature and its effects has triggered a widespread sense of crisis. As it is rightly felt, if continuing unabated, this attack is threatening to destroy not only an external environment but the human habitat, that is, the very condition of human life on earth. As a result, an insurgency or countermovement has emerged in many parts of the world dedicated to reestablishing a proper balance or (what one may call) a symbiosis between humankind and nature. The first requisite of this "ecological" effort is that the rigid divide between "man" and nature be cancelled in favor of wholeness or a more holistic relationship; differently phrased: the wall of separation has to be breached so that humanity can again enjoy the company of nature, and nature the company of humans. The movement in this direction is nurtured by many different resources and traditions. Some of these resources are religious or spiritual in character; others are literary or poetic.[2] All such resources are no doubt helpful and important. However, given that the "man-nature" split was first articulated at the onset of modernity, and especially in the philosophy of Descartes, it seems appropriate also to invoke possible philosophical remedies. After all, a dilemma articulated so forcefully by modern philosophy can hope to find a resolution or settlement only through additional philosophical argument. This, in any case, is the trajectory pursued in the present pages. Traditionally, philosophical inquiry dealing with the natural realm was called "philosophy of nature." More recently, partly in response to the present ecological crisis, the endeavor has come to be termed "ecophilosophy." In this sense, the present pages are meant as contributions to ecophilosophy.

As it happens, philosophical resources wrestling with the dilemma are by no means lacking, even and especially in the context of modern Western philosophy. Although overshadowed and even marginalized by the dominant Cartesian (or rationalist-scientific) perspective, modern Western thought is inhabited by a remarkably rich and fertile undercurrent or countercurrent. Gilles Deleuze, in one of his writings, refers to a "counter-history" of Western philosophy (which prominently includes Spinoza, among many others). While seeming to be part of the history of philosophy, he writes, this counterhistory appears to escape it or has another story to tell.[3] To be aware of this countercurrent—and probably several such countercurrents—means to be aware that modern Western philosophy is by no means a compact, homogeneous doctrine, but an intellectual inquiry inhabited by consensus and dissensus, by agreement and difference, by multiple trajectories—not all of which are equally recognized in standard philosophy textbooks. Today, under the impact of contemporary experiences, some of the less valued or more marginalized philosophical initiatives need to be retrieved, foregrounded, and freshly interpreted. What emerges from this retrieval is the (perhaps surprising) fact that modern Western philosophy provides powerful resources precisely in the domain of natural philosophy, or "ecophilosophy." Without being able exhaustively to deal with all the facets of the countercurrent, the objective of the present study is to lift up at least some of its most prominent strands for renewed appreciation.

The first prominent figure considered is Benedict (or Baruch) Spinoza, who occupies the ambivalent position of being both a Cartesian and an anti-Cartesian and thus hovers on the cusp between the dominant rationalist current and its countercurrent. To some extent, Spinoza in our time experiences a kind of revival or even "revivalism"—but a revival sometimes nurtured by very conflicting, or else confused, impulses. Thus, he is often presented as a radical antirationalist, a naive Romanticist, and even a Darwinian "naturalist."[4] As it seems to me, no recovery is possible without a recognition of the Cartesian strand, in all its ambivalence. In this respect I follow Genevieve Lloyd when she writes that Spinoza's thought "belongs, on the one hand, firmly with the rationalist tradition—with the philosophies of Descartes and Leibniz. . . . Yet his thought also has clear affinities with later attitudes associated with Romanticism." The difference between modern Cartesianism and Spinoza revolves mainly around the issue of holism versus dualism, of wholeness versus fragmentation. In Lloyd's words (with which I again agree): "As a self-contained entity, the Cartesian mind forms part of a whole with neither God nor world." By contrast: "The individuality of the Cartesian self gives way in Spinoza's philosophy to a way of thinking of the self as part of an interconnected totality—as itself, in a new way, part of nature." Differently phrased: while "Cartesian selves are ambiguously located between the separate individuality of their substance (*res cogitans*) and the universality of reason," Spinoza's selves "rejoin nature through the individuality of bodies construed as uniquely differentiated parts of nature."[5] To be sure, the different facets of Spinoza's thought did not immediately concur, but needed time to develop and coalesce. In the present study, the chapter devoted to Spinoza traces this development from some early texts, written in the vicinity of a Mennonite group, to his later and probably most mature work: his *Ethics*.

The discussion of Spinoza is followed in the same chapter by some comments on two thinkers who were both deeply influenced by him and appreciated much of his work: Leibniz and Hegel. As a rationalist and mathematician, Leibniz shared Spinoza's ambivalence regarding the Cartesian system. What attracted him chiefly to Spinoza was the celebration of holism, of the vision of a unified cosmos maintaining the partnership among God, nature, and humanity. Where he departed from this vision was regarding the tendential overemphasis on unity vis-à-vis differentiated particularities—a departure that led to the formulation of a complex fabric of individual entities called "monads," all correlated or coordinated in a "preestablished" (not externally imposed) harmony or symbiosis. In even stronger (perhaps exaggerated) terms, an objection to Spinoza's holism was voiced by Hegel in his *Lectures on the History of Philosophy*. In opposition to all those accusing Spinoza of atheism, Hegel saw in the latter's thought "too much God"—in the sense of a relative deemphasis on distinct individuality. In Lloyd's words, for Hegel, "Spinoza was not up to the challenge of apprehending oneness without letting difference slip; and the result is that his substance is a static and undifferentiated reality." Concurring at least in part, Lloyd adds that "individuality does indeed have a paradoxical character in Spinoza's philosophy" and notes that "Hegel's reading of him—as the philosopher of the abyss [of oneness]—is not fanciful." However, Hegel may have overcompensated for this supposed defect by stressing individual selfhood to the point that the broader God-nature nexus slipped away.[6]

This latter suspected slippage was at the heart of the protest launched by one of Hegel's friends from his student days: Friedrich Schelling. As it happens, as in the case of Spinoza, contemporary philosophy witnesses a kind of Schelling revival—mainly as an antidote to the one-sided rationalism and anthropocentrism frequently attributed to both Descartes and Kant.[7] A main focus of the ongoing revival is on Schelling's "philosophy of nature," a perspective he developed between 1796 and 1802. Through intense critical engagement with fellow idealist philosophers (especially Kant and Fichte), Schelling in successive initiatives articulated a metaphysical vision that, in many ways, recuperated Spinoza's holism, but now on the level of an idealist "identity" of nature and spirit. The chapter on Schelling traces the development of his thought through its successive stages, starting from his *Ideas for a Philosophy of Nature* (of 1797). In this text, Spinoza's holistic vision was reformulated as the ultimate concurrence of subject and object, finitude and infinity, on the level of "spirit." As he explained at the time, spirit necessarily objectifies itself in the world of nature and thereby acquires a dimension of finitude. At the same time, however, spirit retains its infinitely generative and regenerative élan, thus paving the way to the holistic reconciliation of inner and outer, of mind and matter. Going beyond Spinoza (but partly in accord with Leibniz), Schelling saw this reconciliation also as a merger of the universal and particular, of the absolute and contingent. Some of the arguments tentatively sketched in *Ideas* were fleshed out in greater detail in *First Outline for a System of the Philosophy of Nature* (1799), where Schelling presented his outlook as a "speculative physics" designed to overcome Cartesian dualisms and to "grasp the absolute unity in the infinite diversity of action." This text, in turn, was only a prelude to the *System of Transcendental Idealism* (1800), which postulated a merger of reflective and "naturalistic" perspectives and even a "parallelism" of intellect and nature achieved with the aid of "intellectual intuition."

As one should note, Schelling was not only an idealist philosopher, but also a strong devotee of poetry and the arts—a quality that made him a mentor and partial participant in the emerging "Romantic movement" of the time. Contrary to a widespread misconception, that movement was not only literary and emotive in character, but maintained a strong connection with German idealist philosophy. At least during the early phase of the movement, many prominent Romantics wrote philosophical treatises—often inspired by Schelling—as well as novels and lyrical poetry. It was only during the later stages that the symbiosis between philosophical idealism and Romantic sentiment became strained; at that point, the initial union of spirit and nature, of intellect and world, tended progressively to give way to private subjectivism and inward retreat (from the world). The chapter on Romanticism concentrates on those phases when sentiment still paid tribute to idealist thought and also to the linkage of art and nature. The first section focuses on the early German Romantic movement, turning attention especially to the writings of Friedrich Schlegel, Novalis, and Hölderlin—showing that, at least in Schlegel's case, Schelling's "identity" system was transformed into a philosophy of yearning and infinite approximation. A similar outlook is found in early English Romanticism as represented by the works of Wordsworth and Coleridge—both strongly influenced by idealist philosophy. While Wordsworth (in his famous "Preface" to *Lyrical Ballads*) placed the emphasis on unspoiled natural sentiments, Coleridge (in his *Biographia Literaria*) gave to these sentiments a more transformative or "transcendental" cast. The concluding part of the chapter deals with "New England Transcendentalism," whose very name testifies to the legacy of spiritual-idealist (and perhaps Neoplatonic) teachings in America. The discussion here examines Emerson's famous essay "Nature" (1836)—with its vision of cosmic unity and its celebration of a (Schelling-style) parallelism of spirit and nature—and concludes with a review of Thoreau's *Walden* (1858) and its dominant accent on solitary life.

Thoreau's stress on individual solitude was still tamed and mitigated by his holistic conception of nature (and also by his intermittent engagement in social reform). In the later part of the nineteenth century, however, this balanced conception was increasingly challenged and eroded by the advances of the Industrial Revolution and the "rugged individualism" of the emerging capitalist market. As a result of these and related developments, dissatisfaction with Romantic retreat grew among many intellectuals who insisted on a more determined "holism" and especially on the need to reconnect mind with world and nature and hence to supplement individual self-cultivation with "progressive" social reform. There was another strand in this dissatisfaction, namely, the realization of a persistent dualism not properly attacked in the past: the dualism between a static infinity (or transcendence) and the random flux of phenomena. To overcome this polarity, it was necessary to reconceive nature and the world of phenomena as a temporal "process," as the ongoing unfolding of potentialities. Both the emphasis on "process" and the concern with social reform were the hallmarks of American pragmatism as represented by the work of Charles Sanders Peirce, William James, and John Dewey. Mainly because of his extensive comments on nature and society, the chapter on pragmatism focuses on Dewey's evolving thought. It is precisely in Dewey's case that the linkage with German idealism can still be clearly detected—not with Kant or Fichte, but with Hegel. The first section of the chapter deals with the development of Dewey's philosophical position, tracing his movement from an initial Hegelianism to a postidealist pragmatism. In part, this movement was due to his encounter with Charles Darwin—which is the topic of the following section. The chapter is rounded out by a detailed review of Dewey's famous "Paul Carus Lectures" (of 1925), published under the title *Experience and Nature.*

At the time when pragmatism was beginning to recede in America—due to a number of factors (including the return of "pure" theory in the form of conceptual analysis)—an intellectual current arose in Europe that in many ways resembled its American precursor: the current of phenomenology and existentialism. What primarily linked pragmatism with its European counterpart was the disillusionment with traditional philosophical systems and abstract theorizing coupled with a turn to human practice or (what Dewey called) lived "experience." Initially, it is true, the traditional privilege granted to "theory" (in the sense of a detached overview) persisted in the accent of early phenomenology on the inspection of phenomena from the vantage of pure consciousness. Once the accent shifted, however, from aloof inspection to a closer engagement with the world—giving rise to "existential" phenomenology—the parallel with the American precursor came more clearly into view. Nowhere are this shift and this affinity more evident than in the work of Maurice Merleau-Ponty, who collaborated with Jean-Paul Sartre in the French resistance movement. The chapter on Merleau-Ponty follows the development of his thought through three main stages of philosophical articulation. In the first phase—represented by *The Structure of Behavior* (1942) and *The Phenomenology of Perception* (1945)—the philosopher sought to chart his way from transcendental reflection to a more dynamic phenomenology of the "life-world"; in the course of this journey, he discovered the uncanny status of "nature": its refusal to be captured both as a product of mind and as an external physical occurrence. The second phase—marked by a number of prominent essay collections—continues this journey with a steadily deepening insight into the complexity of the lived world. It is in the last phase of his short life that Merleau-Ponty's thought reaches its full maturity: especially in a series of lecture courses on "Nature" offered at the Collège de France and in the posthumously published *The Visible and the Invisible,* with its provocative notions of a "flesh of the world" and a generalized "aesthesiology."

Next to Merleau-Ponty's oeuvre, the depth and fertility of existential phenomenology and ontology are revealed in the work of his great German contemporary: Martin Heidegger. Like the French thinker, Heidegger also made the journey from transcendental reflection—represented by Edmund Husserl's phenomenological idealism—toward a stronger engagement with existential situatedness, an engagement that is at the heart of his definition of human existence (*Dasein*) as "being-in-the-world." Still, despite this explicit focus on worldliness, Heidegger's approach to the topic of "nature" was more halting than that of his French colleague. Especially during the early period of his intellectual development—the phase culminating in *Being and Time* (1927)—nature tended to be seen as a set of phenomena directly available to human experience, as targets either of theoretical cognition (*Vorhandenheit*) or pragmatic utility ("equipment," *Zuhandenheit*). What was not, or only dimly, perceived at the time was how nature could itself be a constitutive premise of human experience. A major breakthrough in this respect occurred about a decade later, first in Heidegger's lectures on Schelling and then in his detailed analysis of Aristotle's concept of "nature" (*physis*). World War II and its dislocations delayed the further development of these insights. It is only in some of his later writings that the status of nature can be more clearly glimpsed; this is true especially of his recuperation of pre-Socratic teachings (with their vision of a primordial holism) and his exegesis of Hölderlin's poetry. The chapter on Heidegger traces this progressive maturation in three steps: first, by examining salient passages in *Being and Time;* next, by turning to the writings on Schelling and Aristotle; and finally, by pondering later texts on Parmenides and on the status and meaning of poetry (seen as a gateway to a more primordial thinking, or *Andenken*).

All the thinkers discussed above—together with a number of others not mentioned (like Giambattista Vico, Herder, and Nietzsche)—form part of what Deleuze has called the "counter-history" or countercurrent of modern Western philosophy. What they all share in com-

mon is the striving to overcome traditional dualisms or bifurcations
in favor of a renewal of wholeness or connectedness (not neglectful
of relevant differences). There is another, still more far-reaching dimension of this antidualist striving: namely, the endeavor to bridge
the ancient divide between (what is loosely called) the "East" and
the "West." As it happens, several members of the Western countercurrent were more or less keenly aware of the affinity of their endeavor with teachings commonly associated with Asian philosophical
and religious traditions. The concluding chapter dealing with Asian
thought highlights the holistic strand in these traditions, a strand not
only eluding the mind-matter (or subject-object) bifurcation but also
transgressing the theory-praxis hiatus in favor of an accent on ethical
life conduct in accordance with the "way" (dharma or *tao*). In the case
of classical Indian thought, the emphasis on wholeness is manifest
in the Uphanishadic celebration of *brahman* as the unifying force of
life—a celebration finding mature expression in the postclassical philosophy of "nondualism" (Advaita Vedanta) yoking together human
life, the natural cosmos, and the divine. In the Buddhist tradition, a
similar outlook (despite subtle modifications) is manifest in the non-
dualist conception of being and nonbeing (*sunyata*), in the stress on
universal interconnectedness (*pratitya samutpada*), and in the accent
on liberating practice along the "noble eightfold path." In traditional
Chinese thought, ethical life conduct is seen as embedded in a complex web of relationships, a web that ultimately links all things and
beings under the aegis of a holistic *tao* expressed in the formula "all-
under-heaven" (*tien-shia*).[8]

The appendices seek to round out the book's overall argument
by adding some supplementary features and considerations relevant
to its theme. The first pays tribute to one of the leading pioneers of
the contemporary ecological movement, Thomas Berry, who passed
away in 2009 at the age of ninety-four. As the essay tries to show,
Berry in an admirable fashion combined a deeply spiritual "ecopiety"—celebrating nature as a "sacred liturgy"—with an astute and
clear-minded "ecophilosophy" (inspired in part by Teilhard de Chardin). The second offers reflections on humanism or "human nature"
presented from the angle of what has come to be known as "philosophical anthropology." Akin in many ways to the goal of ecophilosophy, philosophical anthropology seeks to transgress the mind-matter

or spirit-nature hiatus by situating the locus of human beings in a complex and holistic network of relationships, a network described by Raimon Panikkar as the "cosmotheandric" nexus. The essay first discusses some of the leading proponents of philosophical anthropology in the twentieth century, highlighting especially the work of Max Scheler and Helmuth Plessner. In the next step, attention is shifted to certain "antihumanist" tendencies during the later part of the century, tendencies associated with facets of "postmodernism." The concluding section turns to the still more recent resurgence of philosophical anthropology, a resurgence paving the way to a "chastened humanism" on the far side of both anthropocentrism and antihumanism. In a way, this return links up with Heidegger's postulate of an "other" humanism, as well as with recent developments in biology and neuroscience.[9]

1

Nature and Divine Substance
Spinoza

Among modern philosophers, no one has honored nature more than Baruch (or Benedict) Spinoza by linking and even fusing nature with the divine. To be sure, his famous formula "deus sive natura" (God or else nature) can easily be misunderstood. The formula does not propose a crude "naturalism," which would reduce nature to physical processes analyzed by science; rather, the opposite is the case: physical processes are integrated as mere emblems into an all-embracing divine order. To this extent, the formula is indicative of Spinoza's position as a whole: his location at the cusp between traditional speculative metaphysics and modern natural science wedded to rational analysis. From traditional ontology he inherited the conception of a unified cosmos and also some key categories like "substance" and "attributes." At the same time, he realized that the traditional worldview—having shrunk into rigid, barely intelligible dogma—could no longer be maintained in the old way; hence, new inquiries and new formulations were needed to make sense of the world. In venturing into these new inquiries, Spinoza followed Descartes and a host of modern rationalists and natural scientists; yet he also departed from or went beyond Descartes by seeking to remedy the fissures or splits to which modern reason gives rise: the splits between thought and action, between self and other, between reason and faith, and between God and nature. This striving renders baffling his thought today, like that of many of his contemporaries. In the words of Merleau-Ponty: the "rationalism" of that period "seems full of myths to us: the myth of *laws of nature* vaguely situated between norms and facts . . . and the myth of *scientific explanation,* as if [it] could one day transform the very existence of the world into an analytic and self-evident proposition."[1]

Spinoza's life was brief (1632–1677), but surrounded by a host of dramatic events and developments—in the midst of which he was able to maintain an extraordinary calmness and serenity. In the account of Lewis Feuer, Spinoza's thought was forged or honed in a time of crisis, war, and revolution: it was the time of "Cromwell, the Thirty Years' War, the Levellers, the Quakers, the Catholic Inquisition in Spain"; but it was also the time of a budding liberalism and civic republicanism that flourished especially in his native Holland. As a young man, Spinoza was deeply attracted to the new republican and revolutionary ideas, which provided an antidote to prevailing forms of domination based on wealth, power, or religious privilege. In a way, the ideas promised a return to social and even cosmic unity or solidarity—a return no longer premised on a hierarchical "chain of being," but rather on civic equality, toleration, and public engagement. As Feuer points out, in addition to religious motivations, these sympathies were fostered by several factors. First, one of Spinoza's favorite teachers was Francis van den Ende, who, apart from teaching him Latin, also imbued him with radical political sentiments (which later brought that teacher to grief). Another factor was his close association with Mennonites and Quakers, especially with a group of Collegiant-Mennonites located in Rijnsburg near Leiden. Finally, there was his attachment to the liberal republican movement led by John de Witt, who was a critic of both royalists and the ruling Calvinist party with its theocratic pretensions. Feuer divides Spinoza's intellectual development into three stages: leading from a religious and social utopianism to a mature republicanism and finally to a resigned realism (after the killing of de Witt in 1672).[2] Given the different focus of the present pages—on nature rather than politics per se—I shall proceed somewhat differently, examining first some writings penned in a Mennonite context and then one of his major texts, the *Ethics,* completed in The Hague around 1675.

The Improvement of Understanding

Following his expulsion from the Jewish community in Amsterdam in 1656, Spinoza moved to Rijnsburg near Leiden, where he lived in the vicinity of a pious Mennonite community. By all accounts, that Mennonite group was quite unusual: religiously traditional, while intellectually very progressive. In Feuer's terms, they were wont to employ "Cartesian language" in order to convey their aspiration of a "mystical union with God." They were also socially "communal," or cooperative, and opposed to the aggressive competitiveness of the emerging market economy.[3] In these quiet and peaceful surroundings, Spinoza was able to recover from the Amsterdam drama, to collect his thoughts, and to embark on his chosen path of philosophical reflection. His first objective was to find a reliable and suitable pathway for his thinking, removed from the rampant prejudices and heated ideological posturings of his time. In 1637, René Descartes had published his famous *Discourse on Method*, which was intensely studied by Spinoza and his friends. (The latter may also have been familiar with Descartes's *Rules for the Direction of the Mind*, written around 1628 but not published, and perhaps also with his *Meditations on First Philosophy* of 1641). Thus, after having settled into his new environment, Spinoza around 1662 decided to write down his own methodical "rules" under the title *Treatise on the Improvement of the Understanding* (*Tractatus de Intellectus Emendatione*).

The treatise was clearly Cartesian in inspiration, especially in its search for mental or intellectual clarity; however, from the outset there was also a departure from the Cartesian model. Together with Descartes, the treatise sought to delineate a firm pathway toward philosophical truth; yet this pathway was from the beginning embedded in a more encompassing agenda: the search for the "good life," or the proper ethical way to conduct one's life. In this manner, the quest for truth was intimately linked with the quest for goodness, or theory with practice—thereby revealing Spinoza as a "pragmatist" avant la lettre. The opening paragraphs of the treatise disclose an intense yearning for genuine goodness and a deep discomfort or chagrin over the many false idols misleading human lives. Spinoza declared that after having suffered many troubling ordeals, "I at last resolved to inquire whether there exists and can be found some true good by which alone, to the exclusion of all the rest, the self would be guided and through which, once I had found and understood it, I could enjoy forever continuous and supreme happiness." As one can see, the author speaking here is not so much a Cartesian as an Aristotelian, and the supreme goal aspired to is the classical idea of happiness, *eudaimonia,* or blessedness. The chief false goods or idols misleading human conduct, in Spinoza's text, are economic wealth, public fame or power, and sensual pleasure. "As the actions of men testify," he writes, "wealth, fame, and pleasure are usually regarded as the highest goods. By these three, the mind is so much distracted that it can hardly think of any other good"—or even think at all. Since these goods were the idols almost universally worshipped in his native Holland, Spinoza was faced with a stark alternative: "I realized that if supreme happiness lay in fame and wealth [and pleasure], I was bound to miss it by turning elsewhere. But I also knew that I would equally miss it if I pursued fame and wealth, while supreme happiness did not lie in them."[4]

Spinoza's text is at pains to explicate the defects or disadvantages associated with the mentioned idols. Regarding sensual pleasure, its enjoyment can be so intense or overwhelming—he observes—that it obstructs all other activities and especially intellectual inquiries. Moreover, its satisfaction is often and even habitually followed by "extreme melancholy"—which tends to "distract and dull" the mind. On the other hand, pursuit of wealth or public glory has a built-in momentum that can never be really satisfied. Basically, their pursuit is not usually followed by "remorse," as in the case of sensual desire. Rather, "the more we possess of fame and wealth, the greater . . . is our desire to increase them"; but frustration of that desire, which is likely to happen, "plunges us into despair." The upshot for Spinoza is that, in the case of the cited idols, satisfaction of enjoyment depends entirely on finite things or phenomena, which are perishable, rather than being nurtured or oriented to the infinite source or wellspring of all things and phenomena. This source is infinite being itself, which is also the ground of finite beings. In Spinoza's words: "It is the love of perishable things which causes the misfortunes previously mentioned. But love of an eternal and infinite thing nourishes the mind with pure happiness and is free from sorrow; hence, it is most desirable and to be sought with all our strength." This does not mean that finite or external goods are to be entirely shunned; they have their place in human life, provided they are kept in a subordinate place: "I came to realize that to pursue money, sensual pleasure or glory is harmful only when they are pursued for their own sake and not as a means to other things."[5]

Having indicated what sorts of goods should not be pursued "for their own sake," the text proceeds to elaborate on that infinite being that *does* deserve to be cherished for its own sake and not as a means to other ends. Spinoza calls this end the "true good" or the "supreme good." Since in this world all things are related and in this sense "relative" to each other, the ultimate good sought cannot be one of the relative things, but must be found in insight into the whole relational character of the world—which is nothing else but the divinely instituted order of "nature." Every pathway that facilitates progress toward this end can be seen as a relative good in the service of the higher goal. The supreme good, from this angle, is basically the happiness achieved through insight into the order of nature and practical life-conduct in accordance with this insight. Spinoza at this point describes the highest good in strongly holistic terms: as "the knowledge of the union of the mind with the whole of nature." As a holistic good, this union cannot be achieved by some individuals in isolation from, or to the exclusion of, other human beings. At this point, the sociable or cooperative character of the entire quest comes to the fore. "My pursuit of happiness," we read, "is not complete without the endeavor to have many others achieve the same level of reasoning as myself, so that their reason and desire be fully cooperative with my own." Spinoza in this connection even sketches the contours of a social or political vision congruent with the achievement of the supreme good: "We must establish the sort of society which will enable the greatest number of people to achieve the goal in peace and without undue difficulty." This, he adds (in good pragmatist fashion), "will require the study of moral philosophy as well as the theory of education."[6]

Having established that the pursuit of the supreme good is both a theoretical and a practical endeavor, Spinoza devotes the remainder of his treatise mainly to the cognitive-theoretical side, that is, the "improvement" of mind or intellect—which can only be accomplished through adherence to the right epistemic method or methodology. This part of the treatise—devoted to the conception of "clear and distinct ideas"—is couched largely in Cartesian terms (which is why I abbreviate the account for present purposes). Spinoza initially differentiates among four modes of cognition or knowledge acquisition: namely, cognition through hearsay, through unexamined sense experience, through loose inference, and through comprehension of the "essential" character of a substance or thing. While making some room for the role of inference, the treatise clearly gives preference to the last type, because only this mode of cognition "grasps adequately the essence of things without the risk of error." In order to attain this grasp, one must first of all distinguish between the "idea" or true rational concept of a thing and its instantiation in particular objects. For Spinoza (following Descartes), it is manifest that "certainty consists in nothing but the idea itself, that is, in the way we experience an actual essence"; this has as a corollary that "nobody can know what is the highest certainty unless he has adequate ideas of things." The method for gaining access to true ideas is the "model of systematic thinking and reflection," which is nothing else but "knowledge reflecting upon itself." This method should enable us "to distinguish true [i.e., clear and distinct] ideas from all other ideas," to develop "rules" for the improvement of the mind, and to set up a procedure of inquiry. The highest idea is the concept of an infinite, divine being that encompasses all of nature: "The first principle is a single and infinite being. It is the totality of being(s), outside of which there is nothing."[7]

God and Human Beings

Having discussed the path to true knowledge and real happiness, the task is now to explore the character of that highest and infinite being that is the target of all cognitive and practical striving. While still living in Rijnsburg, Spinoza composed a text on this topic that, in retrospect, appears as a prelude to or sketch for his later *Ethics:* his *Short Treatise on God, Man and His Well-Being (Tractatus de Deo et Homine).* What he endeavors to demonstrate in this treatise is first, that there is only one infinite and all-embracing "substance," which we commonly call "God" (or else nature); and second, that this substance is endowed with a number of infinite "attributes" of which we can know perfectly only two: namely, bodily or spatial "extension" and mind or "thought." By postulating the oneness or unity of the ultimate substance, the treatise undercuts the Cartesian mind-body dualism, which is found to be neglectful of the underlying primordial matrix. By treating extension and thought, however, as infinite attributes, the text in a way validates or makes room again for the Cartesian distinction. Another important distinction introduced in the text is that between "*natura naturans*" and "*natura naturata*," where the former is seen as the creative or active spirit of God/nature, whereas the latter represents finite things or phenomena viewed as receptacles or depositories of this spirit. Expressed in different (more contemporary) vocabulary, the distinction adumbrates the relation between primordial, ontological "Being" and its reflection in "ontic" beings or elements. (As can readily be seen: what is missing in the treatise—as also in the later *Ethics*—is the aspect of "temporality," which is usually associated with the recent formulation.) Spinoza's argument in the treatise starts out in a resolutely Cartesian—or else neo-Scholastic—manner: "Whatever we clearly and distinctly know as belonging to the nature of a thing, we can also truly affirm about that thing. Now [by virtue of our reason] we can know clearly and distinctly that existence belongs to the nature or essence of God." The essence of a thing, however, is "from all eternity" and "unto all eternity shall remain immutable." Hence, "the existence and essence of God are the same."[8]

Here, one may wonder how human reason can have access to, and claim apodictic "knowledge" of, an ultimate substance like God/nature, whose "infinite" character seems to hover forever as an inexhaustible horizon at the border of thought. Leaving this worry aside, the subsequent argument of the treatise is stunning in its rational lucidity—or else its display of what one may call "faithful reasoning" (*fides quaerens intellectum*). From the thesis of the coincidence of essence and existence in God, Spinoza proceeds to the level of the "attributes" of which every one is said to be "infinitely perfect in its kind." Giving some due to the infinite character of God, he acknowledges that his attributes are likewise infinite and that "those which are known to us" are only two: namely, "thought and extension." These attributes are said to inhere in the substance of God/nature and in this sense are neither perishable nor finitely divisible; to the extent that we encounter "particulars" or separate elements, the latter are not attributes, but only phenomenal "modes": "As regards the parts of nature, we maintain that division . . . never takes place in substance, but always only in the 'mode' of substance." What emerges from these comments is a picture of an original unity of God/nature whose dispersal into separate modalities remains closely integrated into the primordial wholeness. In Spinoza's words: "Nature is a being of which all attributes are predicated, and this being so, it cannot be lacking anything wherewith to produce all that there is to be produced." What, in turn, follows from this premise is that "all other things can by no means exist, or be understood, apart from or outside Him," that is, God/nature. Another way of formulating this proposition is to say that "God is the cause [or better: the ground or undergirding matrix] of all things."[9]

Once God/nature is seen as the "cause" or grounding of all things in the world, the question arises how it is still possible to differentiate between the cause and the caused, or between the grounding Being and the grounded beings. It is at this point that Spinoza introduces again the distinction between *natura naturans* and *natura naturata*. As he says: "We shall divide the whole of nature" into these two dimensions (which, of course, is not a real or substantive division, but only an analytical one). By *natura naturans* is meant "a being that we conceive clearly and distinctly through itself," that is, God/nature. On the other hand, *natura naturata* manifests itself on a general/universal and a special/particular level. The general level "consists of all the attributes which depend immediately on God," whereas the particular "consists of all the distinct, particular things which are produced in terms of 'modes.'" As is clear from the preceding, the general concept of *natura naturata* comprises the two basic attributes, namely, extension and thought, or else "motion in matter" and "understanding in the thinking thing" (*res cogitans*). As an attribute, motion or extension is such "that it has been from all eternity and to all eternity will remain immutable" and hence "is infinite in its kind." The same can be said of thought or understanding. The central question of the remainder of the treatise is how "man" or human being is properly related to, or can find fulfillment in, God/nature. For Spinoza, "man" is not a substance, but only participates in the general attributes of motion and thought on the level of particular modes: "All that he has of thought are only 'modes' of the attribute 'thought' which we have attributed to God; and again, all that he has of form, motion, and other things, are likewise 'modes' of the other attribute which we have predicated of God." The clear upshot is that Spinoza's perspective is neither anthropocentric nor crudely "naturalistic" or materialistic, but rather theocentric or God/nature-centric, and never allows finite things to drift too far from this center.[10]

The connection of human beings with their world and ultimately with the God/nature center is nurtured by certain inner dispositions or mental states—of which (in accordance with his earlier formula)

Spinoza distinguishes mainly four: hearsay opinion, unexamined experience, inferential belief, and true knowledge. The first two of those dispositions are oriented toward purely transient things and result in confused attachments. Inferential belief places us on the way but does not reach the goal or God/nature center—to which only clear and distinct knowledge can attain. All the mentioned dispositions are modes of passion, desire, or love; but there is a clear ascending scale of perfection among passions corresponding to the level of the targets of desire. "For," Spinoza states, "we have said that love is a union with an object which our understanding judges to be good and glorious; and by this we mean such a union whereby both lover and the beloved become one and the same thing or together constitute one whole." Now, if the love or desire is oriented toward transient and worthless goods, the desiring being must remain "wretched" and frustrated; and there are even degrees of wretchedness: "If those who desire transient things that have a measure of reality in them are so wretched, how wretched must those be who love honor, riches, or sensual pleasures which have no reality whatsoever!" Hence, in order to find true happiness, it is imperative that love be directed toward a good that is perennially lovable or worthy of love. In terms of the treatise, if we seek to know truly the imperishable good, only genuine love can guide us. For "true love results always from the knowledge that the thing loved is glorious and good. What else can follow but that it can be lavished upon nothing more ardently than upon the Lord our God? For He alone is glorious and perfectly good."[11]

At this point, a quandary emerges precisely with regard to the central God/nature formula (*deus sive natura*). The phrase brings together two aspects that seem to be in tension, if not conflict, with each other. If the accent is placed on nature, we appear to be confronted with a vast network of forces, an anonymous fabric of attributes and modes that entirely lack the quality of personhood. This feature is reinforced if the network is expressed in mathematical-logical formulas, that is, styled as a universal algorithm. In that case, how can nature also be apprehended as God, and in particular, how can Spinoza address it as "the Lord our God" who alone is "perfectly good" and deserving of our deepest love? Is it possible to love and worship an impersonal algorithm? On the other hand, if the accent is placed on a personal deity capable of receiving love, how can the latter be squared with the assumption of a network of anonymous forces inhabiting the cosmos? As it appears at this point, the God/nature formula privileges identity over difference, or universal-unitary substance over differential "entwinement." At the same time, the formula tends to bypass the issue of the personal versus the impersonal character of the divine (what traditional Indian philosophy calls the *saguna* and *nirguna* aspects), as well as the issue of a possibly evolutionary or else dialectical sequence of the nature/divine constellation. The quandary involved in the notion of a substance identical with itself surfaces clearly toward the end of the treatise, in a section dealing with God's love for human beings. Relying on self-identity, Spinoza rejects this notion: "We have said that to God no modes of thought can be ascribed except those which are in His creatures; therefore, it cannot be said that God loves mankind, much less that He should love them because they love Him." He adds: "Properly speaking, there can be in Him no love for something else; since all form only one thing which is God Himself."[12]

Ethics

As previously indicated, the treatise on God was only a sketch for or a prelude to a major philosophical text Spinoza was working on after his relocation to The Hague in 1663: his *Ethics* (*Ethica Ordine Geometrico Demonstrata*). As the title indicates, the study was an ambitious undertaking aiming to demonstrate basic ethical principles deductively or in the (then popular) "geometrical method." In fact, the undertaking was so ambitious that it took the author more than a decade to finish—a decade marked by numerous political upheavals and also by the demands placed on him by other philosophical writings (dealing with theological and political topics). In many respects, even more than his other writings, the *Ethics* can be considered Spinoza's chef d'oeuvre because of its detailed exposition of the God/nature metaphysics and its implications for practical human conduct. The basic premises and axioms of that metaphysics are presented in the first part of the text, titled "Concerning God." In conformity with his earlier writings, Spinoza defines the ultimate substance again as "self-caused," that is, as a substance in which "essence involves existence" and whose very nature is "only conceivable as existent." Closely connected with substance are the (by now familiar) terms *attribute* and *mode,* where the former means a quality "which the intellect perceives as constituting the essence of substance," and the latter refers to "modifications of substance" or aspects "which exist in something other than themselves." The upshot is that God is "an absolutely infinite being," that is, "a substance consisting in infinite attributes of which each is eternal and essentially infinite."[13]

Even more strongly than before, Spinoza insists on the unity or holistic character of the ultimate substance. As he states in a particularly lapidary proposition, "Besides God no substance can be granted or conceived"—which implies as a corollary that "God is one," meaning that "there is but one substance in the universe which is absolutely infinite." The two dimensions stipulated in Cartesian philosophy (*res cogitans* and *res extensa*) are nothing but "attributes of God" or else affections or accidents of such attributes. Closely aligned with these statements are the propositions that "whatsoever is, is in God, and without God nothing can be or be conceived" and that "God and all the attributes of God are eternal." This unitary or holistic conception applies to the entire universe and all distinct beings, because "all things are conditioned to exist and operate in their particular manner by the necessity of the divine nature." In this context, Spinoza again introduces the difference between *natura naturans* and *natura naturata,* calling the first an "active" and the second a "passive" perspective. From what has been said, he notes, it should be sufficiently clear that "by nature viewed as active we should understand that which exists in itself and is conceived through itself or through those attributes of substance which express eternal and infinite essence." On the other hand, "by nature as passive I understand all that which follows necessarily from the nature of God or of any of the attributes of God, that is, all the modes of the attributes of God which can neither exist nor be conceived without God." As before, the two divine attributes that are accessible to human understanding are extension and thought—which are the topics of the second part of the text. As we learn there, human beings have a body and are capable of thinking. However, in both respects they merely participate in the divine attributes, which are eternal. For, we read: "Thought is an attribute of God, or God is a thinking being"; and "Extension is an attribute of God, or God is an extended being."[14]

Rather than pursuing further these metaphysical reflections, I want to turn in the present context to their practical-ethical implications—implications that are spelled out in the remaining parts of the text under the headings of "emotions" and "human freedom." In a slight modification of the distinction between *natura naturans* and *natura naturata,* Spinoza detects in human beings both active and passive dispositions that, in turn, give rise to human emotions. "By emotion," he says, "I mean the modifications of the body whereby the active power of the said body is either increased or diminished, and also the ideas of such modifications." Our ideas are reflections of the modifications of the body; hence, "our mind is in certain cases active and in other cases passive. Insofar as it has inadequate ideas, it is necessarily passive" (which means its power is diminished). The most adequate and active disposition in human beings is the endeavor of self-preservation—which follows from the human participation in the ultimate substance, or the God/nature matrix: "Everything insofar as it is in itself, endeavors to persist in its own being," which means that it expresses "in a given determinate manner the power of God." Given the inherence in the divine substance, the desire to persist in being "involves not finite but indefinite time." Given the rejection of the Cartesian mind-body dualism, preservation in time for Spinoza involves both a physical and a mental disposition: "Whatsoever increases or diminishes, helps or hinders the active power of our body, the idea thereof also increases or diminishes, helps or hinders the power of thought in our mind." The two emotions most likely to increase or else diminish the active direction of human life, in Spinoza's text, are pleasure and pain, attraction and repulsion, love and hatred: "We endeavor to bring about whatsoever we conceive to be conducive to pleasure; but we endeavor to remove or destroy whatsoever we conceive to be truly repugnant thereto or conducive to pain."[15]

What needs to be remembered, however, is that Spinoza's text offers not only an empirical description of emotions but also their normative-ethical assessment. What may mislead observers in this context are passages like the following: "The knowledge of good and evil is nothing else but the emotions of pleasure and pain" or "We call a thing good or evil when it is of service or the reverse in preserving our being." What tends to be forgotten, however, is that to "preserve our being" means precisely to preserve our embeddedness in the divine essence—which, in turn, presupposes an insight into, or understanding of, our place in the God/nature matrix. This is precisely what is meant by the proposition that "every man, by the laws of his nature [that is, his body-mind and his emotions] necessarily desires or shrinks from what he deems to be good or bad"—namely, good or bad for preserving his being. What are called ethical virtues follow from this understanding: "The more every man endeavors and is able to seek what is useful to him—in others words: to preserve his being— the more is he endowed with virtue." This means that virtue cannot be conceived as existing separately from, or in opposition to, human inclinations, especially the inclination "to be." Human mind or reason is able to provide insight into these inclinations and into the connection between human existence and "being." "To act absolutely in obedience to virtue," Spinoza states, "is in us the same thing as to act, to live, and to preserve our being . . . in accordance with the dictate of reason on the basis of which we seek what furthers our self-being." Another way of phrasing this insight is to say: "We know nothing to be certainly good or evil, save such things as really further our understanding, or such as are able to hinder us from understanding."[16]

With the aid of understanding or human reason, we are able to perceive our situation not from a particular perspective or the perspective of idiosyncratic dispositions, but from the vantage of the whole or God-nature—a vantage that is the key to both human happiness and human freedom. In Spinoza's words: "The mind's highest good is the knowledge of God, and accordingly the mind's highest virtue is to know God" (or God-nature). A premise or corollary of this insight is the proposition that human mind is alive or "active" in the endeavor of rational understanding, an endeavor that coincides entirely with the meaning of virtuous action, that is, action geared toward self-being or the coincidence of self-being and God-nature. Another corollary is the insight that things in the world that hamper or obstruct our striving for self-being in union with God-nature can be considered "bad," whereas everything that furthers or is in harmony with this striving inherent in our "nature" is "necessarily good." Among the things that hamper or obstruct the natural striving are base or consuming passions or emotions that are recalcitrant to rational understanding—such as the passions for power, wealth, or sensual pleasure. To the extent that humans are prey to these passions, they are prone to lose their understanding as well as their freedom; more important, they are bound to come into conflict with each other. "Insofar as human beings are assailed by emotions which are passions, they can be contrary to each other"; differently put, they cannot be said "to be naturally in harmony." By contrast, if people live in obedience to reason and find their virtue in the understanding of God-nature, they will "always necessarily agree in nature" or "always live in harmony with each other."[17]

Following this train of thought, Spinoza is led to the vision of a harmonious, well-ordered world—whose concord can be disrupted only by the pursuit of self-seeking ambitions and desires. As he writes: "The highest good of those who follow virtue is common to all, and therefore all can equally rejoice [or find happiness] therein." This derives from the maxim (previously stated) that the pursuit of virtue is the same as the endeavor to know or understand God—a good "which is common to all and can be possessed and enjoyed by all human beings equally." In this striving there is no room for selfishness, since it is a striving for self-being in harmony with God-being (or God-nature). "The good," the text states emphatically, "which every man who pursues virtue desires for himself he will also desire for his fellow-men, and all the more so in proportion as he has greater knowledge of God." The reason is that, when a person loves a good, he (or she) will "love it more constantly if he [she] sees that others love it also"; consequently he (she) will endeavor to bring it about "that others should love it also" and "that all should equally rejoice therein." The joint love of virtue that prevails in the "natural" condition of human beings carries over with still greater force into society or an established social context. According to the *Ethics:* "Whatever is conducive to social human life or prompts men to live together in harmony is good, whereas whatever brings discord into a social state is bad." In close connection with this proposition, Spinoza discusses a number of human dispositions that are either conducive or detrimental to social concord. Thus, we read that "pleasure [or happiness] in itself is not bad but good, whereas pain in itself is bad"; likewise, that "mirth [or joyfulness] cannot be excessive but is always good, whereas melancholy [or dejection] is always bad." Still more important are these maxims: that "love, conceived as sensual desire, may be excessive," though otherwise it tends to be good—while, on the other hand, "hatred can never be good," for "when we hate a person, we endeavor to destroy him," that is, "to do something that is clearly bad."[18]

In addition to these maxims and admonitions, the *Ethics* is a treasure trove of moral insights and sound teachings—not all of which can be detailed here. What pervades and animates the entire text is (what one may call) a cheerful piety, a loving devotion and surrender to the divine God/nature that is the ground of all things and beings. It is this sincere devotion to, and intellectual love of, the divine that earned Spinoza in later times the admiration of some European humanists (including the poet Goethe, who called him a "God-intoxicated" [*Gott-trunken*] thinker). No doubt, this was unexpected praise for a writer-philosopher who, during his life and for a long period afterward, was denounced and even cursed as an apostate and atheist throughout Europe. But denunciations of this kind never touched or affected his mind. Probably, during his lifetime, what most irked his opponents was his cheerful piety, his display of goodwill toward his enemies—even toward those "orthodox" believers who claim to monopolize the divine or to have a proprietary relation to God on the basis of special selection. In opposition to all kinds of pretentious orthodoxy, he put the emphasis on (what is called) "orthopraxis," that is, the cultivation of pious practical conduct. As he writes in the *Ethics:* "Whatever we desire or do . . . in orientation toward the idea or the understanding of God, I call *religion*. And I call *piety* the desire of well-doing which is inspired by a life lived according to such understanding." In both his teachings and his own life conduct, Spinoza seemed to follow and uphold the instruction of the prophet Micah: "He has shown you what is good; and what does the Lord require of you but to pursue justice, to practice kindness, and to walk humbly with your God."[19]

Even more than his writings and elaborate treatises, it is Spinoza's practical conduct that can inspire, and serve as a model for, people in our own time. Although it is possible to quibble with some of his theoretical formulations—especially when offered "*more geometrico*"—it is much more difficult to quibble with his conduct both in private and in social life. Almost all the biographical accounts of Spinoza testify to his personal goodness and friendly disposition. Steven Nadler writes that while he was working on his *Ethics*, Spinoza "spent a good deal of time in his room, working on either his lenses or his writing, or perhaps just reading. . . . Far from being the morose, anti-social recluse of legend, he was, when he put down his work, gregarious and possessed of a pleasing and even-tempered disposition." All in all, "he was kind and considerate, and enjoyed the company of others who in turn seem to have enjoyed his." Even the protean philosopher Pierre Bayle— Nadler adds—who excoriated Spinoza for his atheism, "took note of the virtues of his personal character and his blameless lifestyle."[20] These and other testimonials amply justify the description of Spinoza as a pragmatist avant la lettre. As one should note, however, his ethical disposition and practice of virtue were not limited to private conduct, but extended directly to his conception of social and public life. In this respect, the conclusion of the second part of the *Ethics* is instructive and eloquent. As Spinoza states there: the conception advanced in his text "uplifts social life, inasmuch as it teaches us to hate no man, neither to despise, to deride, to envy or to be angry with any. Moreover, it tells us that each should be content with his own and helpful to his neighbor." Most important, on the political level, the conception "confers no small advantage on the commonwealth; for it teaches how citizens should be governed and led, not so as to become slaves, but so that they may freely do whatever things are best."[21]

Epilogue: Leibniz and Hegel

As indicated before, Spinoza for a long time was an outcast from polite society and orthodox religious circles. Yet even during that dark period, there were intellectuals or philosophers who interacted with him and appreciated his work. One of these was the German philosopher and mathematician Gottfried Wilhelm Leibniz (1646–1716), the designer of the binary system and, alongside Isaac Newton, the inventor of infinitesimal calculus. Like many intellectuals of his time, Leibniz built upon the rationalist legacy of Descartes, while also trying to reformulate or remodel the Cartesian system. It was this latter endeavor that brought him into the philosophical proximity of Spinoza, with whom he both agreed and disagreed on important points. In 1676, during a journey from London to his native Hannover, he actually met and had long discussions with Spinoza, who had then just completed his *Ethics*. Basically, the agreement as well as disagreement between the two thinkers revolved around the issue of the status of the divine substance and its relation to all beings in the world. What Leibniz warmly embraced was Spinoza's holistic approach, that is, his insistence on the ultimate union of God-nature or the cosmos and his rejection of any kind of dualistic division or fragmentation. Where he departed from Spinoza was with regard to the structure of this holistic vision—a structure that Leibniz considered too narrowly restrictive and too neglectful of the integrity and distinct individuality of beings in the world. Throughout his life, Leibniz struggled to find a more adequate formulation of the God-world connection—a struggle that culminated in 1714 in his *Monadology* (of which only the barest outline can be offered here).

In his *Monadology*, Leibniz takes over the substance metaphysics articulated by Spinoza (and earlier by scholastic philosophy)—but with a crucial twist. Whereas Spinoza stipulated one single ultimate substance to which all the attributes and modalities of beings are subordinated, Leibniz postulates an infinite number of distinct substances that he calls "monads"—although their ultimate ground of existence resides in God, seen as primordial substance. As he states at the very opening of his text: "The monads which we shall discuss here are nothing other than simple substances which are contained in composite entities." The term "simple" here means that they are compact, indivisible, and without spatial extension; hence, they can be called "the true atoms of nature and, in a word, the elements of things." More important, monads are self-contained and not affected or controlled by outside factors; although endowed with a view or perception of the cosmos, they do not have "windows through which something could enter into or depart from them." Although self-contained and immune from external causal forces, monads in Leibniz's account are endowed with different inherent "qualities" and thus highly individualized; for "there are never in nature two beings that are perfectly alike and where one could not find a difference that is internal or founded on an intrinsic determination." Another important feature is that monads are liable to continuous change and transformation—with the source of change traceable again not to outside causes, but to an internal principle of movement. Leibniz describes this principle as striving or "appetition," or else "*conatus*," stating that this striving may not always reach "the wholeness of perception at which it aims," but can approximate it and from there proceed to further strivings. Because of this continuous movement, monads exhibit the Aristotelian quality of "*entelechy*": "One could give the name '*en-*

telechies' to all simple substances or created monads; for they all have in them the urge to a certain perfection. They also display a certain self-sufficiency (*autarkeia*) that makes them sources of their own internal actions."[22]

There are some additional aspects where Leibniz departs from, or further radicalizes, Spinoza's metaphysics. As will be recalled, the latter ascribed to divine substance an infinite number of attributes— of which two are most important and cognitively accessible, namely, thought and extension (or extended matter). Leibniz's work breaks entirely with this conception and especially with the notion of extension as primordial attribute. Basically, given the "simple" and unextended character of monads, spatial extension for Leibniz is not at all an ontological reality, but rather—like temporality—an intrinsic quality of monadic perception (a notion that much later gave rise to the idea of the a priori character of space and time). A close corollary of this "internalization" of space is the strong emphasis on the mind-body correlation or synergy—an emphasis going beyond both Cartesian dualism and Spinoza's notion of two separate attributes of being. For Leibniz, both thought and matter, or body, are endowed with inner striving, or *conatus*—although matter lacks consciousness and especially the faculty of temporal retention in memory. As the Spinoza scholar Genevieve Lloyd tells us, it is in terms of *conatus* "that the true distinction between mind and matter is to be understood." Basically, in the Leibnizian version of *conatus*, "mind and matter—kept so firmly apart by Descartes [and to some extent even Spinoza]—draw together." Where the distinction comes in is in the fact that "every body is [only] a momentary mind or one lacking recollection; for it does not retain its own *conatus* and another contrary one for longer than a moment." Differently put: bodies "lack memory" or "the perception of their actions and passions"; hence they are, as it were, "momentary minds, with no continuity through time."[23]

Given the pronounced differentiation of individual monads in his work, the basic question arises how Leibniz was able to maintain the holistic or unitary quality of Spinoza's metaphysics. Here two crucial considerations have to be kept in mind: first, the synchronized or "preestablished" harmony between monadic perspectives; and second, the role of God as the ultimate ground or anchor of monadic existence. Although windowless and in a way self-contained, all monads function in a "relational" universe where all things and beings are mutually adjusted and harmoniously correlated. This basic relationality, or this "accommodation of all created things to each other," Leibniz states, has as a consequence that "each single monad has relations which express all others, and hence each is a perpetual living mirror of the whole universe." By virtue of this correlation, something amazing is accomplished: "the greatest possible variety combined with the greatest possible order—which means: as much perfection as can be." The ultimate source and warrant of this correlation, in Leibniz's view, can be found in a primordial substance, or "primal monad" (*Ur-Monade*). "The final ground of all things," we read, "must be in a necessary substance in which the variety of changes is contained embryonically, as in its source. This substance we call God." Given that this supreme substance—which is described as "unique, universal, and necessary"—cannot have anything "outside or independent of it," one can conclude that "it is incapable of any limitation and hence must contain reality to the utmost possible degree." Leibniz sums up this part of his argument: "Accordingly, God alone is the primal unity (*Ur-Einheit*) or the primal monad (*Ur-Monade*). All the created or derivative monads are its products and originate, so to speak, through continual fulgurations of the deity from moment to moment, confined only by the receptivity of created beings which are essentially limited."[24]

What comes into view here is the central feature and achievement of Leibniz's work: the merger and even coincidence of holism and singularity, of universalism and particularism. This merger, one should note, is not superimposed from above but an emerging quality. This feature is well expressed by Martin Heidegger: "In the simultaneous striving (*conatus*) of the diverse possibilities for existence there emerges a combination of existing beings bringing about the greatest possible sum of perfection. Out of the conflict of beings striving for existence emerges the realization of as many as possible; and this conflict of aspiring existences happens, so to speak, in front of God."[25] The harmonious correlation of all existing (and possible) beings in the world is articulated in the *Monadology* in numerous eloquent passages. Thus, regarding the reciprocal accommodation of monads, we read: "Thus, among created beings, actions and reactions are in a way reciprocal. For, when comparing simple monads, God finds in each reasons which oblige him to accommodate the other to it; and thus, what in certain regards is active is passive from another point of consideration." The most captivating passage, however, can be found a bit later in the text, where Leibniz writes: "Every bit of nature can be conceived as a garden full of plants or a pond full of fish. But each branch of the plant, each member of an animal, each drop of its bodily fluids is, in turn, such a garden or such a pond." And "although the earth and the air surrounding the plants of the garden, or the water surrounding the fish of the pond, are certainly neither plant nor fish, they yet contain more of them, though mostly of a minuteness imperceptible to us." Which leads to the conclusion: "Hence there is nothing fallow, nothing sterile or dead in the world—no chaos, no disorder, save in appearance."[26]

Despite the correlation and even coincidence of natural harmony and the primal monad or God, Leibniz recognizes a certain differentiation in the sense of an ascending scale of awareness. Basically, the sequence leads from inanimate monads via animate monads endowed with "soul" to reflective monads (human beings) endowed with "spirit" or "intellect." As one should note, the sequence does not entail the Cartesian superiority of mind over body, of cogito over extended matter, but only a deepened insight into the God/nature constellation. Expressed in Spinoza's terminology of *natura naturans* and *naturata,* one might say that the sequence involves a progressive ability of the created world (*naturata*) to participate in the designs of God (*naturans*). Leibniz explains: "Among other differences between ordinary 'souls' and 'spirits' (or intellects), there is also the aspect that souls in general are living mirrors or images of the created world, while spirits have the additional faculty to be images of divinity itself, that is, of the creator or ground of nature." This has as a consequence that spirits are capable of "knowing the system of the universe and of imitating it through some constructive samples"—which means in turn that they are capable of "entering into some kind of community with God." Thus, there is dual harmony: one operating in the world of nature, the other obtaining between "the physical realm of nature and the moral realm of divine grace." The conclusion of the *Monadology* is a paean to this overall harmony, culminating in a new formulation or vision of the "city of God": "From all this one can readily conclude that the assembly of all spirits must compose the city of God, that is, the most perfect state possible under the most perfect of monarchs. This city of

God, this truly universal monarchy, is a moral world within the natural world, and it is the most exalted and most heavenly work in which consists the true glory of God."[27]

The post-Cartesian rationalism of Spinoza and Leibniz fell out of favor during the eighteenth century under the influence of "Storm and Stress" and the rise of German idealist philosophy. However, not all thinkers joined this trend. A notable exception was Georg W. F. Hegel (1770–1831), who throughout his life maintained a keen interest in both Spinoza and Leibniz. What attracted him to Spinoza was, above all, the strong holism undergirding his work. As he wrote in his *Lectures on the History of Philosophy*, in Spinoza "the dualism of the Cartesian system was altogether set aside"; for him, "soul and body, thought and Being, cease to have separate existence." In an admiring vein, he added the high praise that "thought must begin by placing itself at the standpoint of Spinozism; to be a follower of Spinoza is the beginning of all philosophy"—for "the soul must commence by bathing in this ether of the One Substance." In a cross-cultural aside, the *Lectures* finds in Spinoza's holism "an echo from Eastern [Asian] lands," of "the Oriental theory of absolute identity." Counterposed to this line of praise, however, the text advances an equally strong criticism, regarding Spinoza's lack of concrete determination and his neglect or deemphasis of singularity or individuality. As a corollary of his accent on unity, Hegel observes, "substance with Spinoza is not yet determined as in itself concrete." As a result, the individual or particular is treated simply as finite and ephemeral, that is, as an emblem of "false individuality." However, "true individuality and subjectivity" are not "a mere retreat from the universal, not merely something finitely determinate," but at the same time "being-for-itself, determined by itself alone." Hence, the grandeur and limitation of Spinoza's thought is that "he is able to renounce all that is determinate and particular, and restrict himself to the One, giving heed to this alone."[28]

The defect of Spinoza's system was remedied to a certain extent by Leibniz through his correlation of particularity and universality. According to Hegel, Leibniz's work stands in opposition to both the atomistic empiricism of John Locke and the substantialism of Spinoza and yet tries "to bind them together again." For, "on the one hand, he expresses in the many monads the real nature of things as distinguished and individual; on the other hand and in contrast to this, he upholds the ideality of Spinoza and the non-absolute nature of all difference." Phrased differently: "While Spinoza asserted the universality, the oneness of substance, and while Locke made infinite determinations his basis, Leibniz by means of his fundamental principle of individuality, brings out the essentiality of the opposite aspect of Spinoza's philosophy, existence for itself, the monad—but the monad regarded only as an absolute concept, perhaps not yet as the 'I'" (in the sense of idealist philosophy). The latter aspect becomes ultimately the basis for Hegel's critique. According to the *Lectures*, Leibniz was only partially able to reconcile particularity and unity and in the end had to rely on a deus ex machina, the intervention of a transcendent deity: "God has the special privilege of having laid upon Him the burden of what cannot be comprehended. The word of God is thus the makeshift which leads to a unity which itself is purely hypothetical; for the progression of the many out of this unity is not demonstrated."[29]

The goal of Hegel's own philosophy was precisely to overcome philosophically the remaining polarity. In a way, he sought to accomplish this goal by translating Leibniz's distinction among inanimate, animate, and spiritual monads into the movement of spirit "coming to itself" through the sequence of being-in-itself, for-itself, and in-and-for-itself—the latter coinciding with absolute spirit or pure subjectivity. This was no doubt a great philosophical gain. But in orienting everything toward absolute spirit, the domain of nature in Hegel's philosophy was progressively deemphasized or placed into a marginal position.[30] It was precisely this marginalization that prompted the insurgence and recovery of the philosophy of nature by Hegel's friend from his student days in Tübingen: Friedrich Schelling (1775–1854).

2

Nature and Spirit

Schelling

"The character of the entire modern epoch," Schelling wrote in 1797, "is idealist and its dominant tenor is to turn inward. The ideal world surges mightily into the limelight, but is still held back by nature's retreat into mystery. The secrets of the latter, however, cannot be truly grasped until nature's mystery is plumbed and expressed."[1] These lines were penned in the midst of Enlightenment optimism and at the height of German idealist philosophy as inaugurated by Immanuel Kant and continued by his successors, notably Fichte and Hegel. Schelling was by no means unimpressed by the upsurge of enlightened idealism; as we know, his youthful writings bore the strong imprint of Kantian as well as Fichtean critical rationality. However, Schelling was also one of the first to detect the Achilles heel of a triumphant rationalism: its expulsion from reason of the entire "outer" world (thematized by Kant as the realm of "things-in-themselves")—an expulsion he astutely perceived as the reaffirmation and even further deepening of the Cartesian bifurcation between mind and matter, subject and object. The chief victim of this expulsion was "nature" in all its manifestations. In many ways, the entire trajectory of Schelling's lifework can be seen as a prolonged effort to rescue nature from this victimization.

In launching his rebellion, Schelling never claimed to be breaking entirely new ground. In several of his early writings, he placed himself squarely in the lineage of two great philosophical mentors: Spinoza and Leibniz.[2] Without embracing either the former's reliance on "substance" or the latter's notion of "monads," he felt kinship with both in their opposition to unmediated dualisms and their search for the prior ground undergirding polar conflicts. In his time, unmediated dualism was prominent especially in the Kantian opposition between "noumenal" and "phenomenal" spheres and in the Fichtean confrontation between "ego" and "non-ego." Although challenging the limits of critical rationality—it is important to note—Schelling's work never exchanged rationalist one-sidedness for its opposite. Despite occasional accusations of antirationalism or irrational mysticism, Schelling never veered from the path of philosophical inquiry, including the path of enlightened reason. In fact, in extending his inquiry to the realm of nature, his work sought to lay a more solid groundwork for human freedom or emancipation and hence to contribute to the comprehensive or holistic flourishing of "spirit" (or *Geist*).[3] In the following I shall concentrate mainly on the period from 1796 to 1802, the period during which Schelling was most intensely preoccupied with the elaboration of a "philosophy of nature." After outlining some of the main arguments presented in his *Ideas for a Philosophy of Nature* and his treatise the "World Soul," I shall proceed to discuss in some detail his so-called *First Outline* and his *System of Transcendental Idealism,* in order finally to turn attention to his dialogue *Bruno* and his *Philosophy of Art*, together with some of their implications.

Ideas and "World Soul"

Nature as a philosophical issue only slowly entered Schelling's range of concerns. His earliest writings invariably paid tribute to "noumenal" or transcendental consciousness (in Kant's sense) and to the constitutive productivity of subjectivity or the ego (in Fichte's sense). Strides in a new direction emerged first in a text of 1796—but then with resolute vigor. The philosophical task for Schelling at the time was to find a standpoint transgressing both a naively reductive realism and a lopsided subjectivism or idealism. How was this possible? "What is required first of all," he notes, "is to find a place where subject and object, vision and visible coincide or are *identical*." This locus can only be the idea of "spirit" (*Geist*) that exists both in and for itself, which means it is not an external thing for consciousness. As he adds: "I call 'spirit' what is only *its own* object. By being an object for itself without being an empirical thing, spirit is at the same time absolute subject for which everything is an object." Here, an intrinsic dynamic or dialectic comes into view. For a merely external thing is something inert, incapable of self-movement. By contrast, spirit (echoes of

Fichtean teachings) is defined by autonomy and active productivity; hence, it exists in the mode of "becoming" (*Werden*) and in fact is nothing "but an eternal becoming." By linking being and becoming, spirit also links finitude and infinity. For, Schelling states, while mere objects are "necessarily finite," spirit in its eternal self-movement cannot be finite. Yet in treating everything as a target of awareness, spirit also objectifies itself and thus enters the realm of finitude: "Spirit is spirit only by objectifying itself and hence becoming finite. It is neither infinite without becoming finite, nor becomes finite without being infinite. Hence, it is neither infinite nor finite, but rather exhibits the most primordial *union* of finitude and infinity."[4]

The vision of a primordial union was buttressed in the cited text by an explicit appeal to Leibniz and Spinoza. In Schelling's words: Leibniz did not talk about external "things-in-themselves" far removed from conscious awareness; he "did not know of any entities or beings except those which recognize themselves or are recognized by spirit." External things for him were not inert or lifeless objects; rather, "he endowed his monads with faculties of understanding and portrayed them as knowing and representing . . . beings. Immortal mind," Schelling exclaims, "what has become among us of your teachings!" A few pages later, the same text invokes the legacy of Spinoza, in fact the "inevitability of Spinozism"—although the latter in a new guise or formulation. Whereas Spinoza himself spoke of "substances," thus giving the impression of inert things or objects, a proper reformulation had to focus on the primordial union of subject/object, finitude/infinity—which is the level of "spirit." "Finitude and infinity," Schelling reiterates, "are primordially united only in the being of a spiritual nature." In actual life, to be sure, the same unity unfolds and also differentiates itself in an ongoing process of objectification—a process that reveals the productive self-movement of spirit and also its self-limitation in the world. In Schelling's presentation, the unfolding movement of spirit involves a dialectical interplay of infinite and finite moments—where the former can be described as "positively" active and the latter as "negatively" reactive or passive. Once raised to the level of awareness, he states, consciousness can distinguish between two sides of the movement, where the one side has a "positive or enhancing" character, the other side a "negative or limiting" character: "In the measure in which spirit limits [or objectifies] itself, it is simultaneously active (*tätig*) and passive (*leidend*); and since every action also promotes human consciousness, the nature of individuality must also display this juncture of action and passivity."[5]

While clearly accentuating the "primordial union," the cited text does not fully explore the process of "becoming," that is, the unfolding of union into difference or polarity and its subsequent possible restoration on a new level. This exploration was the topic of the first mature statement of Schelling's position: his *Ideas for a Philosophy of Nature* of 1797. As Robert Stern observes in his introduction to the English translation, Schelling, having just moved from Tübingen to Leipzig, "plunged into a study of medicine, physics and mathematics, and arrived at a picture of nature that emphasized its polarity and dynamism"—a picture that strongly departs from Kantian and Fichtean themes. In his own introduction to the text, Schelling offers in bold strokes a sketch of his view of nature and the latter's relation to reflection and spirit. As he writes, his objective is not to present a deductive system, but to show how experience guides us in this domain, disclosing a developmental process. Initially, he notes, humankind was embedded in nature and lived in "a philosophical state of nature." The first stirring of conscious reflection, however, disrupted this union—and this not accidentally; for "human spirit whose element is freedom, inevitably seeks to free or disentangle itself from the fetters of nature and her tutelage." Hence, with the advancement of internal reflection, humans are placed in conflict with the external world (subject-object split), and philosophy begins: "reflection separates from now on what nature had always united." Yet, Schelling adds, this separation is not an end or goal, but only a "means" of emancipation. For the real essence of human beings is action (*Handeln*), and action means the objectification of spirit in the world—a process that does not aim at the suppression of that world, but at the recovery and self-finding of spirit in action. Thus, between spirit and world "no rift must be established; rather, contact and reciprocity must be possible between them, for only in this manner does 'man' become 'man.' Originally, there is in humans an absolute equilibrium between [natural] forces and consciousness. Humans can upset this balance through freedom—in order to reestablish it again through freedom."[6]

Relentless reflection without such recovery, in Schelling's view, constitutes a troublesome mental pathology, an illness that—by seizing control of human beings—destroys human spiritual life "at the root." At this point, diremption or alienation triumphs. Such pathology, he writes, "makes the separation between humans and the world permanent by treating the latter as a 'thing-in-itself' which neither intuition nor imagination, neither understanding nor reason can reach." Opposed to this illness stands (what he calls) "genuine philosophy," which regards reflection as merely a means. This philosophy takes full account of this basic division—but only "in order to reunite through freedom what in human spirit was originally and necessarily united, that is, in order to remove forever this diremption." Unsurprisingly, the text here heaps praise again on Spinoza and Leibniz for holding fast to this insight. "The first," we read, "who with complete clarity saw mind and matter as one, thought [*cogito*] and extension [*res extensa*] as mere modifications of the same principle, was Spinoza. His system was the first bold outline of a creative imagination which perceived the finite directly in the idea of the infinite, purely as such, and recognized the former only in the latter." Proceeding from this outline and correcting some of its shortcomings, Leibniz developed still more fully the idea of coincidence, the insight into the basic connection and parallelism between mind and matter, inside and outside. Although largely ostracized and treated like "a stranger among us," Schelling insists that the time was ripe to restore Leibniz's philosophy as an antidote to prevailing tendencies. For he belonged to the few "who treated even knowledge as a free activity" and who exuded in his work "a universal world spirit (*Geist der Welt*) revealing itself in the most manifold forms." Above all, nothing could be further removed from his thought than "the speculative chimera of a world of 'things-in-themselves' which, unknown and unseen by any mind, are supposed to affect and produce our ideas."[7]

To establish a connection between mind and matter, modern philosophy often relies on the principle of causality—thus either treating ideas as the result of external material causes or else treating matter (or the outside world) as a pliant instrument of mind. For Schelling, this approach was thoroughly deficient, as it presupposed in essence the basic separation or duality that it sought to remedy. A prominent endeavor of modern philosophy, he writes, is "to place object and idea into the relationship of cause and effect." Although seemingly promising at a first glance, the endeavor ultimately fails and even backfires.

Since modern critical reflection treats objects as external "things-in-themselves," it is inconceivable how one could make "things into the effects of our ideas." Hence, the only alternative remaining is "to make the ideas dependent upon things and to regard the latter as causes, the former as effects." It is patently clear, however—Schelling adds—that with this move "we cannot really achieve what we wanted." For if things are the causes of ideas, then they precede the ideas as outside forces: "Consequently, the division between the two becomes permanent." Thus, the causal approach not only fails to elucidate the linkage between thought and object but renders it entirely unintelligible. But it is precisely the goal of philosophy to further understanding: its task is to show how, after having been reflectively separated through freedom, object and idea "can be united again through freedom," that is, how "originally there was no separation between them."[8]

The linkage sought by philosophy thus cannot be explained causally, nor can it be construed mechanically as part of an external mechanical process. For "what is caught up in a mere mechanism cannot step out of it and ask: how has all this become possible?" Hence, the only promising line of explanation is to assume a continuity or parallelism between nature and mind, between the forces (*Kräfte*) operating in the natural universe and the forces animating our mind or spirit. What this brings into view is the insight that the movement and sequence of ideas "comes about and arises together or in tandem with the movement of things, and vice versa." Put differently: "the succession of ideas is as little possible without the things as things without the succession"—which means that "both are in mutual relation and mutually necessary in regard to each other." As Schelling writes in a lapidary formulation: "There is then no alternative but to try to derive the necessary sequence of ideas from the nature of mind (and from finite mind as such), and in order that this sequence be truly objective, to have the things themselves arise and come into being with this sequence." Among all previous philosophical systems, he adds, "I know of only two—those of Spinoza and Leibniz—which not only undertook this attempt, but whose entire work is nothing but this attempt." What needs to be done—and this is Schelling's own line of endeavor—is to pursue their insights and to bring them more clearly in accord with the modern ideas of spirit and freedom. What recent philosophy has properly underscored is that infinite ideas have no life apart from human thought and its natural substrate and that human spirit is anchored precisely in this originary union. Sequestered from human understanding, the meaning of ideas, concepts, or affects is unfathomable—which means that "nothing infinite can dwell in us without finitude." Hence, "the necessary union of the ideal and the real, of the absolutely active and the absolutely passive . . . exists in me originally without my prodding and thus constitutes my very nature."[9]

This argument leads Schelling to an organic (not mechanical) conception of nature whose rise and evolution correspond to the inner movements of mind. "Organicism" here means that nonhuman nature is governed by the interplay of form and matter in the same way as human life obeys the interplay of spiritual and natural-material forces. In the organic world, we read, no mechanical linkage of cause and effect can be found, since every organism "exists for itself," carrying the "ground of its existence" in itself. Accordingly, in every organism the shaping or organizing principle coheres with its very existence, with the result that "form and matter here are inseparable"; the "unity" of the organism lies in its own being (not in some external whim). What follows from this point is that awareness of organic unity is indeed a "judgment" of spirit, though not an externally superimposed judgment, but one manifest in the "purposiveness" of organisms themselves. Differently put: organic unity entails that the idea of form is empty without its natural substrate, just as the concept of matter is void without an indwelling, organizing idea. In Schelling's account, it is possible to pursue this view of organic unity from inanimate and animate beings through a "stage sequence" (*Stufenfolge*) all the way to the complexity of human life. In the latter, too, the connection of real existence and purposive idea attests to the "original union of mind and matter," now surfacing in the linkage of "idea and action, design and execution." In customary (though inadequate) language, human life is seen as the conjunction of "mind and body," all animated by the internal life-spring called "soul." Summing up the gist of "stages" of life, Schelling concludes with this poignant statement: "Nature should be seen as visible spirit, spirit as invisible nature. Here then, in the absolute identity of spirit in us and nature outside of us, the problem of the possibility of a self-contained nature must be resolved."[10]

The actual body of *Ideas* examines the forces and processes of nature as such, moving from the phenomena of light and electricity to the dynamic processes of attraction/repulsion and finally to the science of chemistry—an examination that falls outside the scope of these pages. Rather than delving into these analyses, I want to turn briefly to another study penned about a year later, called "On the World Soul" (1798). As we know, the study greatly impressed the poet Goethe, who saw in it a parallel to his own organic view of nature (inspired in many ways by Spinoza). The subtitle of the study presents it as an attempt at "the explanation of the universal organism"— certainly a broad and comprehensive endeavor. Attached as a preamble to the study is another text dealing with the general relation "between the real and the ideal in nature," a text that focuses once again on the "original union" between form and matter, between finitude and infinity. As Schelling observes, the infinite cannot be added to the finite, nor the finite to the infinity, like a mere supplement; rather, "both must be united through an original and absolute necessity or need." This link or necessity can be called an "absolute bond, or else their copula." The essence of this bond is "the absolute negation of nothingness, or the absolute affirmation of itself in all of its forms." What is important to realize is that the uniting bond—in ancient times called "world soul"—and what it unites are not separate dimensions; for between the two we cannot find any other connection but "the law of identity." Adopting a slightly different language, Schelling invokes the quasi-Platonic idea of love or sympathy:

> Basically we can express the uniting bond as the infinite love for itself (the highest in all things) or the infinite desire to manifest itself—with the proviso that the absolute must not be seen as separate from this desire but rather as the infinite will-to-itself (*Sich-selber-wollen*). . . . The imprint of this eternal and infinite will-to-itself is the world.[11]

As was the case in *Ideas,* the study on the "world soul" makes a plea for an organic conception of nature prevailing or taking precedence over any mechanical features that might be found. In Schelling's words: "The world is an *organism,* and a universal organism is the very condition or presupposition of mechanism." Again as in *Ideas,* the bulk of the study traces the processes of nature through a sequence of stages (*Stufenfolge*), from inorganic to organic and finally to human life.

While the discussion of inorganic nature ranges over the phenomena of light, air, electricity, and magnetism, the section on organic and human life focuses on the aspects of self-organization, sensibility, and attraction/repulsion. A common thread running through the sequence is the tension or interplay of two opposed but mutually dependent forces, especially the dark force of finite gravity (*Schwere*) and the exhilarating infinity of light. What needs to be noted is that this interplay manifests itself in the greatest variety of forms. "The eternal or infinite," we read, "affirms itself not only as the unity of all beings, but extends this affirmation to all beings in their particularity, that is, it is unity in difference, totality in particular identity." While the principle of unity is in some ways associated with gravity, light allows for the infinite profusion of diversity; only the two in their combination generate "the beautiful appearance of life." The highest goal of the philosophy of nature, Schelling adds, is to grasp "the living existence of God both in the unity and particularity of beings"; to this extent, Spinoza's saying remains true that "the more we know individual beings the more we are able to know God."[12]

First Outline and Transcendental Idealism

Having obtained a professorship in Jena as a result of his previous writings, Schelling decided to flesh out in greater detail his philosophy of nature and especially to spell out more clearly some aspects *Ideas* had left ambiguous. As an accompaniment to extensive lectures on the topic, he published in 1799 his *First Outline for a System of the Philosophy of Nature,* together with an elaborate "Introduction" to this *Outline.* In the words of Keith Peterson, the English translator of the text, the *First Outline* "provides perhaps the most inclusive exhibition of Schelling's early thought and method in the philosophy of nature"; by presenting the latter as a "speculative physics," Schelling endeavored to demonstrate how "in our investigations into nature we already employ certain ideas or acts of mind" and that "without these conditions [modern] natural science itself would not have achieved anything thus far."[13] Building on his previous writings, the beginning of *First Outline* powerfully reasserts the coincidence of unity and diversity, totality and difference, infinity and finitude. According to the very first axiom of the text: "The unconditioned [infinite] cannot be sought in any particular [ontic] thing nor in anything of which one can say that it [ontically] is. For what 'is' only partakes of being and is only a particular form or kind of being. Conversely, one can never say of the unconditioned that it [ontically] exists; for it is *Being itself* which does not fully exhibit itself in any finite product." Since Being, however, is not a dead or inert entity, but rather spirit in action, a second axiom immediately follows, namely, that "absolute activity cannot be exhibited by a finite product, but only in an infinite process." Hence, the task of a philosophy of nature, seen as a "speculative physics," must be "to grasp the absolute unity in the infinite diversity of action, and thus to find the point where the multiplicity of diverse actions can be unified in nature."[14]

As sketched earlier in *Ideas,* the unfolding process of nature is not simply an external mechanism, but rather exhibits tension and reciprocal interaction between opposed but linked elements. "The activity," we read, "which inner spirit opposes to externality displays its receptivity of the outside world, showing that the same activity really depends on this receptivity." Hence, natural organisms in their stage sequence are basically modes of reciprocal action on different levels and in different guises. As Schelling explains in his own "Introduction," such a view of nature is radically different from a purely "transcendental" philosophy, which, relying only on internal consciousness, subordinates the real to the ideal, the finite to the infinite. In opposition to this kind of transcendentalism, natural philosophy has the task of deriving "the ideal from the real," that is, to show the embeddedness or inherence of the infinite in the finite. To this extent, this philosophy can be called a "speculative physics" or else a "Spinozism of physics." The governing maxim of this philosophy or speculative natural science must be "to explain all phenomena on the basis of forces of nature"—taking the latter phrase in the widest possible sense and thus extending it even "to that region where interpretation of nature has until now been accustomed to stop: namely, those organic phenomena which seem to presuppose an analogy with mind or reason." Continuing this line of thought, Schelling adds in a bold extrapolation (fleshed out more fully in *First Outline*):

> For, granted that there is really something which presupposes such analogy in the actions of animals, what follows from the

standpoint of realism is that what we call "mind" or "reason" (*Vernunft*) is also a play of higher and necessarily unknown natural forces. For, inasmuch as thinking is lastly a mode of acting and reacting (producing and reproducing), there is nothing impossible in the thought that the same activity by which nature reproduces itself anew in each successive phase, is reproductive also in thought through the medium of the organism (just like, through the action and play of light, nature—which exists independently of it—is created *immaterially* and as it were for a second time).[15]

The reference to an immaterial dimension in a way refers back to the opening maxim of *First Outline:* the correlation of the unconditioned and the conditioned, the infinite and the finite. In the unfolding process of nature seen as a "becoming," the infinite externalizes or objectifies itself in the real or finite—but without simply collapsing into the latter. As Schelling states, elaborating on the first maxim, infinite spirit or creativity and finite (or ontic) products both coincide and remain different, or coincide in their tensional difference. His "Introduction" delves more deeply into this tensional relation. "Inasmuch as everything of which we can say that it [ontically] is," we read, "is of conditioned character, it follows that only Being itself can be unconditioned." But, "seeing that every particular conditioned being can only be thought as a limitation of creative activity—the sole and ultimate ground of all reality—Being itself must be thought as that unlimited [or infinite] creative activity." This insight leads Schelling to formulations reminiscent of Spinoza's arguments. "Insofar as we regard the totality of beings not merely as a product," he writes, "but simultaneously as creative, it becomes *nature* for us, and it is precisely this identity of product and creativity (or productivity) which is designated by the term 'nature' even in ordinary language." Now, nature seen as a mere product (*natura naturata*) "we call nature as object (the target of empirical science)," while nature seen as creativity (*natura naturans*) "we call nature as a subject (the sole target of philosophy)." Of nature seen as an object, he adds, "we can say that it [ontically] is," whereas we cannot say this of nature seen as a subject "which is Being or creativity itself." With the idea of an absolute creativity we associate the notion of "ideal infinity." But such infinity should also be concrete or real; hence, "concrete infinity is an infinite becoming."[16]

As in *Ideas*, the *First Outline* pursues the dynamic becoming of nature through successive stages of development and manifestation, dwelling again on such phenomena as magnetism, light, electricity, attraction/repulsion, and chemical processes. An important feature of the text is the emphasis on the linkage of inorganic and organic nature in an unfolding continuum of becoming. As we read toward the end of the "Introduction": "Nature viewed as a whole is absolutely organic," and "the result to which genuine natural science must lead is this: that the difference between organic and inorganic nature exists only in nature as object [*natura naturata*], whereas nature as originally creative [*naturans*] soars above both." The entire process of dynamic becoming is summarized late in *First Outline* in these terms: "The process presupposes an evolution of the universe from one original being, but also a dispersion of this being into ever new beings or products. The ground of this infinite dispersion must have been placed in nature by an original duality"; yet the same diremption must be seen "as having emerged from an originally identical being"—which is not thinkable "unless that identical being is posited as an *absolute involution, as a dynamic infinity*." Another important feature of Schelling's text is its connection of ontological and ethical concerns. Keith Peterson notes that the evolution portrayed in the book involves, in its stress on infinite action, "the engagement of human freedom in transcending mechanism from the start. Not only epistemological and ontological, the philosophy of nature is an expressly ethical project."[17]

In the aftermath of the *First Outline*, Schelling felt challenged to expand his horizons further by seeking to correlate and even reconcile his philosophy of nature with the then-dominant Kantian and Fichtean idealist conceptions. The result was his *System of Transcendental Idealism* (of 1800). As he writes in the "Foreword" of the book: "The purpose of the present work is simply this: to enlarge transcendental idealism into what it really should be, namely a system of all possible knowledge, and thus to demonstrate the viability of such a system, not merely generally but in actual fact, through the real extension of its principles to all possible domains" of inquiry. The means employed to achieve this extension, he adds, consist "in presenting every part of philosophy in a single continuum and the whole of philosophy as what in fact it is: namely, a progressive history of self-consciousness." Undergirding the effort is Schelling's long-standing ambition to correlate and harmonize ideal and real, infinite and finite dimensions of life. "The author's chief motive," he confesses, was to demonstrate "the parallelism between nature and [higher] intelligence which he had sought for a long time and for whose depiction neither transcendental philosophy nor philosophy of nature are adequate by themselves, but only both together." Michael Vater, introducing the English translation of the text, states that the work correlates or parallels "the transcendental system [of Kant and Fichte] with a co-equal system of natural science or natural philosophy, and contemplates joining the two through a transcendental logic, a metaphysical theory of identity and difference."[18]

In its attempted linkage of transcendental and "naturalistic" perspectives, *System* is less coherent or persuasive than some of Schelling's other writings. Vater rightly describes it as a "transitional work" or an *"entr'acte"* between Schelling's earlier texts and his subsequent formulation of an "identity system" merging idealism and realism (as first outlined in his *Presentation of My System of Philosophy* of 1801). In the 1800 text, the "parallelism" of nature and intellect often seems to amount to nothing more than a juxtaposition of opposing positions. As we read in the opening paragraphs: "The essence of everything merely objective we may call '*nature*,' while the essence of everything subjective may be called 'I' or '*intelligence*.' Both concepts are mutually opposed." Philosophy hence is left with two options: "Either the objective is made primary and one asks: how can something subjective be added which coincides with it." Or else: "The subjective is made primary and the problem then becomes how something objective can be added which coincides with it." If the objective is made primary and the subjective derivative, we are in the domain of "nature-philosophy." To the extent that there is something like "transcendental philosophy," the latter has to pursue the opposite path, namely, that of "proceeding from the subjective as primary and absolute and letting the objective arise from it." A complete or comprehensive philosophy hence would consist in the parallelism of the two approaches and the effort to find their possible coincidence: "Nature-philosophy and transcendental philosophy have divided themselves into these two approaches." In the end, all philosophy is faced with the task "either to make intelligence out of nature, or else nature out of intelligence."[19]

For present purposes, the interest of the 1800 text resides mainly in those passages that seek to move beyond the subject-object split in order to explore the prior ground undergirding this division. In this respect, two themes are chiefly relevant: "intellectual intuition" and the work of art. The notion of "intellectual intuition" has its origin in the question of how intellect can know the world without objectifying both itself and the world, that is, "how the ultimate ground of the harmony between subject and object becomes accessible to intellect [spirit] itself." What one has to assume or postulate here is that intellect is capable of an "intuition" (*Anschauung*) "whereby in one and the same act it is at once conscious and unconscious for itself," that is, simultaneously active and passive. "The intuition we have postulated," Schelling elaborates, "is to bring together what exists separately in the act of freedom and the intuition of nature: namely, the identity of the conscious and the unconscious in the intellect, together with the consciousness of this identity." Accordingly, the target of this intuition "will veer on the one hand toward nature and on the other toward freedom, in order to unite in itself the character of both." What intellectual intuition shares with the act of freedom is that it is consciously enacted; what it shares with nature is that it is unconsciously produced. The two aspects have to be initially separate because otherwise consciousness would vanish; however, they cannot be infinitely separate (as in a totally free act) because then a full manifestation of identity would be impossible. Hence, there must be a point "where the two merge into one"; and conversely, where the two merge, the result can no longer be the pure result of conscious freedom. Schelling at this juncture appeals to a Leibnizian metaphor, stating that the point of merger is "nothing but that absolute Being which contains the common ground of the pre-established harmony between the conscious and the unconscious."[20]

For Schelling, the most prominent illustration and manifestation of intellectual intuition is the work of art, as seen from the angle of "aesthetic intuition." In his words: "The work of art (*Kunstwerk*) presents to us the identity of conscious and unconscious activities." Thus, "the basic character of the art work is that of an *unconscious infinity* (synthesis of nature and freedom). Apart from what he or she has put into the work with manifest intention, the artist seems instinctively, as it were, to have depicted an infinity which no finite mind is capable of fully developing." Hence, the domain where intellectual intuition manifests itself concretely is the domain of art and especially poetic art. Schelling adds that going beyond the competence of reflective philosophy, art alone is able "to accomplish the impossible: namely, to reconcile an infinite contrast in a finite product, and it is the gift of poetry which reveals in intense manner the primordial intuition." At this point, the text offers some concluding observations on the relation among philosophy, art, and poetry, observations that clear a new and profound path to the domain of nature. "Art," we read, "is the only true and eternal organon which continuously and ever anew portrays what philosophy cannot depict: the unconscious in action and its identity with the conscious." For this reason, art is "the summit for the philosopher because it opens to him, as it were, the holy of holies where, as in a single flame, burns in eternal and original union what is divided in nature and history, and what in life and action forever flies apart." In the medium of art, Schelling adds, nature itself is able to speak to us, but it does so in riddles, fables, and metaphors: "What we call nature is a poem lying secluded in a wondrous and mysterious script. If the riddle could reveal itself, we would recognize in it the odyssey of the spirit, a spirit which, strangely deluded, seeks itself and in seeking flees from itself. Thus, through the world of sense there glimmers—as does meaning through words—as through half-transparent fog the land of phantasy which we seek."[21]

Bruno and Philosophy of Art

As it appears, Schelling was quickly dissatisfied with the 1800 text, mainly because of its juxtaposition—and only loose coordination—of types of philosophy: naturalistic and transcendental. In response to this perceived shortcoming, he quickly embarked on a new and more ambitious project: the project of an identity philosophy or "identity system" in which spirit and nature, subject and object, would be more thoroughly integrated and fused. The first step in this direction was the *Presentation of My System of Philosophy* of 1801, a work written in a deductive-axiomatic style (strongly influenced by Spinoza). The highest point of union in this text is designated as "absolute spirit or reason" (*absolute Vernunft*), a spirit that is said to be neither subjective nor objective, but a synonym for the "absolute indifference" between subject and object, ideal and real dimensions of life. In formal-logical terms, the same union is expressed as "identity" and even as "identity of identity" to underscore the indissoluble connection of elements. The differences found in the real world are said to be not so much outside the original union, but contained in it as latent potentialities. The dynamic forces embryonically present in the union allow for the steady unfolding of these potentialities into a vast array of differences—but without ever canceling the original bond. The gradual development of self-consciousness, in particular, promotes the differentiation and even division between ideal and real elements in a multitude of combinations. In the words of a prominent Schelling scholar: "Absolute spirit in its potentialities involves identity in totality (or unity in multiplicity), just as each of its manifestations represents totality in concrete identity (or unity in particularity)."[22]

Due to its deductive-axiomatic style, *Presentation* appealed only to a small circle of professional philosophers, rather than the general public. In order to reach that broader audience, Schelling shortly afterward composed a more accessible text written in the form of a dialogue, titled *Bruno; or, on the Divine and Natural Principle of Things*. As he wrote to his parents, the text was meant "to provide in all brevity a clear and definitive conception of my philosophy." As the subtitle indicates, the vantage point of the text is again the basic tenet of identity philosophy, that is, the ultimate coincidence of spirit (or God) and nature, of divine and natural components of the world. This coincidence is expressed in numerous passages, but especially in the formulation that "nature is not outside of God but in God." In its style, the text is patterned on Platonic dialogues, and especially on the dialogue "Timaeus," with which Schelling had been occupied for some time. However, in contrast to Plato's separation of form-giving spirit and unformed matter, the dialogue insists on a much closer union between a matter-friendly spirit and a spiritually pregnant matter. In this respect, the substance of the dialogue follows more closely in the footsteps of Spinoza, while also embracing some of the pantheistic ideas of the Italian Renaissance philosopher Giordano Bruno (as expressed especially in the latter's "De la Causa, Principio e Uno," which Schelling had studied). To quote again the scholar mentioned before,

Schelling quickly perceived the "affinity" between his work and some of Bruno's ideas: "Influenced by pre-Socratic philosophy of nature, by Plotinus's doctrine of emanation, and the *docta ignorantia* of Nikolaus Cusanus with its principle of *'coincidentia oppositorum,'* Bruno saw matter not as formless stuff, but as a living, intelligible substance which produces all forms in successive evolution. In this manner, the unity of the divine and natural principles is guaranteed."[23]

The dialogue is actually a conversation among four main participants representing different philosophical perspectives. The character called "Alexander" articulates a kind of speculative materialism and pantheistic naturalism that, in many ways, resembles the views of the historical (and preidealist) Giordano Bruno. The character "Anselmo" defends a speculative intellectualism and transcendentalism familiar from Plato's theory of "ideas," from neo-Platonic teachings, and in part from Leibniz's "monadology." The character "Lucian" is basically a stand-in for Fichte's critical-rationalist philosophy, while the character "Bruno" shoulders the task of formulating Schelling's own "identity system," or realist-idealist philosophy. The most interesting part of the dialogue is the debate between Lucian and Bruno, between a critical rationalism anchored in ego-consciousness and an identity philosophy moving beyond the subject-object bifurcation. On many occasions in the dialogue, Lucian challenges Bruno's alleged precritical pantheism and his insufficient attention to the constitutive function of human consciousness (a challenge repeating almost verbatim Fichte's actual attacks on Schelling). In his defense, Bruno acknowledges the undeniable role of consciousness, yet assigns to the latter not a constitutive or a priori status, but only a derivative function in a complex evolutionary process. The basic stages in this evolutionary process are familiar from Schelling's earlier writings. In the dialogue, the process leads broadly from the original union to the formation of the heavenly bodies and the constitution of space and time; from there the sequence moves to the formation of inorganic matter, the evolution of organic nature, and finally to the emergence of human consciousness and the human soul. In Bruno's words: "But inasmuch as a soul has the character of the intrinsically infinite, while the body is finite (though infinitely finite, and capable of representing the universe), the individual temporal being reveals the mystery hidden away in God—the absolute identity of the infinite, which is prototype, with the infinitely finite, which is the copy."[24]

In its conclusion, the dialogue offers perhaps the most eloquent and captivating expression of Bruno's (and Schelling's) worldview. To discover the original union or indifference, we read, means "to come to know the absolute center of gravity and, as it were, the original metal of truth, the prime ingredient in the alloys of all particular truths." To be sure, the discovery of this center is difficult, and there are many ways of straying from the proper path (ways represented by some of the competing perspectives in the dialogue). "To penetrate into the deepest secrets of nature," Bruno states (paraphrasing his historical forebear), "one must not tire to explore the opposed and extreme polar end points of things: the greatest challenge is not to find the point of union but rather to develop out of this union its opposite elements; this is the genuine and deepest secret of art." Elaborating on this comment, Bruno-Schelling outlines the strategy of his own mode of philosophizing. Following this strategy, he notes, "we shall first discern in the absolute identity of matter and form the way both the finite and the infinite spring forth from its womb, the one necessarily in and with the other." Next, we shall grasp "how that simple ray of light that shines forth from the absolute appears divided into difference and indifference, into finite and infinite dimensions." Finally—and here the language becomes panegyric—"we shall, pursuing this path, reach the point where absolute identity appears divided into two strands, and we shall recognize in the one the origin of the real or natural world, and in the other that of the ideal or divine world. Within the first world, we shall celebrate the eternal incarnation of God (*Menschwerdung Gottes*); in the second the inevitable divinization of humankind (*Gottwerdung des Menschen*)." In this manner we shall in the end perceive "nature within God and God in nature."[25]

As in the earlier *System of Transcendental Idealism*, the celebration of original union is linked in the dialogue with the praise of art, seen as the manifestation of infinite truth in finite form. As we read in a passage articulated by Anselmo: "Just as truth without beauty cannot be truth, so also beauty without truth cannot be beauty"; and just as there is unity of truth and beauty, so also "there is unity between philosophy and poetry."[26] In the fall of 1802, Schelling started a series of lectures in Jena on the topic of aesthetics and art, lectures that were subsequently fleshed out and amplified in many ways and finally co-alesced into his *Philosophy of Art* (only posthumously published). Building on his preceding writings, the text inserts art into the context of identity philosophy, locating it on one of its highest levels. Reaffirming as the core of identity the absolute spirit (or God), the book starts out with a series of lapidary maxims, of which the following seem most important. "The absolute or God," we read, "is that with regard to which being or reality follows immediately from the idea, that is, by virtue of the simple law of identity." Differently put: "God is the immediate affirmation of himself." From this follows, with regard to the reality of nature: "The infinite self-affirmation of God in the cosmos, or the imprint of his infinite reality as such, is what we call eternal nature." On this level, one can distinguish between the actual appearance of nature, that is, *natura naturata,* seen as the mere copy or reflection of the cosmos, and "nature as such" (*naturans*), which is "dissolved into the absolute and hence is God in his infinite self-affirmation." Going beyond the mere juxtaposition of ideal and actual or real dimensions, it is possible to find a point of mediation and indifference that is precisely that of art: "The indifference of the ideal and the real *as* indifference manifests itself on the ideal level as art."[27]

Reiterating a comment in *Bruno* and firmly adopting a Platonic (or Neoplatonic) stance, Schelling insists on the convergence of truth, goodness, and beauty, seen as the three coequal dimensions of the absolute. Elaborating on the meaning of beauty—on the level of both natural and artistic beauty—he states that it is found everywhere "where light and matter, ideal and real are linked." Beauty in this sense is neither the merely cognitively universal (or truth) nor the practically real; rather, it involves "the complete interpenetration and union of both." Differently phrased: beauty is found "where the particular real is so commensurate with its ideal concept that the latter, though infinite, enters into the finite and is perceived *in concreto.*" What should not be forgotten at this point is that, behind some very traditional formulations, there lurks an idea that as such cannot be found in Platonic (or Neoplatonic) teachings, namely, the coincidence of the ideal and the real, the absolute spirit and nature. Deriving basically from Spinoza and Leibniz, this idea transgresses ancient cosmology, as well as a trancendentalist idealism, thus paving the way to a recovery of nature in the context of modern philosophy. To conclude with a passage from Schelling's text that points beyond both natural and artistic beauty: "The entire universe is formed in God as an absolute work of art, in eternal beauty."[28]

3

Nature and Sentiment

Romanticism

"We *seek* the absolute everywhere and only ever *find* [finite] things."
This statement was penned by Friedrich von Hardenberg, known as
Novalis, in 1797 in his *Miscellaneous Observations*.[1] In terse language,
the statement pinpointed in uncannily lucid form the central tenet
of an intellectual trend emerging at that time, called the "Romantic
movement." As one will note, the phrase does not in any way reject
the notion of the "absolute" so prominent in German idealist philosophy, from Fichte to Schelling and Hegel. Rather, it foregrounds an
aspect that was deemphasized by idealism (though foreshadowed in
Kant's stipulation of the limits of reason): the aspect of a certain tension between human mind and the absolute, a tension rendering the
absolute a target not so much of cognition as of longing or fervent
yearning.[2] With this changed accent, a tradition of reflection reen-
tered European thought that had been entirely shunned by mainline
Enlightenment philosophy: the legacy of Neoplatonism, of Böhme,
Nikolaus of Cusa, and Giordano Bruno. The reemergence of this legacy introduced a dynamic imbalance into idealist philosophy, by moving the focus from the "originary union" of spirit to its dispersal into
discordant elements—though without canceling union as a distant vision. The same shift also involved the valorization of sentiment vis-à-
vis pure reason—where "sentiment" does not denote sentimentalism,
but rather inner sensibility and creative engagement.

This does not mean that philosophy, especially idealist philosophy, and Romanticism were at loggerheads. On the contrary, at least
during the early phase of the movement, philosophy and Romantic
sentiment were closely linked. Most of the early Romantics wrote
philosophical treatises (or at least fragments) as well as novels and po-

etry. On the other hand, several idealist philosophers—most notably Schelling—insisted on the intimate connection between systematic philosophical inquiry and poetic imagination (note Schelling's ability to write in quick succession the dialogue *Bruno* and his *System of Transcendental Idealism*).[3] It was only during later stages of the movement that the symbiosis between classical idealism and Romantic sentiment became strained and tended to dissolve. Several factors accounted for this strain: the fading memory of the French Revolution, the Napoleonic wars, the political "Restoration" after 1815, and (last but not least) the Industrial Revolution and its social repercussions. As a result of this battery of factors, the idealist union of spirit and nature, subject and object, progressively gave way in Romantic literature to subjectivism and inward retreat. In the following I shall concentrate on those phases of Romanticism when sentiment still paid tribute to idealist thought and also to the linkage of art and nature. Without trying to offer a comprehensive survey, I first discuss high points of the movement in Germany, then proceed to parallel developments in England, in order finally to explore its offshoots in America, especially among so-called transcendentalist writers. If nothing else, the sequence of settings should disclose the unity in diversity that itself is a major legacy of both idealist philosophy and Romantic poetry.

Early German Romanticism

The phrase "early German Romanticism" usually refers to the period between 1794 and 1808 and a group of thinker-poets centered in Jena and Berlin including the Schlegel brothers (Friedrich and August Wilhelm), Caroline Schlegel Schelling, Friedrich von Hardenberg (Novalis), Ludwig Tieck, Wilhelm Wackenroder, and to some extent Friedrich Hölderlin.[4] In Germany, the Romantic movement had been preceded by the earlier period of "Storm and Stress" (*Sturm und Drang*) represented by such thinkers as Johann Georg Hamann and Johann Gottfried Herder. By and large, the dividing line between the two movements was the publication of Kant's critical treatises. While "Storm and Stress" figures wrote on the eve of and mainly in opposition to these treatises, Romanticism arose in their aftermath and sought not so much to counter as to build on, deepen, and transform Kantian (and Fichtean) initiatives.[5] This was particularly true of German Romanticism. The early circle was a gathering of idealist philosophers and artist-poets who, with different emphases, shared many common aspirations and convictions. A prominent example was Friedrich Schelling, who, though chiefly an idealist philosopher, greatly influenced and was in turn influenced by other members of that circle. For present purposes, I select a limited number of poet-writers who exemplify this confluence; given the primary focus of these pages, the accent will be not on their overall worldview, but on their attitude toward nature.

Among early German Romantics, pride of place is usually accorded to Friedrich Schlegel (1772–1829), the close friend and sometimes antagonist of Schelling. As befits a Romantic thinker, Schlegel had a somewhat turbulent career and went through several, sharply contrasted intellectual phases. During his earliest period he was greatly attracted to classical idealism and especially to the prevalent Weimar "classicism" with its predilection for Greek and Roman culture and art. During his second phase (1796–1808) he was an active member of the Romantic circles in Jena and Berlin and articulated some of the pioneering statements on Romantic art and poetry. His later period, spent mostly in Vienna, was marked by a pronounced shift toward religion and political conservatism. In the present context, the middle period is most relevant, especially as it emerged from the previous "classical" phase. During that earlier phase, Schlegel's outlook bore the imprint not only of Weimar classicism but also of Kant's conception of historical progress and enlightenment—although this conception was tempered from the beginning by borrowings from Herder as well as Rousseau.[6] Together with Kant (and Rousseau), he distinguished between a "natural" social condition or "natural" civilization, on the one hand, and an "artificial" or rationally constructed civilization, on the other. In the natural condition, human life was still embedded in a harmonious cosmos and guided by unspoiled, prereflective inclinations and motivations. In the artificial condition, by contrast, the rise of reflection and individual competitiveness puts an end to natural harmony and replaces it with the conflicts or diremptions between instinct and intellect, reason and imagination, self and other. The issue that remained open at this point was whether the diremptions created by artifacts could be overcome and reconciled at another, still higher stage of development where reason and imagination, nature and civility would finally be joined—pretty much in the way this prospect had been intimated by Rousseau and spelled out more clearly in Schelling's *First Outline*.

In a way, Schlegel's move to Jena and later Berlin signaled his breakthrough to intellectual independence—a breakthrough greatly facilitated by his close affiliation with the early Romantic circle. An immediate manifestation of the change was the turn from historical narratives to more spontaneous literary outpourings, preferably captured in aphorisms and fragments. A first collection of such aphorisms appeared in a journal called *Lyceum* (edited by C. F. Reichhardt). One of the opening fragments in that journal clearly pinpoints Schlegel's shift from a classical to a "Romantic" style. "My [early] essay on the study of Greek poetry," we read there, "is a mannered prose hymn to the 'objective' quality in poetry. The worst thing about it, it seems to me, is the complete lack of necessary irony" (that is, a critical distance to poetic perfection). In subsequent fragments, wit or irony is defined as "absolute social feeling or fragmentary genius"—with the addendum that, in poetry, "every whole can be a part and every part really a whole." Judged by the standards of fragmentary genius or imagination, "all the classical poetical genres have now become ridiculous in their rigid purity." An important ingredient of Schlegel's turn or shift is the deprecation of philosophical "knowledge" in favor of aspiration and yearning. As we read: "Whoever desires the infinite does not *know* what he desires. . . . One can love something deeply precisely because one does not possess it." Unfortunately, however, "there are writers who drink the absolute like water, and books in which even dogs refer to the infinite." Together with the retreat of absolute knowledge, nature too is placed in quotation marks and seen as the target of imagination and sensibility: "Spirit is 'natural' philosophy," while "a poem is only a product of 'nature' which wants to become a work of art."[7]

Following his move to Berlin, Schlegel began to publish with his brother August Wilhelm a journal named *Athenaeum*. That journal became a rich reservoir for the collection of Romantic fragments and aphoristic observations. Friedrich's contributions to the journal can be read as a kind of Romantic manifesto. Most famous in this respect is Fragment 116, which states:

> Romantic poetry is a progressive, universal poetry. Its aim is
> not merely to reunite all the separate species of poetry and
> put poetry in touch with philosophy and rhetoric. It tries to
> and should mix and fuse poetry and prose, inspiration and
> criticism, the poetry of art and the poetry of nature. . . . Ro-
> mantic poetry is in the arts what wit is in philosophy, and what
> society and sociability, friendship and love are in life. Other
> kinds of poetry are finished and are now capable of being fully
> analyzed. The Romantic kind of poetry is still in the state of
> becoming; that, in fact, is its real essence: that it should forev-
> er be *becoming* and never be perfected. . . . It alone is infinite,
> just as it alone is free; and it recognizes as its first command-
> ment that the will of the poet can tolerate no law above itself.

Although affirming the affinity between philosophy and poetry, Schlegel's statements clearly subordinate philosophical reflection to poetry,
or accept philosophy only to the extent that it embraces Romantic
nonperfection. The poet, Schlegel writes at another point, "can learn
little from the philosopher, but the philosopher much from the poet."
A precondition of symbiosis, however, is the relinquishment of absolute philosophical cognition: "One can only *become* a philosopher, not
be one. As soon as one thinks one *is* a philosopher, one stops becoming one." The problem is that, so far, "philosophy is still moving too
much in a straight line and is not yet cyclical enough." In order to
break away from rational linearity, one thing is required: "Intellectual
intuition is the categorical imperative of any theory."[8]

The fragments collected in the journal are full of disdain for linear
philosophers—and full of praise for thinker-poets displaying spiritual
élan and a yearning for the infinite. The former type includes Kant
and even Schelling. "Duty," we read, "is Kant's alpha and omega,"
and "only out of a sense of duty did he become a great man." By
the same token, Schelling's philosophy might be termed a "criticized
mysticism" that ends "in earthquake and ruins." Curiously, despite
this criticism, Schlegel embraces some of Schelling's philosophical
mentors: above all Spinoza and (to a lesser degree) Leibniz. "Every
philosophy of philosophy," he asserts, "that excludes Spinoza must be
spurious." Although demonstrating "how far one can get with philosophy and morality unaided by poetry," Spinoza all the while insists on

not "isolating poetry" from the spirit of his system. While Leibniz was generally a practitioner of "scholastic prose," his work also consists of some "fragments and projects that are witty [that is, spirited]" in the proper (Romantic) sense. What matters most are the inner, creative spirit and the unstinting commitment to the pursuit of infinite ends. "A transcendental perspective on life still awaits us," we are told; "only then will it become really meaningful for us." In the same vein one might say that "someone for whom the inner divine service is the end and occupation of life is a priest" and that "this is how everyone can and should become a priest." As Schlegel affirms in his last *Athenaeum* fragment: "The life of the 'universal spirit' is an unbroken chain of inner revolutions; all individuals—that is, all original and creative ones—live in him." To this might be added a phrase from his novel *Lucinde:* "Only in yearning (*Sehnsucht*) do we find rest."[9]

The notion of yearning or infinite longing immediately brings into view the life-work of another prominent early Romanticist: Friedrich von Hardenberg, or Novalis (1772–1801), a participant in the Jena circle around Schlegel. Among the members of that circle, Novalis was perhaps most deeply imbued with the spirit of Neoplatonic mysticism—a legacy he somehow managed to combine with Spinoza's "pantheism" as well as Fichte's accent on creative inwardness. In the words of one scholar: "Belief in spirituality, the conviction of human distinctness as against the animal and inanimate world, is the grounding axiom of Novalis's thought. . . . The realm of spirit, the repository of truth, is conceived as the end of all philosophical and creative thought."[10] In line with Schlegel's "manifesto," Novalis was firmly committed to the Romantic agenda, stating at one point that "making absolute, making universal," while respecting the particular, is "the authentic essence of *making Romantic.*" Together with Schlegel, he shared a preference for aphorisms and fragments and also the emphasis on the incompleteness of philosophy and its relative subordination to poetry. As we read in one of his later fragments: "The idea of philosophy is a mysterious tradition"—and since all learning is a progression, "philosophy will never be complete." On the other hand, poetry is "representation of the mind, of the *inner world* in its entirety"; in fact, the poet is "truly bereft of his senses: everything takes place within him." From this inward turn comes "the infinity of a good poem, eternity"—which is closely related to "the sense of prophecy

and the religious, the seer's sense itself." Like Schlegel again, Novalis expressed great admiration for Spinoza's outlook, seen not as a
godless naturalism but as a gateway to spiritualism: "Spinozism is a
supersaturation with the divine; unbelief is a lack of divine sense and
of the divine."[11]

By comparison with Schlegel, Novalis was more willing to elaborate on a Romantic conception of "nature"—where the latter appears
like an embryonic antechamber foreshadowing the progressive unfolding of spirit. As he writes plainly in one of his "logological fragments": "What is nature? An encyclopedic index or plan of our spirit."
This plan has to be cultivated and developed—something that was entirely forgotten in modern science, where nature came to be seen as
purely physical or mechanical. "The modern view of the *appearances*
of nature," he adds, "was either chemical or mechanical"; but the genuine scholar of physics "considers nature as at once independent and
self-modifying, and as harmoniously at one with the spirit." It is the
task of both the scientist and the "higher" philosopher to forge a path
of progression leading to "the marriage of nature and spirit"—a path
in which spirit has the guiding role. From this insight follow the tenets
that God ultimately is "the goal of nature," or differently phrased:
that nature "is to become moral" and that "we are its *teachers,* its
moral stimuli." His later fragments insist even more pointedly on the
issue of progression. "Plants, animals, stars, human beings," we read
there, "are already assembled products of nature"; but nature itself
is "a church of infinite natures." Rigorously and relentlessly pursued,
the path of progression leads to the spiritualization and eventual eva-
nescence of nature. As Novalis stipulates, the first and last chapters of
physics belong to the spiritual realm: "Nature cannot be explained as
static; it can only be explained as *progressing*—toward morality. One
day there will be no nature anymore: it will gradually turn into a spirit
world."[12]

Another thinker-poet linked with the early Romantic circle—but
in a more loose and episodic way—was Friedrich Hölderlin (1770–
1843), a friend of both Schelling and Hegel from his student days
in Tübingen. Given his affiliation with the circle, one can assume a
certain convergence of intellectual perspectives. Like other members
of the circle, Hölderlin was exposed to the powerful impact of Enlightenment philosophy and especially of Kant's and Fiche's idealist

systems; like others, he sought to extricate himself from an arid rationalism or abstract conceptualism by turning to art and poetry. Beyond
this point, however, paths diverged. By contrast to certain extreme
Neoplatonic tendencies in the circle, Hölderlin was not willing to
surrender nature entirely to spirit or experience to inner subjectivity.
Moving along lines paralleling those of Schelling, he sought precisely
to overcome the modern diremptions of spirit and matter, subject and
object—an effort that led him in the direction of the "originary (or
primordial) union" undergirding reflective dichotomies, a dimension
he preferred to call "Being" (*Seyn*). As one should note, however,
Hölderlin's notion of "Being" did not at all involve a conceptual philosophical synthesis (in a Fichtean or Hegelian vein), but rather pointed
to a precognitive dimension amenable only to "intellectual intuition"
in the sense of recollection or memory work. In the words of the
Hölderlin-scholar Thomas Pfau: "Hölderlin challenges the possibility of ever [cognitively] determining the primordial ground of Being"
since the latter is seen "to precede any synthetic unity to which cognitive reflexivity remains confined." Accordingly, his assessment of a
primordial ground has the character of "an analeptic (quasi-Platonic)
anamnesis," which poses "a serious challenge to the possibility of an
integral subjectivity, that is, to the continuity of a 'self' as such."[13]

Pfau's comments refer particularly to one of Hölderlin's early essays or fragments titled "Judgment and Being" (*Urtheil und Seyn*, of
1795). In this essay, Hölderlin is first of all intent on elucidating his
terms. "Judgment" here means basically the exercise of critical rationality, an exercise that cannot avoid partitioning (*teilen*) or separating
related elements, such as reason and imagination, spirit and nature,
self and other. In his words: "*Judgment*, in the highest and strictest
sense, is the original separation of object and subject which are most
deeply united in intellectual intuition—a separation through which
alone object and subject become possible, the *arche*-separation." Yet
separation can only divide what is somehow related or linked; hence,
it already implies "the concept of the reciprocity of object and subject
and the presupposition of a whole of which object and subject form
parts." This leads to the notion of "Being," which expresses "the connection between subject and object" where both are firmly joined,
that is, "united in such a manner that no separation can be performed
without violating the essence of what is to be separated." What needs

to be noted, again, is that the union intimated here is not a conceptual synthesis and "must not be confused with identity"; hence, "identity is not equal to absolute Being." What comes into view here is a notion of Being that coincides neither with conceptual synthesis nor with divisiveness, but carries the sense of a unity in diversity or a nondivisive "difference" (such as has been articulated by some recent "postmodern" thinkers).[14]

The differentiated unity or linkage marking "Being" vis-à-vis "Judgment" carries over into Hölderlin's view of the relation between nature and art. In many ways, "nature" here resembles the amorphous, not yet conceptually streamlined entelechy of "Being" (a domain sometimes designated by Hölderlin as *aorgisch*), while "art" designates a constructive form-giving effort (sometimes designated as *organisch*). The tensional relation between nature and art constitutes the central theme of the tragic poem "Empedocles"—as Hölderlin explains in a text penned a few years later (1799). "In pure life," we read there, "nature and art are only opposed harmoniously. Art is the blossom, the perfection of nature; nature only becomes divine in conjunction with the differentiated yet harmonious art." When everything is as it should be and "one combines with the other," then "there exists perfection, and the divine rests between the two." Yet, Hölderlin cautions, this perfection exists "only in sentiment" and not on the level of rational knowledge. For when rational reflection takes over, a split arises: on the one hand, reason generates "an excess of inwardness," while nature descends into "the extreme of the 'aorgic,' the incomprehensible, the unlimited"—until through the progression of reciprocal effects nature and art "meet again as in the beginning," though on a new level. The dramatic relation is illustrated or exemplified in the figure of Empedocles, "a son of tremendous oppositions of nature and art." In the tragic poem, the tension is exacerbated to the breaking point, but not without preserving hope for reconciliation. In Hölderlin's words: "The more powerful the destiny, the more art and nature are opposites, the more it is their potential to individualize themselves, to gain a foothold—and this situation seizes all participants, challenges them until something is found where their unknown need and their secret tendency manifests itself visibly—from which point forward the yearned-for solution must transcend into the universal."[15]

English Romanticism

The idea of a nature-spirit symbiosis, coupled with a pronounced inward turn, can also be found in a parallel movement that emerged in England at the same time—and partly under German influence. The leading representatives of early English Romanticism are William Wordsworth (1770–1850) and Samuel Taylor Coleridge (1772–1834). Like many of their contemporaries, the two poet-writers underwent the strong impact of developments on the European Continent, including the revolutionary events in France and the upsurge of philosophical and literary idealism in Germany. Caught up in the revolutionary fervor, Wordsworth in 1791 visited France to experience directly the turbulent scenery—although the ensuing "reign of terror" quickly dampened his revolutionary sympathies. A few years later, the two poets met and immediately formed a close bond of friendship; they also began to live in close proximity, in two adjoining villages or hamlets in northwest England (the so-called Lake District). During 1798, the two collaborated in publishing a joint volume of poetry, called *Lyrical Ballads,* which is commonly considered to be the starting point of the English Romantic movement. During the fall of the same year, Wordsworth and Coleridge (joined by the former's sister) took an extensive tour of Germany, visiting some of the famous hubs of idealist philosophy and Romantic German poetry. Having studied the language before, Coleridge actually translated some German poetry into English (including Friedrich Schiller's dramatic trilogy "Wallenstein").

For present purposes, what is of primary significance is the volume *Lyrical Ballads,* for which Wordsworth (in unison with Coleridge) wrote a famous "Preface" that is often called the "manifesto" of English Romanticism. In his "Preface," Wordsworth clearly demarcates the emerging Romantic poetry from earlier, more heavily stylized forms of literature. What is said to be innovative and even revolutionary in the emerging genre is the emphasis on human "sentiment" and the "real language of men"—a sentiment available to ordinary human beings and not only to literary or intellectual elites. "The principal object," he writes, "which I proposed to myself in these poems was to choose incidents and situations from common life, and to relate or describe them throughout, as far as was possible, in a selection of language really used by men," while at the same time giving them "a certain coloring of imagination." By choosing as their topic ordinary human situations and experiences, poems, in Wordsworth's view, are able to get in touch with an unspoiled or "natural" way of life, in opposition to the artificial and stratified customs of the past. "Low and rustic life was generally chosen," he adds, "because in that condition the essential passions of the heart find a better soil in which they can attain their maturity" and because in that state "the passions of men are incorporated with the beautiful and permanent forms of nature." People living in rustic surroundings, we are told, are unaffected by the pomp and pretense of polite society and, "being less under the influence of social vanity," are able to "convey their feelings and notions in simple and unelaborated expressions." This stands in stark contrast to the ornate and stilted language of some poets "who think that they are conferring honor upon themselves and their art in proportion as they separate themselves from the sympathies of men and indulge in arbitrary and capricious habits of expression."[16]

As can be seen, poetry for Wordsworth is able to gain access to "nature" by concentrating on, and giving expression to, unspoiled human sentiments. As he writes in a famous passage: "Poetry is the spontaneous overflow of powerful feelings; it takes its origin from emotion recollected in tranquility." This does not mean that the expression of feeling is completely devoid of thought or reflection; but the latter derives from the former, not the other way around. Nor does it mean that poetic expression is purely personal or idiosyncratic; rather, expression discloses something general. Agreeing with Aristotle, he states that "poetry is the most philosophic of all writing" because "its object is truth, not individual and local, but general and objective"—which means that poetry discloses the truth of humanity and, beyond that, the truth of the universe. Here is Wordsworth's lapidary statement: "Poetry is the image of man and nature." Proceeding from this insight, the "Preface" develops in bold strokes the notion of a basic synergy or parallelism between nature and humanity (closely reminiscent of Schelling and Schlegel). Poetry, we read, "considers man and nature as essentially adapted to each other, and the mind of man as naturally the mirror of the fairest and most interesting qualities of nature." Prompted by feelings of sympathy or synergy, poetry "converses with general nature with affections akin to those which, through labor and length of time, the man of science has raised up himself." In order to accomplish their task, poets have to feel all the sentiments of ordinary people, but at the same time have the special gift of expressing them with imaginative power. "What is a poet? To whom does he address himself?" Wordsworth asks finally and answers:

> He is a man speaking to men: a man, it is true, endowed with more lively sensibility, more enthusiasm and tenderness; who has a greater knowledge of human nature, and a more comprehensive soul than are supposed to be common among mankind; a man pleased with his own passions and volitions, and who rejoices more than other men in the spirit of life that is in him; delighting to contemplate similar volitions and passions as manifested in the goings-on of the universe, and habitually impelled to create them where he does not find them.[17]

As previously indicated, Wordsworth's "Preface" to *Lyrical Ballads* reflected—or was meant to reflect—both his own and Coleridge's views. At the time of the writing, the assumption of such a convergence appeared more or less correct—although a simmering dissonance emerged soon enough. For one thing, *Lyrical Ballads* contained mostly poems written by Wordsworth, while relegating Coleridge's contributions to a minor role—an arrangement not conducive to stabilizing friendship. In subsequent years, Coleridge's reservations regarding *Lyrical Ballads* were steadily deepened by the growing alienation between the two former friends and, more important, by Coleridge's recurring bouts with serious illness. As a result of these developments, Coleridge conceived the idea of writing a sequel or rather a counterpiece to Wordsworth's "Preface," a piece that would set forth in detail his own views regarding the meaning of Romantic poetry and of poetry in general. Due to unfavorable circumstances, the execution of this idea proved to be onerous and time-consuming, and it was not until 1815 that the projected work finally appeared under the title *Biographia Literaria*. The text, as it stands, comprising two volumes and twenty-two chapters, is obviously much more than a mere sequel to Wordsworth's essay, but aims to provide a general theory of poetry and literature, relying for this purpose on both literary and philosophical sources. In comparison with his friend's essay, *Biographia Literaria* shifts the accent to a more "transcendental" and transformative (perhaps Neoplatonic) plane and away from the replication of "ordinary" sentiments of "rustic" people. Reflecting on Coleridge's earlier association with Wordsworth, the text distinguishes between two basic types of poetry. In one type, topics are "chosen from ordinary life," and the characters and incidents are such "as will be found in every village and its vicinity." In the other type, clearly preferred by Coleridge, "the incidents and agents [are] to be, in part at least, supernatural, and the excellence aimed at consists in the interesting of the affections by the dramatic truth of such emotions."[18]

Apart from its transcendentalist leanings, a distinguishing feature of *Biographia Literaria* is its eminent erudition, evident in its extensive invocation of ancient and modern philosophers and especially of the teachings of German idealist writers. Among modern philosophers, the text pays attention first to Descartes's rigid dualism of mind and matter, finding the opposition basically untenable. Once the defect of dualism is recognized, the "essence of matter" is seen to be "an act of power which it possesses in common with spirit," with the result that "body and spirit are no longer absolutely heterogeneous, but may without absurdity be supposed to be different modes, or degrees of perfection, of a common substratum." Initial attempts to dislodge dualism were undertaken by Spinoza and Leibniz, but without lasting effect. More resolute efforts in the same direction were made by Giordano Bruno, Jakob Boehme, and all the followers of Neoplatonism (or the *"theologia Platonica"*) whose writings had of late attracted new attention. "The writings of these mystics," Coleridge notes, "acted in no slight degree to prevent my mind from being imprisoned within the outline of any single dogmatic system" and "contributed to keep alive the *heart* in the *head*." The culmination of these developments came with German critical-idealist philosophy and especially with "the illustrious sage of Königsberg," whose work "took possession of me as with a giant's hand," and which, "after fifteen years of familiarity, I still read with undiminished delight and increasing admiration." Transformed in a quasi-dualistic manner by Fichte, the inner truth of Kant finally bore fruit in Schelling's "nature philosophy" and his *System of Transcendental Idealism,* where—Coleridge adds—"I first found a congenial coincidence with much that I had toiled out for myself, and a powerful assistance in what I had yet to do."[19]

The reference to Schelling's "nature philosophy" brings into view Coleridge's own conception of nature and its relation to poetry, literature, and spirit. Over long stretches, *Biographia Literaria* offers a detailed exegesis of Schelling's early writings and especially his *System of Transcendental Idealism.* Unfortunately, the exegesis does not always reach up to the German thinker's deeper insights (and often falls short of Coleridge's own initial antidualist observations). Basically, the exegesis accentuates Schelling's spiritual-idealist leanings, while side-stepping or slighting his notion of "primordial union"; as a result, "nature" for Coleridge comes to signify at best a prelude or backdrop to the unfolding of human self-consciousness and spiritual inwardness. Thus, while starting out from a critique of Cartesianism, the poet ultimately settles for a neat bifurcation of "knowing" and "being," or of the *"ratio cognoscendi"* and *"ratio essendi."* This argument is developed mainly in a section titled "Requests and Premonitions," where we read initially that "all knowledge rests on the coincidence of an object with a subject"—only to be told a bit later that "the sum of all that is merely objective we will henceforth call *nature,* confining the term to its passive and material sense. . . . On the other hand, the sum of all that is *subjective* we may comprehend in the name of the *self* or intelligence." Proceeding from this premise, the text develops a number of "theses" of which the following are most relevant: first, that "absolute truth" cannot be a "thing or object," but must be found "in that which is neither subject nor object exclusively but is the identity of both"; second, that this coincidence is found in the *"Sum* or I am," which "I shall indiscriminately express by the words spirit, self, and self-consciousness"; and finally, that truth can be found "only in the act and evolution of self-consciousness," at a point where "we are not investigating an absolute *principium essendi,"* but "an absolute *principium cognoscendi."*[20]

New England Transcendentalism

From Germany and England Romanticism in due course made its way to America—notwithstanding the country's determination to extricate itself from European entanglements. Given the remoteness and democratic tenor of the "New World," American Romanticism was bound to take on novel and distinctive features—without rupturing the linkage with its European counterparts. On the surface, American pragmatic inclinations, dictated in part by the needs of an untamed continent, seemed likely to provide a more congenial soil to Wordsworthian "naturalism"—his stress on unspoiled, ordinary life— as compared with deeper philosophical ruminations. Yet this is only part of the story. Among leading American authors, concern with philosophical motivations was in fact intense. Above all, Romanticism's predilection for spiritual and often Neoplatonic leanings surprisingly found a home in the rougher American context, where it tended to clash with efforts to subdue the vast wilderness. This spiritual-idealist predilection found prominent expression in the very name or self-description chosen by New England authors: "transcendentalism" or "transcendentalist movement." As one should note, "transcendentalism" here did not (or not necessarily) refer to transcendental or a priori principles in the Kantian sense (although this reference was not lacking); basically the term stood as a protective shield against the perils of brute empiricism or materialism. To this extent, couched in a more accessible idiom, Schelling's and Coleridge's "transcendental idealism" resurfaced on American shores.[21]

Among American authors, Ralph Waldo Emerson (1803–1882) is usually recognized as the leading representative, if not the original founder, of the "transcendentalist movement." Educated at Harvard College and initially serving as a Unitarian minister, Emerson soon underwent the profound impact of various European trends, including Neoplatonism, Kantian idealism, and German and English Romantic literature. In late 1832, he left America for an extensive tour of Europe, where he made the acquaintance of such prominent literary figures as Wordsworth, Coleridge, Thomas Carlyle, and John Stuart Mill. On his return he settled in Concord, Massachusetts, and became active as a lecturer in the Boston area. During this time, in connection with his lecturing obligations, Emerson devoted himself to the serious study of philosophical and religious texts, immersing himself with particular fondness in Hindu and Buddhist sacred scriptures. His studies increasingly alienated him from the rigid qualities of Unitarian orthodoxy and convinced him of the need to develop a more intimate and personal relation with the divine. In 1836, on the occasion of the bicentennial celebration of Harvard College, a number of kindred spirits assembled in Boston and decided to continue their discussions subsequently in regular meetings at private homes. Initially referred to as "the Symposium" or else "Hedge Club" (after Frederic Henry Hedge), the gatherings eventually came to be known as "the Transcendental Club." One of the first prominent writings giving voice to the group's perspective was penned by Emerson and published in the same year (1836) under the title "Nature."

The text is justly acclaimed as one of Emerson's literary masterpieces. In bold strokes and with profound insight, "Nature" introduces the reader to the deeper aspirations and intellectual vision of the transcendentalist movement. At the same time—and with particular significance in the present context—it offers a vivid account of the transcendentalist view of nature and the cosmos, an account hardly matched elsewhere in Romantic literature. Like Wordsworth's "Preface," Emerson's text starts with a call for new beginnings and an emancipation from the past. "Our age is retrospective," he complains. "It builds the sepulchers of the fathers." While previous generations "beheld God and nature face to face," at present one only finds repetition of past formulas. But "why should not we also enjoy an original relation to the universe? Why should not we have a poetry and philosophy of insight, and not of tradition, and a religion by revelation to *us,* and not the history of theirs?" To make a new beginning, for Emerson, a primary need is for the living generation to open its own eyes and to behold the wonders of nature and the cosmos: "Embosomed for a season in nature, whose floods of life stream around and through us, and invite us by the powers they supply to action proportioned to nature, why should we grope among the dry bones of the past?" The opportunity for a fresh experience was there and only waiting for human hearts and minds to seize it. For "the sun shines today also. . . . There are new lands, new men, new thoughts. Let us demand our own works and laws and worship." To give meaning to the fresh experience, of course, there was a need for new interpretation, for a fresh reading of the "book of nature," which is not hidden or concealed. In Emerson's words, "nature is already, in its forms and tendencies, describing its own design. [Hence] let us interrogate the great apparition that shines so peacefully around us. Let us inquire: to what end is nature?"[22]

As it happens, Emerson's inquiry or interrogation starts somewhat lopsidedly: namely, from the assumption of a certain dualism that the remainder of his text is at pains to correct or overcome. Taking a leaf from some idealist teachings, the text asserts that "philosophically considered, the universe is composed of Nature and the Soul." This means that, strictly speaking, "all that is separate from us, all which philosophy distinguishes as NOT ME, that is, both nature and art, all other men and my own body, must be raked under this term, NATURE." Stated differently, "nature" refers to "essences unchanged by man," such as space, the air, the river; although art involves the admixture of human will to these essences, human operations taken together remain comparatively "insignificant." In the following pages, this "philosophical" or cognitive view is quickly replaced by a more "poetic" and inward view of nature. By a poetic view, Emerson means the "integrity of impressions" made by nature on sensitive and creative beings, especially poets; for the person "whose eye can integrate all the parts" of the world is "the poet." Unfortunately, Emerson continues, "few adult persons can see nature"; most cannot even see the sun. By contrast, the lover of nature is "he whose inward and outward senses are still truly adjusted to each other; who has retained the spirit of infancy even into adulthood." For such a person, "intercourse with heaven and earth becomes part of his daily food." When roaming in the forests or woods, this person "casts off his years, as the snake his slough," and "at whatever period soever of life is always a child." At this point, the text launches into a breathtaking paean on nature and its possible meaning for human life: "Within these plantations of God, a decorum and sanctity reign, a perennial festival is dressed." Being placed in this sanctified realm, human beings are simultaneously all and nothing: "Standing on the bare ground . . . all mean egotism vanishes. I become a transparent eyeball; I am nothing; I see all; the currents of the Universal Being circulate through me; I am part or parcel of God."[23]

This vision of cosmic unity is maintained throughout the rest of the essay—only to be interrupted or disrupted occasionally by concessions to a more oppositional, anthropocentric stance. "In the wilderness," Emerson continues, "I find something more dear and connate than in streets or villages"; in fact, the fields and woods suggest "an occult relation between man and nature," even "between man and the vegetable"—in the sense that "they nod to me and I to them." In a distinctly Wordsworthian vein, the text stresses "the advantage which the country-life possesses, for a powerful mind, over the artificial and curtailed life of cities." The poet, above all, "bred in the woods," will not "lose their lesson altogether, in the roar of cities or the broil of politics." The closeness between humanity and nature is manifest in the origin and development of human language, which is never a mere artifact. "As we go back in history," the text states, "language becomes more picturesque, until its infancy, when it is all poetry, or all spiritual facts are represented by natural symbols. . . . And as this is the first language, so it is the last." The lesson to be learned here, for Emerson, is that—prior to any conscious analysis—nature and the world display a poetic and "emblematic" character that is difficult but not impossible to decipher. Here is a remarkable passage that eloquently expresses this view:

> Have mountains and waves and skies no significance but what we consciously give them when we employ them as emblems of our thoughts? The world *is* emblematic. Parts of speech are metaphors, because the whole of nature is a metaphor of the human mind. The laws of moral nature answer to those of matter as face to face in a glass. The visible world and the relation of its parts is the dial plate of the invisible. . . . The visible creation is the terminus or the circumference of the invisible world.[24]

In boldly anti-Cartesian strokes, "Nature" underscores the parallelism or rather the correlation and mutual interdependence of mind and matter, spirit and world. In Emerson's words: "The relation between the mind and matter is not fancied by some poet, but stands in the will of God, and so is free to be known by all men"—provided the mind is purged of pretense and superstition. A major implication of this outlook is the linkage of nature with ethics and religion, bringing into view the contours of a "natural" (though not naturalistic) ethics and a "natural" religiosity. Several brilliant sections of the text are devoted to elaborating these contours. "All things are moral, and in their boundless changes have an unceasing reference to spiritual nature," we read; "therefore is nature ever the ally of religion, lends all her pomp and riches to the religious sentiment." As one should note, ethics and religion here are seen not as opponents, but as allies and even twins: "The ethical character so penetrates the bone and marrow of nature as to seem the end for which it was made." Still more pointedly stated: "Every natural process is a version of a moral sentence. The moral law lies at the center of nature and radiates to the circumference." Once this is grasped, nature also reveals its religious or spiritual quality—provided "religion" is taken in its original meaning of rebinding or reconnecting. "All things with which we deal, preach to us," we read. "What is a farm but a mute gospel? The chaff and the wheat, weeds and plants, blight, rain, insects, sun—it is a sacred emblem." In even more captivating language, Emerson adds: "The aspect of nature is devout . . . The happiest man is he who learns from nature the lesson of worship." Beyond intellectual cognition, "the noblest ministry of nature is to stand as the apparition of God."[25]

Relying on this elevated vision, Emerson chides some types of idealism and Neoplatonism for placing an excessive stress on spirit to the neglect of nature. Idealism carried to an extreme, he writes, "acquaints us with the total disparity between the evidence of our own being and the evidence of the world's being." Such an outlook, he complains, "makes nature foreign to me, and does not account for the consanguinity which we acknowledge to it." The same goes for an "other-worldly" religiosity where the devotee "flouts nature" and even shows "a certain hostility and indignation towards matter"—as did Plotinus, who "was ashamed of his body." Countering this extremism again, the text affirms: "I have no hostility to nature, but a child's love to it. . . . I do not wish to fling stones at my beautiful mother, nor soil my gentle nest." Notwithstanding this celebration of unity or harmony, a number of passages proclaim the ascendancy and even supremacy of human mind over nature, to the point of endorsing the "modernist" conception of human dominion: "Every rational creature has all nature for his dowry and estate. . . . It is his, if he will. He may divest himself of it; he may creep into a corner and abdicate his kingdom, but he is entitled to the world by his constitution." As one will note, the human "I" at this point is no longer "nothing," but rather everything—in fact, a Promethean maker and ruler of the world. "Every spirit builds itself a house," the text concludes, "and beyond its house a world, and beyond its world a heaven. Know then that the world exists for you. For you is the phenomenon perfect."[26]

The ambivalence that emerges here was not restricted to Emerson's "Nature," but characterized his later writings—and in fact, became a hallmark of the ensuing "transcendentalist" movement (where harmony with nature was juxtaposed with growing fervor to a Promethean individualism). The fluctuation can be illustrated with reference to several of Emerson's subsequent lectures and essays. His lecture "The Transcendentalist"—delivered in Boston in late 1841—basically pays tribute to philosophical and poetic "idealism" (without dwelling on the nuances of his earlier essay), stating that the idealist, by contrast to the materialist, "has another measure which is metaphysical, namely the *rank* which things themselves take in his consciousness." From this idealist vantage, "nature is transcendental" (that is, beyond matter); and idealists typically are "lonely": they "repel influences, shun general society; and incline . . . to live in the country rather than in the town and to find their tasks and amusements in solitude." In even stronger terms, individualism and anthropocentrism are extolled in the essay "Self-Reliance" (of roughly the same time). "Trust thyself," Emerson admonishes there; "every heart vibrates to that iron string. Accept the place the divine providence has found for you." To which he adds: "It is only as a man puts off all foreign support and stands alone that I see him to be strong and to prevail. Is not man better than a town?" Despite its chosen title, transcendentalist ambivalence surfaces with full force in the essay "The Over-Soul," which initially appeals to "that unity, that over-soul within which every man's particular being is contained and made one with all other"—and which ends with this tribute to singular uniqueness: "Great is the soul and plain. It is no flatterer, no follower. It never appeals from itself. It . . . gives itself, alone, original and pure, to the lonely, original, and pure."[27]

The attachment to nature and individual distinctness was carried forward and even intensified by Emerson's younger friend Henry David Thoreau (1817–1862). Like the former, Thoreau was educated at Harvard College, from which he graduated in 1837, soon after the publication of Emerson's "Nature." Partly under the influence of this inspiring text, he sought the company and became associated with the members of the "Club," which gathered in and around Boston during this period. Perhaps even more than the poet-philosopher of Concord, Thoreau relished contact with unspoiled natural environments. In 1839, he undertook with his brother an extended and exciting canoe trip (which later became the topic of his celebrated diary titled "A Week on the Concord and Merrimack Rivers"). A bit later, he moved into Emerson's home in Concord, where he contributed as a gardener and handyman to the upkeep of the property, while also giving lectures to, and writing articles for, the "transcendentalist" group. In 1845, in order to be even closer to nature, he moved to a crude hut that he had himself built and largely furnished on the northern shore of Walden Pond near Concord. There, for several years, he managed to provide the bulk of his foodstuff through the cultivation of beans, potatoes, peas, wild berries, and apples. Living a simple life, he also sought to integrate himself as unobtrusively as possible into his natural surroundings. In the words of one scholar, he "cultivated a tolerant relationship with local animal, bird, and fish life such that several individuals from these species came at his call, forgot their fear of man, and became tame and even affectionate."[28] In 1846 he began writing down his experiences, which culminated in his major work *Walden* (finally published in 1858).

Thoreau's text opens with these famous lines: "When I wrote the following pages, or rather the bulk of them, I lived alone, in the woods, a mile from any neighbor, in a house which I had built myself, on the shore of Walden Pond, in Concord, Massachusetts, and earned my living by the labor of my hands only." Although stressing his distance from neighbors, the reclusive poet was not entirely isolated, as he was periodically visited by curious acquaintances and friends. As he writes at one point: "I had three chairs in my house: one for solitude, two for friendship, three for society." Still, the main accent of the text is on personal solitude and alone-ness—which is a solitude of individual consciousness. Thus, although immersed in nature, the individual ego is by no means bracketed. As Thoreau states: "In most books, the *I* or first person, is omitted; in this [text] it will be retained; that, in respect to egotism, is the main difference. We commonly do not remember that it is, after all, always the first person that is speaking." Somewhat later, he quotes with approval an unnamed poet as saying about nature: "I am monarch of all I *survey;* my right there is none to dispute." Being removed from close social contacts allowed Thoreau to cultivate and hone not only his practical or artisan talents but also his mind and literary capacities. As we read in another famous passage: "For more than five years I maintained myself thus solely by the labor of my hands, and I found that by working about six weeks in a year, I could meet all the expenses of living. The whole of my winters, as well as most of my summers, I had free and clear for study."[29]

Simultaneous accent on self-cultivation or individual distinctiveness and thorough immersion of self in nature constitutes the dominant tenor of *Walden*—a tenor that accounts for both its indelible allure and its philosophical complexity (or perplexity). The double emphasis is articulated particularly clearly in the section "Solitude," which starts out with the description of an evening "when the whole body is one sense" and in unison with its surroundings: "I go and come with a strange liberty in nature, a part of herself. As I walk along the stony shore of the pond in my shirt sleeves, though it is cool as well as cloudy and windy, and I see nothing special to attract me, all the elements are unusually congenial to me." A little later, however, the immersion in nature gives way to the accent on separateness and private dominion. "For what reason," Thoreau asks, "have I this vast range and circuit, some square miles of unfrequented forest, for my privacy, abandoned to me by men?" And he adds: "I have my horizon bounded by woods all to myself. . . . For the most part it is as solitary where I live as on the prairies. . . . I have, as it were, my own sun and moon and stars, and a little world all to myself." As Thoreau confesses, he once, early on, felt alone in his solitude at a time of rain; but his mood changed when he became "suddenly sensible of such sweet and beneficent society in nature, in the very pattering of the drops, . . . an infinite and unaccountable friendliness all at once like an atmosphere sustaining me." These comforting comments are followed a few paragraphs later by a passage that is often singled out by students as expressing the very gist of *Walden:* "I find it wholesome to be alone the greater part of the time. To be in company, even with the best, is soon wearisome and dissipating. . . . I never found the companion that was so companionable as solitude."[30]

Both during and after his stay at Walden Pond, Thoreau repeatedly had occasion to encounter "society"—and often its depressing and debasing side. At one time, he was arrested and imprisoned for the nonpayment of a poll tax—an experience that provided inspiration for another famous text: the essay "Resistance to Civil Government" (of 1849), which is also, and perhaps better, known by the title "Civil Disobedience." The essay opens with these celebrated lines: "I heartily accept the motto 'That government is best which governs least'; and I should like to see it acted upon more rapidly and systematically. Carried out, it finally amounts to this which I also believe: 'That government is best which governs not at all.'" Although frequently taken as a manifesto of radical anarchism, the essay might also—with due caution—be read as a plea for a better democratic regime in which individual rights are more fully implemented and respected. As Thoreau writes toward the end of the essay: "Is democracy, such as we know it, the last improvement possible in government? . . . There will never be a really free and enlightened state until the state comes to recognize the individual as a higher and independent power, from which all its own power and authority are derived, and treats him accordingly. I please myself with imagining a state at last which can afford to be just to all men, and to treat the individual with respect as a neighbor."[31] The latter reading, in my view, finds support in some of Thoreau's distinctly "social" engagements after his return from Walden Pond, especially his engagement in the emancipation movement, his opposition to the Fugitive Slave Law, and his speech in defense of the abolitionist John Brown.[32] As can be seen in his conduct, "laissez-faire" for him did not simply mean leaving things alone or preserving the status quo. More important, one can wonder how his views would have evolved in light of the expanding Industrial Revolution and the rise of corporate capitalism—when individualism became increasingly linked with economic privilege and power and when the charm of individual life in the woods tended to lose its innocence.

4

Nature and Experience
Dewey

Notwithstanding Romanticism's captivating and elevating élan, its turn toward "transcendentalism" and individual self-assertion exacted a price: the price of the tendential alienation from the pressing social and political concerns of the time. This alienation was all the more grievous given the steady transformation of America from an agrarian to an industrial and urbanized society, a transformation carrying in its wake a pronounced social stratification tearing at the very fabric of an ostensibly "democratic" country. To be sure, there is no denying that New England transcendentalists were often involved in social experimentation—witness the attempts at communal living at Brook Farm and Fruitlands; but these attempts were typically designed as "utopian" alternatives, rather than efforts to affect society at large. In the wake of the Civil War, dissatisfaction with individual retreat grew among many intellectuals who insisted on the need to supplement (if not replace) self-cultivation with social reform. This shift of accent was buttressed by another, more genuinely philosophical consideration: the conviction that the validity or truth of general principles—transcendental or otherwise—can only be discerned in practice, that is, in the concrete conduct or practical behavior to which principles give rise. More than anything else, it was this conviction that accounts for the move from the "idealist" philosophy undergirding much of Romantic literature to the more reform-oriented outlook of American pragmatism.[1]

Despite the undeniable shift of accent, it is well to remember points of contact or continuity between Romantic poet-thinkers and later pragmatists. One point of contact is the "progressive" spirit animating both movements. As mentioned earlier, the writings of both

Wordsworth and Emerson reflected a profound dissatisfaction with stale traditional formulas, coupled with a spirited plea for (inner and outer) renewal. In an emphatic manner, this plea for renewal was shared by all the main representatives of American postbellum philosophy—which accounts in no small measure for the close association of pragmatism and "progressivism." Another point of contact—still more salient in the present context—is the pragmatic rebellion against Cartesian dualisms, especially the bifurcation between mind and matter, self and other, theory and practice. This rebellion is most clearly and dramatically manifest in the work of John Dewey (1859–1952), to whose writings I shall confine myself here. Given the sprawling character of that philosopher's opus—and the primary focus of the present pages—my presentation in the following will be somewhat circumscribed. In a first section, I shall briefly delineate Dewey's philosophical position, mainly in an effort to differentiate it from Romantic-idealist assumptions. Next, I turn to an intellectual event that decisively shaped his subsequent outlook toward nature and the world: his encounter with Charles Darwin. Finally, I shall discuss in some detail Dewey's major contribution to the topic of present concern: his famous "Paul Carus Lectures" (of 1925), published under the title *Experience and Nature*.

Dewey's Pragmatism

In a poignant manner, both continuity with and departure from Romantic idealism are manifest in Dewey's philosophical orientation. As it happens, the philosopher himself on repeated occasions told the story of his intellectual or philosophical development, delineating in the process the contours of his pragmatism vis-à-vis alternative approaches. A particularly instructive account is provided in his essay "From Absolutism to Experimentalism" (penned in 1930). In that essay, Dewey goes back to his early student days at the University of Vermont, commenting especially on the growing influence of German philosophy on that campus. As he observes, one of his teachers there was "almost the first person in the United States to venture upon the speculative and dubiously orthodox seas of German thinking—that of Kant, Schelling, and Hegel." The venture or excursion in this case (as in many others) was undertaken "largely by way of Coleridge" and

English Romanticism. The phrase "dubiously orthodox" refers to a brewing conflict between German "enlightened" thought and standard "Christian theological doctrines" deriving from Puritan or Reformed teachings. In Dewey's words, at that time "a controversy was carried on between the Germanizing rationalizers and the orthodox representatives of the Scottish school of thought" (concentrated then chiefly at Princeton). To illustrate the prevailing dominance of the Scottish school, and its clash with enlightened reason, the essay gives the example of a Vermont professor—"a man of genuinely sensitive and cultivated mind"—who stated at one point: "Undoubtedly pantheism is the most satisfactory form of metaphysics intellectually; but it goes counter to religious faith."[2]

A main emphasis of Christian theology at the time was not only on religious faith but on nonrational "intuition" in general. In fact, a firm alliance had been established "between religion and the cause of 'intuition,'" to the point that "the cause of all holy and valuable things was supposed to stand or fall with the validity of intuitionism." Curiously, as previously indicated, intuitionism was also a facet of German idealism, especially as it was developed by the Romantic movement. But this was clearly not the aspect that fascinated Dewey. As he writes: "I learned the terminology of intuitional philosophy, but it did not go deep, and in no way did it satisfy what I was dimly reaching for." A new intellectual trajectory—and a way to transcend the earlier controversy—opened up for Dewey when he went to Johns Hopkins University in 1884 to enter upon graduate studies. The time— postbellum America—was ripe for new social and intellectual departures. In Dewey's words: "The eighties and nineties seem to mark the definitive close of our pioneer [or frontier] period, and the turn from the civil war era into the new industrialized and commercial age." Intellectually, the decades were "a time of new ferment in English thought; the reaction against atomistic individualism and sensationalistic [Lockean] empiricism was in full swing." In many ways, Johns Hopkins stood at the forefront of these developments. There Dewey encountered among other teachers a Dr. W. T. Harris, a "well-known Hegelian and editor of the 'Journal of Speculative Philosophy.'" He also met another, more systematic Hegelian named George Morris, who was animated by belief in "the 'demonstrated' truth of the substance of German idealism" and in "its competency to give direction to a life of aspiring thought, emotion, and action." As Dewey confesses, the memory of Morris's teaching was "an enduring influence" on his life. He adds, in a comment that throws light on the specific character of German idealist influence: "He [Morris] came to Kant through Hegel instead of to Hegel by way of Kant, so that his attitude toward Kant was the critical one expressed by Hegel himself." Moreover, he was sufficiently imbued with "common-sense" realism so as to be able to combine "a logical and idealistic metaphysics with a realistic epistemology" and even to uniting "Aristotelianism with Hegelianism."[3]

What attracted Dewey to this "common-sense" Hegelianism was its ability to link theory with practice, that is, rigorous philosophical reasoning with "incidents of personal experience" and practical life. In concrete terms, Hegelianism (cum a dose of Aristotle) provided an antidote to the profound fissures and diremptions characterizing modern life, diremptions deriving largely from the prevailing Cartesian worldview. In Dewey's words, the perspective "supplied a demand for unification that was doubtless an intense emotional craving, and yet was a hunger that only an intellectualized subject-matter could satisfy." In addition to the impact of Cartesian dualisms, the craving was fueled and intensified by the tensions marking Dewey's own New England background. He elaborates on this point: "The sense of divisions and separations . . . [was] I suppose, borne in upon me as a consequence of a heritage of New England culture—divisions by way of an isolation of self from the world, of soul from body, of nature from God"; in their combined effect, these conflicts "brought a painful oppression or, rather, they were an inward laceration." It was into this condition of intellectual and emotional turmoil that the encounter with Hegel's philosophy introduced a prospect of healing and wholeness in both a theoretical and a practical sense. In experientially charged language, the essay pays tribute to this prospect: "Hegel's synthesis of subject and object, matter and spirit, the divine and the human was no mere intellectual formula; it operated as an immense release, a liberation." Above all, "Hegel's treatment of human culture, of institutions and the arts, involved the same dissolution of hard-and-fast dividing walls, and had a special attraction for me."[4]

To be sure, the attraction was never doctrinaire and not immune to change or transformation. As Dewey confesses in the same essay, he "drifted away from Hegelianism" in subsequent decades—without, however, erasing its influence as a "permanent deposit" in his thinking. "Were it possible for me," he adds, "to be a devotee of any system, I still should believe that there is greater richness and greater variety of insight in Hegel than in any other single systematic philosopher—though when I say this I exclude Plato."[5] As we know, the drift mentioned by Dewey led him to embrace a perspective that came to be known as "pragmatism" or else "experimentalism" and that traced the validity of theories and cognitive insights (in a not un-Hegelian fashion) to their bearing on social life and practical conduct. As we also know, the turn was encouraged and promoted by his encounter with the works of Charles Sanders Peirce and William James, especially by the latter's 1898 lecture "Philosophical Conceptions and Practical Results." Quoting from or paraphrasing that lecture approvingly, Dewey states in an essay of 1925 ("The Development of American Pragmatism"): "The ultimate test for us of what truth means is indeed the conduct it dictates or inspires. But it inspires that conduct because it foretells some particular turn to our experience which shall call for just that conduct from us. . . . [Hence] the effective meaning of any philosophic proposition can always be brought down to some particular consequence, in our future practical experience, whether active or passive." Elaborating further on James's argument, Dewey in the same context offers his own assessment or interpretation of the new perspective: "Pragmatism, thus, presents itself as an extension of historical empiricism, but with this fundamental difference, that it does not insist upon antecedent phenomena but upon consequent phenomena; not upon the precedents but upon the possibilities of action."[6]

As interpreted by Dewey, the distinctive feature of pragmatism is not simply an emphasis on action or (mindless) activism, but rather its stress on the learning experience undergone in the process of action or practical conduct. Quoting or paraphrasing James again, he underscores that "the whole function of philosophy ought to be to find the characteristic influences which you and I would undergo at a determinate moment in our lives, if one or the other formula of the universe were true." As can be seen, pragmatism in Dewey's view does not disparage thought or philosophizing per se, but only its reduction to a passive function of "mirroring" reality, to the exclusion of its creative participation in ongoing practical life. What matters most from a pragmatic perspective is "the human and moral importance of thought and of its reflective operation in experience." This outlook stands in opposition both to an abstract "intellectualism" or self-contained rationalism and to a brute empiricism content with gathering atomistic sense data without an interpretive intervention. Finding himself again in full agreement with James, Dewey notes the opposition of pragmatism to the empiricist "atomism of Locke and of Hume," as well as "the *apriorism* of the synthesis of rational principles by Kant and his successors." In comparison with traditional sense-data empiricism, the pragmatic outlook favors a more "radical" empiricism rooted in the concrete experiences of human beings in search of meaning. By comparison with abstract intellectualism, the same outlook stresses the role of an "emergent" reason or of an operative rationality "at work." In Dewey's words, the pragmatic orientation involves "a critique of the theory of knowledge and of a logic which has resulted from the theory proposed by neo-Kantian idealism and expounded in the logical writings of such philosophers as Lotze, Bosanquet, and F. H. Bradley."[7]

What all these observations point to or corroborate is the centrality of the notion of "experience" in Dewey's thought—a notion, by the way, that also was quite central in Hegel's philosophy (and especially his *Phenomenology of Spirit*).[8] On repeated occasions, Dewey felt compelled to explain or elucidate the precise meaning of the term. Important in this regard is an essay of 1905 titled "The Postulate of Immediate Experience." As he observes there, the distinctive difference between pragmatism—seen as a "radical" or "immediate" empiricism—and alternative positions resides in a basic presupposition: "a presupposition as to what experience is and means." As previously indicated, experience for Dewey is not just an inductive procedure, a gathering of random facts or sense data; nor is it deductively derived from abstract premises. Rather, it is a relation to the world as such. In Dewey's concise formulation: "Immediate empiricism postulates that things—anything, everything, in the ordinary or non-technical use of the term 'thing'—are what they are experienced as." This postulate applies to practical conduct as well as to acts of knowing or theorizing; for knowing is "one mode of experiencing," and the primary philosophical issue is to find out "*what* sort of an experience knowing is— or concretely, how things are experienced when they are experienced *as* known things." This argument leads Dewey to a crucial formulation (with epistemic as well as ontological implications): "There are two little words through explication of which the [radical] empiricist's position may be brought out—'*as*' and '*that*.'" What is indicated or implied in these terms is "that things are what they are experienced *as* being; or that to give a just account of anything is to tell what *that* thing is experienced to be." (No doubt, students of Continental philosophy will find here a clear parallel to the phenomenological and hermeneutical emphasis on understanding something "as.") For Dewey, there is no need to go behind experience to an absolutely "external" reality or a Kantian "thing-in-itself." From the empiricist's point of view, he notes, there is "no need to search for some aboriginal *that* to which all successive experiences are attached, and which is somehow thereby undergoing continuous change."[9]

About a decade later, Dewey elaborated further on the crucial "postulate" of radical or pragmatic empiricism, sharpening at this point its contours vis-à-vis earlier philosophical approaches. If one wanted to grasp these contours or salient differences, he states, then a focus on experience provides a "natural point of departure." The contrast that immediately jumps into view is that, traditionally, experience was treated chiefly as a "knowledge-affair" tied to induction or deduction. In British sensationalism, experience was split asunder into sensory data; but this doctrine of sense data was derived "neither from observation nor from experiment." By contrast, Kantianism invoked rational principles or universal bonds; but in so doing, it accepted sensory randomness and simply "proceeded to supplement it from non-empirical sources." Investigation of experience, however, provides a warrant for neither of these views. Other contours have to do with the focus of traditional empiricism on static or "given" data, to the exclusion of future prospects or possibilities, and the positivist stress on fact-gathering, to the exclusion of theoretical interpretation. But, Dewey remonstrates, "experience, taken free of the restrictions imposed by the older concept, is full of inference. There is, apparently, no conscious experience without inference; reflection is native and constant." What is missing in past forms of empiricism, above all, is an awareness that experience involves the "ongoing intercourse of a living being with its physical and social environment." This realization gives to the term a concretely lived or existential quality. In Dewey's words: "Experience is primarily a process of undergoing: a process of standing something; of suffering and passion, of affection, in the literal sense of these words." This does not mean that experience is purely "inner" or psychic, or involves "slipping along in a path fixed by inner consciousness"; rather, "private consciousness is an incidental outcome of experience of a vital objective sort." Above all, experiencing as an undergoing is "never mere passivity," since even "the most patient patient is more than a reactor," namely, a patient-agent: "Experience, in other words, is a matter of simultaneous doings and sufferings."[10]

The Influence of Darwin

As can be seen, experience for Dewey means basically (what some have called) "being-in-the-world," where "world" includes not only the human or social world but also (and prominently) nature. It was the extreme turn toward inwardness and private subjectivity in the later Romantic movement that prompted him to embrace a more solidly experiential and "transactional" perspective attentive precisely to the nonsubjectivist dimension of nature. As he writes in an essay of 1927: "No matter how much one may draw upon contrasting phases of life—Greek and Indian with [George] Santayana, or The Golden Age of Emerson, Thoreau, and Whitman with [Lewis] Mumford— for aid in understanding [our world], it is also true that without an understanding of natural science and technology in their own terms, understanding is external, arbitrary, and criticism is 'transcendent' and ultimately of one's own private conceit." It is not the case (as is sometimes asserted) that Dewey was unaware of the dangers of "scientism," or the thoughtless abuse of technology for the pursuit of purely instrumental or anthropocentric goals dismissive of ecological needs. However, the correction of such abuse, for him, could not proceed through a disdainful rejection of natural inquiry, but only through a more responsible transactional approach, that is, through an "*immanent* criticism of existing industrialism and of the dead weight of science" where "instruments are made into ends" and hence "deflected from their intrinsic quality and thereby corrupted."[11]

It is against the background of these and similar considerations that one needs to understand Dewey's turn to Darwin and evolutionism at a certain point of his life. Charles Darwin's *The Origin of the Species* had been published in 1859 and exerted a profound impact among both natural scientists and philosophers. Dewey early on detected an affinity between Darwin's study and his own emerging "radical" empiricism: namely, in the rejection of fixed, transempirical essences behind the flux of phenomena. To pinpoint this affinity, and also its significance for pragmatism, Dewey in 1910 published a book-length text titled *The Influence of Darwin on Philosophy* (which was preceded by an essay with roughly the same title in 1909). As the opening chapter noted, the very title of Darwin's book marked a rupture with, or departure from, traditional metaphysical epistemology. "That the combination of the very words 'origin' and 'species,'" we read, "embodied an intellectual revolt and introduced a new intellectual temper is easily overlooked by the [scientific] expert." The conceptions that had dominated epistemology and the philosophy of nature for two thousand years, and had become "the familiar furniture of the [Western] mind," rested on the assumption of the superiority of the permanent and the defectiveness of change. "In laying hands upon the sacred ark of absolute permanency," the text states boldly, "in treating the forms that had been regarded as types of fixity and perfection as originating and passing away, *The Origin of Species* introduced a mode of thinking that in the end was bound to transform the logic of knowledge, and hence the treatment of morals, politics and religion." Despite the wide attention it attracted, the innovative quality of the study was for some time concealed by an "anti-Darwinian clamor" that left the impression that the issue was between science and religion or theology. But the latter was not the case, for the real issue "lay primarily within science itself" and within philosophy and its underlying worldview.[12]

In the remainder of the chapter, Dewey elaborates in greater detail on the sea change effected by Darwin's work. In ancient Greek thought, he notes, the permanent aspect of things and phenomena was captured in the word *species*; Aristotle coined the term *eidos,* which the Scholastics translated as "species." This view became canonical in subsequent centuries: "The conception of *eidos,* species, a fixed form and final cause, was the central principle of knowledge as well as of nature. Upon it rested the logic of science." Basically, science was assumed to aim "at realities lying behind and beyond the processes of nature" and to pursue this aim by means of "rational forms transcending ordinary modes of perception and inference." The first stirrings of innovation occurred in the sixteenth and seventeenth centuries, when scientists like Kepler and Galileo began to transfer interest "from the permanent to the changing." However, their focus was on astronomy, physics, and the inorganic universe, leaving aside the organic world, the "kingdom of plants and animals," which provides the gateway from the inorganic to the human world. It was the accomplishment of Darwin to open this gateway and thereby also to provide a new "access to mind and politics." "The influence of Darwin," we read, "resides in his having conquered the phenomena of [organic] life for the principle of transition, and thereby freed the new logic for application to mind and morals and life." When Darwin said of "species" what Galileo had said of the earth—"*e pur si muove*"—"he emancipated, once and for all, genetic and experimental ideas as an organon of asking questions and looking for explanations."[13]

Apart from involving the relation between permanence and change, Darwin's innovation—for Dewey—affected a number of salient issues, especially the issues of intelligent design versus contingent evolution and of the role of mind versus matter as primary causal variables. In large measure, the classical notion of "species" was predicated on the idea of prior design, that is, of a "purposive regulative principle" that, though not visible, operates as an "ideal or rational force" pursuing its own ultimate manifestation. Seen from this angle, matter and sensory experience were only external or marginal features subordinated to a higher purpose. Starting in classical thought, this idea persisted through the Middle Ages into modernity; even into the late eighteenth century, it functioned as "the central point of theistic and idealistic philosophy." Viewed against this background, Darwin's novelty emerges into plain view, for his principle of natural selection "cut straight under this philosophy." Dewey at this point takes pains to guard against misreadings of Darwin's work, especially readings that claim that the accent on "process" eliminates "intelligence" from the universe and ethical standards from human and social life. Charges of this kind, often advanced by "hostile critics," are non sequiturs. What is involved in the Darwinian (and pragmatist) turn, Dewey notes, is not a dismissal of intelligence, but rather a shift "from a [prior] intelligence that shaped things once and for all to the particular intelligences which things are even now shaping"; that is, "from an ultimate goal of good to the direct increments of justice and happiness that intelligent administration of existing conditions may beget." Likewise, what Darwinian pragmatism calls into question is not ethics as such, but an ethics immune from concrete learning experiences: "Philosophy foreswears inquiry after absolute origins and absolute finalities in order to explore specific values and the specific conditions that generate them." Instead of seeking justification for ultimate values "in the remote and transcendent," pragmatic philosophy "humbles its pretensions to the work of projecting hypotheses for the education and conduct of mind, individual and social." The point is "to improve our education, to ameliorate our manners, to advance our polities" by having recourse to "specific conditions of generation."[14]

The following two chapters of the book explore the implications of Darwin's thought for ethics, while later chapters concentrate more on its implications for logic and epistemology. In the second chapter, titled "Nature and the Good" (presented in the form of a conversation), Dewey adumbrates a kind of "natural" or (rather) experientially nurtured ethics that finds its standards in concrete situations. As the pragmatist interlocutor says: "Personally, I don't need an absolute to enable me to distinguish between the good of kindness and the evil of slander, or the good of health and the evil of valetudinarianism. In experience, things bear their own specific characters." Strictly speaking, this statement does not imply that "nature" as such has ethical concerns—since "literally it has no mind of its own." Such concerns emerge only—and emerge "naturally"—with the generation of human intelligence. Hence, nature exhibits regard for ethical value only "when it produces a living organism that has settled preferences and endeavors." The argument is continued in the chapter "Intelligence and Morals." This chapter traces the development of moral theory from the ancients through the Middle Ages to modernity and up to the present. Traditional moral theories are again criticized for their abstractness: "They all alike assumed the existence of *the* end, the *summum bonum,* the final goal; and of *the* separate moral force that moves to that goal." With the Darwinian innovation, such doctrines fade into the background. What is emerging in their stead is "the growing belief that the proper business of intelligence is discrimination of multiple and present goods and of the varied immediate aims of their realization, not search for the one remote aim." Hence, having learned what it cannot do, moral theory becomes responsible "for the better performance of what needs to be done" and what only a broadly equipped intelligence *can* undertake: namely, "study of the conditions out of which come the obstacles and the resources of adequate life, and developing and testing the ideas that . . . may be used to diminish the causes of evil and to buttress and expand the sources of good."[15]

Some of the themes discussed in subsequent chapters—such as those of epistemology and truth theory—have already been sketched previously and hence can be briefly summarized here. Thus, the chapter entitled "The Experimental Theory of Knowledge" contrasts pragmatism with metaphysical realism, stating that traditional epistemology makes knowledge a problem by assuming behind cognition factors incompatible with actual experience: "These assumptions are that the organ of knowledge is not a natural agent but some ready-made state of mind or consciousness, something purely 'subjective'" in comparison with which everything else is an external "objective" reality. The next chapter—titled "The Intellectualist Criterion of Truth"—is an attack on F. H. Bradley's idealist contention that "the philosophical conception of reality must be based on an exclusively intellectual criterion, a criterion belonging to and confined to theory"—a conception that Dewey terms "intellectualism" because of its neglect of practice and concrete experience. The emphasis on the linkage between thought and practice is continued in the chapters "Belief and Existences" and "Experience and Objective Idealism." The latter essay takes to task philosophers who claim that only "Reason" (with a capital R) can provide access to permanent reality, a source of pure and innate ideas, and the means of ordering sense data in a coherent framework. In the chapter "Consciousness and Experience," a certain kind of "psychologism" is criticized to the extent that the latter assumes a pristine "internality" removed from practical conduct. The concluding chapter—"The Significance of the Problem of Knowledge"—admirably sums up the gist of Darwinian pragmatism by presenting that approach as the exit route from the stalemate between "sensationalism," on the one side, and "rationalism" or "intellectualism," on the other: "The reason then that neither school can come to rest in itself is precisely that each one abstracts one essential

factor of conduct. . . . The result, if we remain at this point, is practically a deadlock. Each can make out its case against the other. To stop
at such a point is a patent absurdity. If we are to get out of the cul-de-
sac, it must be by bringing into consciousness the tacit reference to
action which all the time has been the controlling factor."[16]

Experience and Nature

In 1925 John Dewey delivered the "Paul Carus Lectures" in Chicago,
a series of talks that subsequently were assembled in revised form under the title *Experience and Nature*. Building upon the long string of
his previous writings and studies, the lectures offer a grand overview
and summation of Dewey's "nature philosophy" or what might better
be termed his pragmatic and humanistic "naturalism." As he states in
the opening preface of the book: "I believe that the method of empirical [or pragmatic] naturalism presented in this volume provides the
way, the only way . . . by which one can freely accept the standpoint
and conclusions of modern science: the way by which we can be genuinely naturalistic and yet maintain cherished values, provided they are
critically clarified and reinforced." Although sometimes chastised as
being antiethical or antihuman, this kind of naturalism is "not destructive" or nihilistic; it is "rather a winnowing fan" that "inspires the mind
with courage and vitality to create new ideals and values in the face
of the perplexities of the new world." The opening chapter—dealing
with philosophical method—asserts firmly the experiential character
of theoretical knowledge and hence the close linkage between experience and world and especially between experience and nature. The
pragmatic approach, we are told, upholds faith in experience "when
intelligently used as a means of disclosing the realities of nature." Diligently pursued, the approach shows that "nature and experience are
not enemies or alien"; that experience is "not a veil that shuts man off
from nature," but a means of penetrating continually further into the
heart of nature." Seen from this angle, pragmatism is not so much a
"study of philosophy" in itself, but rather "a study, by means of philosophy, of life-experience."[17]

The following chapter—"Existence as Precarious and as Stable"—reads like a European "existentialist" tract of roughly the same
period. The basic point here is that human existence is not a solitary

venture, but is embedded in the contexts of "history, life, and culture." Generally speaking, these contexts are not usually stable or
predictable: "The world is a scene of risk; it is uncertain, unstable,
uncannily unstable. Its dangers are irregular, inconstant, not to be
counted upon as to their times and seasons." In order to tame or control irregularity and to achieve security, human beings and societies
have tended to fasten upon a realm of permanence immune from flux.
This tendency is abundantly manifest in traditional metaphysics and
metaphysical philosophies. "One of the most striking aspects of the
history of philosophic thought," we read, "is the recurrent grouping
together of unity, permanence (or the 'eternal'), completeness and rational thought, while upon another side stand full multiplicity, change
and the temporal, the partial, defective, sense and desire." The division is obviously just an urgent attempt to separate "the precarious
and unsettled from the regular and determinate, guided by the need
for security." The form commonly taken by the division is the bifurcation of the world into "a superior, true realm of being and a lower,
insignificant or phenomenal realm," or the splitting of existence into
"the supernatural and the natural." As before, Dewey finds the division operative both in crude sensationalism (or materialism) and in
idealism or "intellectualism." As he writes: "Spiritualistic idealism and
materialism alike treat the relational and functional distinction [be-
tween stable structure and change] as something fixed and absolute.
One doctrine finds structure in a framework of ideal forms, the other
finds it in matter. They agree in supposing that structure has some
superlative reality"—which is "another form taken by preference for
the stable over the precarious and incompleted."[18]

The next two chapters take up again the issue of design and
contingency and especially the role of "ends" or purposes in natural
processes. Traditionally, the argument from design relied on a preordained trajectory or a linear teleology in which "ends" are implied in
initial premises. Attention to natural contingency disturbs or disrupts
this linearity. To the extent that purposes are retained, they take at
best the form of a complex inquiry, of difficult learning processes that
can be grasped, if at all, only in narrative accounts, in stories or histories of encountered and undergone events. In Dewey's words: "The
foundation for value [or purpose] and the striving to realize it is found
in nature, because when nature is viewed as consisting of events rath-

er than substances, it is characterized by *histories,* that is, by continuity of change proceeding from beginnings to endings." Hence, it makes sense to say that "initiations and consummations occur in experience." Another traditional way of formulating the design argument is in terms of an ontological "chain of being," a hierarchical ordering of substances in which higher and lower levels are related in an ascending and descending scale. "The hierarchy," Dewey states, "was explicit in Greek thought: first and lowest are vegetative ends, normal growth and reproduction; second in rank come animal ends, locomotion, and sensibility; third in rank are ideal and rational ends, of which the highest is blissful contemplative possession in thought of all forms of nature." In this gradation, "each lower rank, while an end, is also a means or preformed condition of higher ends." The text sharply criticizes this scheme from the perspective of a pragmatic (and democratic) progressivism: "Such a classificatory enterprise is naturally consoling to those who enjoy a privileged status, whether as philosophers, as saints or scholars, and who wish to justify their special status."[19]

The stress on narratives and natural processes might give the impression that mind or consciousness is somehow marginalized or erased. As Dewey insists, however, this impression is mistaken and largely the result of the Cartesian separation of mind (cogito) from world and social interaction, including linguistic communication. But if language is recognized as the means of social cooperation and mutual participation, then "continuity is established between natural events and the origin and development of meanings." From this non-dualist angle, Dewey writes, mind is seen "to be a function of social interactions, and to be a genuine character of natural events when these attain the stage of widest and most complex interaction with one another." These observations have a bearing also on the status and role of individualism and subjectivity in human life. Just as in the case of "mind," Dewey does not see the individual as a fixed entity, but rather as an agency developing and maturing in encounters. "Existentially speaking," the text states, "a human individual is a distinctive opacity of bias and preference conjoined with plasticity and permeability of needs and likings. One trait tends to isolation, discreteness; the other trait to connection, continuity." On the one hand, the opacity of private bias may lead to "blind solitariness" and even aggression; on the other hand, the connecting trait—unless critically channeled—

may lead to conformism. At this point, Dewey remembers Hegelian teachings and especially the importance of recognition. "Here is the ultimate dialectic," he writes, "of the universal and individual. One no sooner establishes his private and subjective self, than he demands it be recognized and acknowledged by others, even if he has to invent an imaginary audience . . . to satisfy the demand." Experience is again an important taskmaster: "No person taught by experience ever escapes the reflection that no matter how much he does for himself, what endures is only what is done for others."[20]

One of the most probing and instructive chapters deals with the so-called mind-body problem—an issue that has troubled Western philosophy at least since the onset of modernity. As Dewey observes, the problem was not really present in antiquity because Greek thought, as well as Greek religion and art, was "piously attentive to the human body." Things began to change in the Middle Ages and took a sharp turn with the rise of modern science. At this point, nature came increasingly to be seen as "wholly mechanical"; at the same time, the presence within nature of a creature "possessed of life, manifesting thought and enjoying consciousness" was a mystery. Once science replaced the older terms of potentiality and actuality with those of mechanical causality, "mind and matter stood over against one another in stark unlikeness." Causal science and abstract Cartesian dualism here merged into close symbiosis. Since early modernity, it is true, efforts have also been afoot to resolve the dilemmas created by the mind-body bifurcation. The efforts range from "the materialism of Hobbes, the apparatus of soul, pineal glands, and animal spirits of Descartes," all the way to "pre-established harmony, occasionalism, parallelism, epiphenomenalism, and the *élan vital*"—a "portentous array." For Dewey, the problem resides not so much in the attempted "solutions," as in the underlying metaphysical and ontological assumptions. The real philosophical task hence lies in the "reconsideration" of these assumptions or presuppositions. Going beyond the confines of dualism and mechanical causality as such, these assumptions have to do with deeper issues, especially "the denial of quality in general to natural events," the neglect of temporality or "temporal quality," and the dogma of "the superior reality of 'causes.'"[21]

Dewey's own approach to tackling the problem is to reformulate the traditional "chain of being" in a new way: one relying no longer on

a hierarchy of substances (or essences), but on a sequence of qualitative interactions and relationships. As he notes, it makes sense to
differentiate between "the qualities of situations in which organisms
and surrounding conditions interact." Once this approach is followed,
it becomes possible to distinguish among three main levels of qualitative relations: "The distinction between physical, psycho-physical, and
mental is one of levels of increasing complexity and intimacy of interaction among natural events." This formulation does away with the
notion that matter, life, and mind are different entities or "beings"—a
mistake deriving from a "substantiation of eventual functions." For
Dewey, "matter" or "the physical" is "a character of events when they
occur at a certain level of interaction." It is more than a "bare essence"
or thing-in-itself, for it is the "property of a particular field of interact-
ing events." To be sure, when dealing with "inanimate things," qualities as such may be safely disregarded, for they present themselves
as "intensities and vector directions of movement" capable of mathematical statements. In the case of organic life and mind, however,
qualities acquire "natural existential status"; both psycho-physical and
higher mental phenomena may be grasped as qualitative interactions
without a "dualistic breach in historic, existential continuity." Summa-
rizing this conception, the text offers this formulation:

> In general, three plateaus or fields may be discriminated. The
> first, the scene of narrower and more external interactions,
> while qualitatively diversified in itself, is physical; its distinc-
> tive properties are those of the mathematical-mechanical
> system discovered by physics and which define matter as a
> general character. The second level is that of life. Qualitative
> differences, like those of plant and animal, lower and higher
> animal forms, are here even more conspicuous. . . . The third
> plateau is that of association, communication, participation.
> This is still further internally diversified, consisting of indi-
> vidualities. It is marked throughout its diversities, however,
> by common properties which define mind as intellect, posses-
> sion of and response to meanings.[22]

In one of its concluding chapters, the book turns to an important
dimension of a pragmatic or humanistic naturalism: the role of art.

Despite his reservations regarding Romanticism, Dewey at this point endorses a central Romantic idea: that art and poetry constitute the privileged locus of the reconciliation of nature and humanity. As he states in his preface: "The highest because most complete incorporation of natural forces and [creative human] operations in experience is found in art." The chapter steers a course between an abstract aestheticism celebrating private enjoyment and instrumental production centered on the labor of the artisan invested in the shaping of materials. Cutting through this bifurcation, pragmatism holds that "art is practice" and that "the only distinction worth drawing is not between practice and [aesthetic] theory, but between those modes of practice that are not intelligent, not inherently and immediately enjoyable, and those which are full of enjoyed [or consummatory] meanings." Once this insight dawns and is accepted, Dewey argues, it will be commonplace that art is "the complete culmination of nature (and that 'science' is properly a handmaiden that conducts natural events to this happy issue)." At this point, one would find the disappearance of those separations or diremptions that trouble present thinking: "division of everything into nature and experience, of experience into practice and theory, art and science, of art into useful and 'fine,' mental and free." From this angle, art does not just exist for itself (*l'art pour l'art*), but carries a deeper, existential, and transformative significance: it is "a device in experimentation carried on for the sake of education." Viewed in this manner, art "solves more problems which have troubled philosophers and resolves more hard and fast dualisms than any other theme of thought."[23]

Experience and Nature was not Dewey's final word on the theme of a pragmatic naturalism. Some fifteen years later, on the occasion of his eightieth birthday, he presented in New York a talk entitled "Nature and Experience" that, in part, was meant to answer some of his critics and, more important, highlighted again the significance of experience in overcoming "hard and fast dualisms." Dewey notes, with some chagrin: "Presentation of a view of experience which puts experience in connection with nature, with the cosmos, but which would nevertheless frame its view on the ground of conclusions reached in the natural sciences, has trouble in finding ways of expressing itself." To make some headway, what needs to be avoided is both an abstract "cosmic idealism" and a "mechanistic materialism." From a pragmatic perspective, it is important to stress that qualities or ends are not "extra-natural" or "super-natural," but rather continuous with natural experience. Only in this manner is it possible to overcome the crisis resulting from "the dualistic opposition of subjective and objective, mind and matter, experience and nature." For this purpose it is imperative to formulate "a theory of nature and of the connections of man *in* (not *to*) nature on the basis of a temporal continuum."

Once nature is seen not simply as a causal system of mechanical laws but also as a qualitative dimension responding to human needs and aspirations, another traditional separation falls by the wayside (or is at least greatly softened): that between theory and practice, between science and ethics. This point—although perhaps not directly relevant to science as such—is crucial for pragmatic philosophy, which, in finding "value-considerations" in experience, inevitably has "a practical, that is, a moral" orientation. While making room for a great diversity of concrete ends and judgments, the final test or criterion of such a philosophy has to be "what is done in the living present, what is done in giving enriched meaning to other things" in the broader social and political context.[24] This statement clearly pinpoints the gist of an experientially grounded naturalism with ethical and political connotations.

5

Nature and Life-World

Merleau-Ponty

While pragmatism was beginning to ebb in America, an intellectual movement arose in Continental Europe that in many ways resembled—but also reformulated—its basic motivations and themes: the movement of phenomenology and existentialism. What chiefly linked pragmatism with its European counterpart was the disillusionment with traditional philosophical systems and the pretense of abstract theory coupled with a turn to human practice and (what Dewey called) "experience." Initially, it is true, the traditional privilege granted to *theoria* (in the Greek sense of "oversight") persisted in the accent of early transcendental phenomenology on the visual perception of phenomena from the vantage of pure consciousness. Once this accent shifted, however, from visual perception to a broader encounter with the world—giving rise to existential and "genetic" phenomenology—the parallel with the American precursor came more clearly into view. Nowhere are this shift and this affinity more evident than in the work of Maurice Merleau-Ponty, one of the collaborators with Jean-Paul Sartre in the French resistance movement. The American philosopher John Wild has astutely remarked that in reading Merleau-Ponty's writings, "the American reader will be reminded, at many points, of the social behaviorism of George Herbert Mead" (the pragmatist ally of Dewey). Moreover, in the background of Merleau-Ponty's thought one discovers the legacy of a thinker who also influenced early pragmatism: Hegel. In the words of another observer: "There is no contradiction between [his] existentialism and the deeper aspiration which animated Hegel, above all the Hegel of the *Phenomenology of Spirit.*"[1]

Despite the short span of his life (1908–1961), Merleau-Ponty's

oeuvre covers a broad range of philosophical initiatives and transfor-
mations. His early writings reflect the struggle involved in his attempt
to move from early transcendental phenomenology to his own brand
of "experiential" philosophy. The main works of this phase are *The
Structure of Behavior* (1942) and *The Phenomenology of Perception*
(1945). The English title of the first book is somewhat odd and unfor-
tunate as it gives the impression of providing a defense of psychological "behaviorism" (which it actually criticizes); a better translation (of
the French *comportement*) might have been "conduct" or "practice."
In the second book, the term *perception* needs to be extended beyond
strictly visual confines to the experiences garnered by living-in-the-
world or in the "life-world." The second phase of his work contains
some overtly political texts (which I shall bypass), together with such
broadly philosophical works as *Sense and Non-Sense* (1948) and *Signs*
(1960), collections of essays of which some are pertinent here. The
last phase of his life was incredibly productive, but cut short by ter-
minal illness. For present purposes the most significant texts are *The
Visible and the Invisible* and *Nature: Course Notes from the Collège de
France,* both posthumously published. In a way, all his investigations
culminate in these final works, his inquiries into nature in the *Course
Notes.* The following presentation accompanies Merleau-Ponty's oeuvre through its consecutive stages, while keeping its eyes pinned on
his final excursus into the philosophy of nature.

The Primacy of Perception

Although written and published during the turbulence of World War
II, Merleau-Ponty's first book, *The Structure of Behavior,* displays a
steadiness and soundness of judgment befitting more tranquil surroundings. To understand the motivation and gist of the work, it is
good to return to John Wild's prefatory comments. With regard to
background, Wild notes correctly that Merleau-Ponty was "thoroughly trained in the discipline of phenomenology" and that he had
"carefully studied the writings of [Edmund] Husserl, not only the published works but also the later unpublished manuscripts at Louvain."
Yet, although admiring Husserl's initiatives, he never treated them
as finished doctrines, but rather as invitations to further inquiry into
lived experience. Hence, turning away from an abstract or "worldless

consciousness," he preferred to investigate "historical man as he is engaged and existing in the world." In pursuing this investigation, he found himself starkly at odds—just like Dewey's pragmatism before—with the tradition of Cartesian dualism. Seeking to overcome this dualism, his phenomenology was bound to "cut through the traditional oppositions between realism and idealism, body and soul, sense and reason, subjectivism and objectivism." Although perhaps misleading, the term *behavior* (*comportement*) was chosen precisely because of its presumed "neutrality with respect to the traditional distinction between mind and body." For Merleau-Ponty, the term designated "neither a series of blind reactions to external 'stimuli,' nor the projection of acts motivated by the pure ideas of a disembodied, worldless mind," thus pointing beyond both "an objective behaviorism" and "a vitalistic psychism." In this manner, his thought was progressively led into the arena of a primordial "life-world" seen as a precognitive and "pre-conceptual world."[2]

In his own "Introduction," Merleau-Ponty states the aim of his study concisely: "Our goal is to understand the relations of consciousness and nature: organic, psychological or even social." Traditionally, the term *nature* designates an objective causal nexus: "a multiplicity of events external to each other and bound together by relations of causality." This conception is opposed by critical (Kantian or neo-Kantian) thought, for which external things exist only as objects "for" consciousness. From this angle, there is no nature "in-itself": "There is nothing in the world which is foreign to the mind" because "the world is the ensemble of relations borne by consciousness." This conflict can be found in physics and biology and even in the more recent discipline called "psychology," where the dispute rages over the status of mind. "To the extent that it has attempted to be a natural science," Merleau-Ponty states, "psychology has remained faithful to realism and to causal thinking"; as a result, mind appears as a "particular sector" of the objective world or sector of the brain endowed with the peculiar property of existing "for-itself" (*pour soi*). The opposing "mentalistic thesis" presents consciousness as a productive or constitutive source of meaning. Accordingly, two philosophies appear to exist side by side: one that makes nature a target constituted by consciousness and another that treats organism and mind as simply two modes of one and the same natural reality. To make some headway in this situation, Merleau-Ponty proposes to tackle the pertinent questions "by starting from below," that is, from the actual experience garnered in everyday human "behavior"—the latter term taken in a broad sense and not coinciding with the stimulus-response model of John Watson and his followers.[3]

The opening two chapters present in effect a detailed analysis and critique of Watsonian behaviorism, including its modifications through Pavlovian "reflexology" and the complex role of the cerebral cortex. Despite increasing sophistication, behaviorism—in Merleau-Ponty's view—never exits from the dilemmas of empirical sense perception according to which human behavior is simply a reaction to random external stimuli. What is missing in this doctrine is the advent of intelligible meaning from sense data. Partly relying on Gestalt theory, Merleau-Ponty remedies the behaviorist defect by showing that behavior is never an isolated reaction, but rather a patterned conduct occurring in a "form" or "structure," that is, in a distinct frame of reference allowing for the emergence of "sense" from sense data. In his words, such structured frameworks permit learning processes to occur: "Since they establish a relation of meaning between situation and response, they explain the fixation of adapted responses and the generality of the acquired aptitude." What emerges at this point is an insight that is not far removed from Deweyan pragmatism: namely, that natural life-forms and modes of conduct are not "substances" existing "in-themselves," but rather sets of patterned relationships in distinct frameworks. Merleau-Ponty in this context distinguishes between different types of patterned relations ranging from frameworks completely enclosing behavior to more open-ended frameworks allowing for broad learning experiences (in his terminology, the range leads from "syncretic forms" over "non-movable" to "symbolic forms"). In the last case, the world ceases to be a "material plenum consisting of juxtaposed parts" and rather opens up a space "where behavior can manifest itself as such." The basic point of the argument so far is the defense of a midpoint between realism and idealism: "Behavior is not a thing, but neither is it an idea. It is not the envelope of a pure consciousness and, as witness of behavior, I am not a pure consciousness." This precisely is meant by the statement that "behavior is a form."[4]

Building on these comments, the next step of the argument is the broad differentiation between "orders" or levels of being, called respectively the "physical," the "vital," and the "human" orders. By-passing the stark opposition between materialism and mentalism, the text here maintains that "matter, life, and mind" should be under-stood not as substances, but as "three orders of significations." The notion of "form" or gestalt here is a guiding motif, with form provid-ing in a sense "the solution to the antimony of which it is the occasion: the synthesis of matter and idea." Reminiscent again of Dewey—but more directly influenced, it seems, by the work of Max Scheler—the layered scheme gives rise in the end to a crucial philosophical ques-tion: the role and status of consciousness in the structurally patterned world.[5] Construed no longer as an overseer or external spectator, con-sciousness can only participate in the contextual configurations from a concrete perspective or in a perspectival manner. In actual or lived experience, Merleau-Ponty observes, "this perspectival character of my knowledge is not perceived as an accident, as an imperfection due to the existence of my body and its distinctive point of view"; similarly, "knowledge by 'profiles' is not equal to a degradation of true knowledge which would grasp the totality of the possible aspects of phenomena all at once." Far from introducing a "coefficient of sub-jectivism," perspective provides us on the contrary with the assurance of "communicating with a world which is richer than what we know if it." Using quasi-Hegelian language, the text adds that the phenom-enal word from this angle is grasped simultaneously "as 'in-itself' (en soi), that is, as gifted with an interior which I shall never have finished exploring" and "as 'for-me' (pour moi), that is, as given 'in person' through its momentary aspects." The upshot of this argument is that, to do justice to direct experiences, it will be necessary to maintain "against empiricism" that they are "beyond their sensible manifesta-tions" and "against intellectualism" that they are not sequestered in the realm of judgment but are "embodied in their apparitions."[6]

The latter insight is clearly a move beyond Descartes and his mind-matter or mind-body bifurcation. What is missing in the Car-tesian formula is the entry into consciousness of something that is "given" and not constituted. "There is an existential index," we read, "which distinguishes the perceived object from an idea and which manifests 'something' in them not coterminous with my mind." Dif-ferently put: "The intellection which the cogito had found in the heart of perception does not exhaust its content." These considerations lead

Merleau-Ponty to the final question: whether there is not perhaps "a truth of naturalism." Resorting again to the notions of gestalt and structure, he wonders whether there is not a "joining of an idea and an existence," a "contingent arrangement by which materials begin to have meaning in our presence, intelligibility in the nascent state." This possibility puts into question the assumptions of "intellectualism," which asserts an overview of the world "from one end of knowledge to the other," showing instead how consciousness experiences "its inherence in an organism at each moment" and how "mind *comes into the world*." Seen from this angle—to repeat an earlier point—the relation between mind and body is radically reformulated. What is involved is not "a duality of substances," but rather a layering of patterned forms or structures and their intersection: "The body is the acquired dialectical soil upon which a 'higher formation' is accomplished, and the soul is the meaning which is then established." In a formulation reminiscent again of Hegel and Dewey, the text adds: "By a natural development the notion of *Gestalt* led us back to its Hegelian meaning, that is, to the concept before it has become consciousness of self. Nature, we said, is the exterior of concept; but precisely the concept as concept has no exterior and the *Gestalt* still has to be conceptualized as the unity of interior and exterior, of nature and idea."[7]

The arguments of *The Structure of Behavior* were carried forward in Merleau-Ponty's second text, *Phenomenology of Perception*, with greater attention to the participation of consciousness in world experience. Pondering Husserl's motto "To the things themselves," the preface explains that the motto suggests indeed a turning or returning, but a "return to that world which precedes knowledge, of which [rational] knowledge always *speaks,* and in relation to which every scientific schema is an abstract and derivative sign-language." Thus interpreted, Husserl's call is "absolutely distinct from the idealist return to [pure] consciousness." In opposition to the Cartesian self-enclosure of the *cogito,* phenomenological reflection in the proper sense "does not withdraw from the world toward the unity of consciousness," but rather "steps back to watch the forms of transcendence fly up like sparks from a fire." With regard to Husserl's central notion of "reduction"—the bracketing of the "natural attitude"—further phenomenological inquiry teaches "the impossibility of a complete reduction." What such inquiry ultimately discloses is "not a consciousness at home with itself, but rather one aware of its own dependence on an unreflective life which is its initial situation, unchanging, given once and for all." This insight into dependence explains the progressive move of phenomenology in the direction of what Husserl called the "life-world" (*Lebenswelt*)—but the latter now seen in a more concrete, temporal, and contextual sense. In Merleau-Ponty's words: "The self-evidence of perception is not adequate thought or apodictic self-evidence. The world is not what I think, but what I live through. I am open to the world; I have no doubt that I am in communication with it, but I do not possess it. It is inexhaustible."[8]

The opening chapters of the book delineate, once again, the distinctive character of phenomenological experience by contrasting it both to sense-data empiricism and to abstract intellectualism. "What we object to in empiricism," the text states, "is not its having taken [the natural world] as its primary theme of analysis. For it is quite true that every cultural object refers back to a 'natural' background against which it appears." The problem is that the "nature" about which empiricism talks is "a collection of stimuli," and we cannot assume that nature thus conceived is the actual target of experience. Hence, phenomenology has to "rediscover the natural world and its mode of existence" (as distinguished from the "scientific object"). On the other hand, in seeking to discover the "significance" of sense experience, intellectualism does not hold the adequate key; for significance is not equivalent to rational or conceptual understanding. For Merleau-Ponty, the "real sin of intellectualism" resides in leaving untouched the realm of sense data and then superimposing a preconceived meaning upon it. At this point, Gestalt theory is again introduced as a possible remedy—provided it does not slide back into a causal or explanatory psychology. It is precisely Gestalt theory, the text insists, that has brought home to us "the tensions which run like lines of force across the visual field and the system constituted by my own body and the world, and which breathe into it a secret and magic life by exerting here and there forces of distortion, contraction, and expansion." What limits or handicaps Gestalt theory is the lack of "new categories" to give adequate expression to its insights. For what is needed is "a complete reform of understanding": more specifically, the notion of "a *non-positing* consciousness, that is, a consciousness not in possession of fully determinate objects," of "a *logic lived through* which

cannot account for itself, of an *immanent meaning* which is not clear
to itself."[9]

As in Dewey's case, a major aspect of the reform of understanding involves a rethinking of the mind-body or subject-object binaries.
In seeking to overcome these binaries, the text affirms, we need to
discover "the origin of the object at the very center of our experience," that is, we must seek to grasp the "emergence of being and
understand how, paradoxically, there is *for us* an *in itself.*" The task
applies with particular urgency to the "lived body." Once ceasing to
function as part of the Cartesian *res extensa,* the body begins to carry
with it "the intentional threads linking it to its surroundings" and finally to reveal or disclose "the perceiving subject as [an index of] the
perceived world." An important aspect of this perceived world is the
world of nature or "natural world," a domain that is a crucial topic of
the concluding chapters. "I am thrown into a nature," Merleau-Ponty
declares, "and that nature appears not only as outside me, in objects
devoid of history, but it is also discernible at the center of subjectivity."
In addition to the consciously measured time of recorded history, he
notes, there is another recessed temporality that may be called "natural time": "Hence, my voluntary and rational life knows that it merges
into another power which stands in the way of its completion and
gives it a permanently tentative look. Natural time is always there."
The fact that prenatal existence and the earliest years of infancy hover
in the back like an unknown territory is not due to a failure or lapse of
memory: "there is nothing to be 'known' in these unexplored lands."
In order to have some inkling of the amorphous existence preceding
conscious life, one only has to look at the recessed temporality eluding conceptual grasp: "Because I am borne into personal existence
by a time I do not constitute, all my perspectives stand out against a
background of nature."[10]

The theme of nature and the natural world leads, in *Phenomenology of Perception,* to an elaborate discussion of the "human world,"
of the relation to "other people," and hence of intersubjectivity—a
discussion I bypass at this point. What is common to the experience
of all the various dimensions of "world" is the excess of experience
over cognition, the fact that perceptual encounter steers a course
beyond or beneath the categories of the cogito and extended matter. "Whether we are concerned with my body, the natural world, the

past, birth or death," we read, "the question is always how I can be open to phenomena which transcend me, and which nevertheless exist only to the extent that I take them up and live them." Differently put, the question is "how the presence to myself (*Urpräsenz*) which establishes my own limits and conditions every alien presence is at the same time de-presentation (*Entgegenwärtigung*) and throws me outside myself." From this angle, both idealism and realism—the former by making the world immanent, the other by making it an external nexus—falsify experiential relations and render them "unintelligible." For if the natural and social worlds exist, they must be theoretically "immanent"—they can only be "what I see behind and around me"—*and* factually "transcendent"—they exist before and outside of being targets of conscious acts. This insight leads ultimately to a mode of reflection "more radical" than empirical science, namely, to a "phenomenology of phenomenology": "We must return to a *cogito* in search of a more fundamental *Logos* than that of objective thought, one which endows the latter with its relative validity, and at the same time assigns to it its place."[11]

The Turn to Ontology

The preceding comments in a way chart and foreshadow Merleau-Ponty's subsequent path of inquiry. Taken rigorously, the reference to a "more radical" reflection points beyond a "phenomenology of perception" and even beyond phenomenology in the traditional sense (as the "intentional" exploration of phenomena). In the same way, the search for a "more fundamental *Logos*" points toward an arena no longer surveyed by a Cartesian cogito: an arena antedating and overarching both subject and object, both active intentionality and passive receptivity. Small wonder that, in the writings penned after World War II, the name of Martin Heidegger surfaces with increasing frequency and usually in connection with the quest for deeper "ontological" underpinnings. In the perceptive words of Hubert Dreyfus and Patricia Dreyfus, introducing the postwar text *Sense and Non-Sense* (of 1948): "From the *Gestaltists*, Merleau-Ponty learned that we *discover* meanings by responding to solicitations already in our experience; thus we are not the absolute source of meaning." At the same time, in Heidegger he found "a philosophical version of the view that meanings are not [externally] *given* to experience but received from it." Hence, following Heidegger, he "calls the activity of organizing the world by responding to it from within 'being-in-the-world' or 'existence.'" The search for deeper underpinnings does not cancel, but rather reinforces the earlier critique of epistemological dualism, of the resort to either sense-data realism or a priori knowledge. Dreyfus and Dreyfus tell us that academic disciplines have become "stultified by trying to understand their subject matter either in terms of mechanical causation or in terms of the working out of a conscious idea." What needs to be recovered here is (what one may call) the "sub-linguistic structure" or the "spirit" of a life-form—where "spirit" is taken in a quasi-Hegelian sense. For it was Hegel who had shown the emergence of meaning from nonmeaning, of "sense" from "nonsense," and that "time and tragic sacrifices are required for reason to become manifested in history."[12]

In the book itself, the significance of Hegel for contemporary philosophy is elucidated in a chapter titled "Hegel's Existentialism." Referring to Jean Hyppolite's comments on *Phenomenology of Spirit,* Merleau-Ponty agrees that all the great ideas of the twentieth century had "their beginnings in Hegel"; for it was he who started the attempt "to explore the irrational and integrate it into an expanded reason which remains the task of our time." It was Hegel who, without lapsing into relativism, initiated a broader view of understanding that can respect "the variety and singularity of individual consciousnesses, of civilizations and ways of life," but never cease to detect a coherent sense in them. Thus today, if we do not despair of "a *truth* above and beyond divergent viewpoints," then no task in philosophy and cultural education can be more urgent than reestablishing "the connection between, on the one hand, the thankless doctrines which try to forget their Hegelian origin and, on the other, that origin itself." In Merleau-Ponty's opinion, the *Phenomenology of Spirit* is relevant precisely for a postidealist type of inquiry because it offers an account "not only of ideas, but of all the areas which reveal the mind at work: customs, economic structures, and legal institutions as well as works of philosophy." Referring specifically to the struggle for recognition between master and slave, he interprets this struggle as a general metaphor for social evolution or development, in the sense that "learning the truth about death and struggle is the long maturation process" of human history. Viewed from this angle, the heart of existentialism resides not so much in talk about anxiety and aporias, but in the idea of a shared commonality "which human beings affirm or imply by the mere fact of their being and at the very moment of their mutual opposition."[13]

As one should note, of course, the Hegel celebrated here is the author of the *Phenomenology,* not of the system of absolute idealism or "absolute spirit" (who, in Kierkegaard's famous phrase, had ensconced himself in a "palace of ideas"). On the whole, *Sense and Non-Sense* remains faithful to the trajectory of moving beyond idealism and objectivism, a path that leads into an uncharted, precognitive arena—which is not the same as a mystical escape. As Merleau-Ponty observes at one point, defending him against such a charge, the "whole point" of Heidegger's thought is that he "wants to reflect on the unreflected." This is why he deliberately proposes "to study the being-in-the-world which is always presupposed by reflection and is anterior to predicative operations." In this manner, Heidegger—like Hegel before him—makes "spirit" and holistic unity "a future and a problem," wishing to see them "emerge from experience," not taking them for granted beforehand. The same orientation can also be found in the later Husserl when he put aside his earlier transcendental idealism. At that point, Merleau-Ponty writes, Husserl "kept getting a clearer and clearer picture of the residue left behind by all reflexive philosophy, and of the fundamental fact that we exist before we reflect." At this juncture, precisely in order to obtain "complete clarity" about the human condition, he ended up by defining, as the primary task of phenomenology, "the description of the lived world or life-world (*Lebenswelt*) where Cartesian distinctions have not yet been made." Thus, while having started with a "static phenomenology," Husserl finally moved toward a "genetic phenomenology" that traces the emergence of meaning from obscurity.[14]

A similar tribute to the later Husserl can also be found in a series of essays penned in the 1950s and assembled in the volume titled *Signs* (1960). There, the chapter "The Philosopher and His Shadow" traces again the complex trajectory that Husserl's thought traversed on the way toward the life-world. "By moving to the pre-theoretical, pre-thetic, or pre-objective order," we read, Husserl "upset the relationships that obtain between the constituted and the constituting." The submerged and prereflective domain of "Being" from now on "draws its truth from a 'layer' where there is neither absolute spirit nor the immanence of intentional objects in that spirit, but only incarnate minds which through their bodies 'belong to the same world.'" This move does not signal the replacement of philosophy by empirical psychology or anthropology; rather, it involves the search for a deeper *"Fundierung"* beneath the operation of the Cartesian cogito. This search, in turn, does not cancel the cogito, but inserts it into a deeper, ontological matrix. "Logical objectivity," Merleau-Ponty comments, "is not self-sufficient"; it is limited to "consecrating the labors of the pre-objective layer, existing only as the outcome of the *'Logos* of the aesthetic world' and having value only under its supervision." Against this background it becomes possible to grasp some of the more cryptic formulations found in Husserl's later writings. Between the deeper, ontological layer and the "higher" level of constitution, one can detect the operation of that kind of "self-forgetting" (*Selbstvergessenheit*) that Husserl had already named in *Ideen II* and that he took up again later in the theory of "sedimentation." Thus, "the forces of constitution do not move in one direction only; they turn back upon themselves."[15]

In light of these reflections, it becomes understandable why the tribute to the later Husserl is joined in the same volume by a tribute to a very different group of thinkers not mentioned by either Husserl or the earlier Merleau-Ponty: thinkers like Spinoza, Leibniz, and Malebranche. Surprisingly (or perhaps not surprisingly), a chapter in *Signs* comments favorably on an older type of rationalism, found in the seventeenth century, which was not yet truncated in the manner of later scientific philosophy. What is amazing and appealing in that earlier rationalism is its connection of nature and culture, of "natural laws" in the sense of physical laws and of normative standards. This rationalism, Merleau-Ponty states, "seems full of myths to us: the myth of *laws of nature* situated halfway between norms and facts, and according to which, it was thought, this blind world has been constructed; the myth of *scientific explanation* which . . . could one day transform the very existence of the world into a self-evident proposition." This older rationalism, he adds, was still "rich with a living ontology." To this extent, the seventeenth century was "that privileged moment when natural science and metaphysics believed they had discovered a common foundation." The science of nature it fostered did not yet make "the object of science the rule of ontology." At that time, Spinoza, Leibniz, and Malebranche—and to some extent even Descartes—recognized "beneath the chain of causal relations another type of being which sustains that chain without breaking it." Broadly speaking, "Being" then was not yet "reduced or flattened out" to the level of causal objectivity. What all the mentioned thinkers recognized was that "there is also the being of the subject or the soul, the being of ideas, and the inner relation of truth. And the latter universe is as extensive as the former, or rather it encompasses it."[16]

Despite the lapse of time and an obvious difference of emphasis, the older rationalism in Merleau-Ponty's view still finds resonance and traction in some modes of contemporary philosophy. To be sure, the latter cannot recapture the sweeping holistic scope of the older tradition; but it can and does retrace some of the steps of that tradition. In his words: today's philosophy "will never regain the conviction of holding the keys to nature or history in its concepts"; but it cannot and will not "renounce its radicalism, that is, the search for presuppositions and foundations which had produced the great [older] philosophies." A recent example is Heideggerian ontology, where "Being" hovers behind or beyond "the empirical multiplicity" of existing things and yet remains always "intended through them"—because separated from beings "it would only be a lightning flash or darkness." To be sure, it seems difficult if not impossible to reaffirm the plenary rationality animating an earlier age, because this confidence has become infested with doubt and shadows: "The established human community feels problematic, and the most immediate life has become 'philosophical'" (in the sense of being shot through with questions). Hence, Merleau-Ponty concludes, "we cannot conceive of a new Leibniz or Spinoza entering life today with their fundamental trust in its rationality." Above all, present-day and future philosophers will not be able to repeat or reanimate the conceptual systems of their forebears. But they will continue to learn in Leibniz and Spinoza "how happy centuries thought to tame the Sphinx, and in their own less figurative and more curt fashion, they will keep on giving answers to the many riddles she puts to them."[17]

Nature and the "Flesh" of the World

At the time of the publication of *Signs*, Merleau-Ponty was at the height of his productivity and full of intellectual zest. Due to his untimely early death (in May 1961), many of his later writings were published only posthumously; in particular, this includes important texts dealing with the specific topic of these pages. In this context, one needs to remember that Merleau-Ponty was not only a famous author but also a great teacher whose academic career led him from Lyon and the Sorbonne to the pinnacle of French academic life, the Collège de France (to which he was elected in 1952). It was as a teacher at the Collège that he offered three yearlong lecture courses collectively titled "The Concept of Nature": the first in 1956–1957; the second in 1957–1958; and the third, after a one-year hiatus, in 1959–1960. The content of these courses is available today in two forms: first, in the form of summaries or synopses (*"Resumés de cours"*) that were presented to the pertinent ministry; and second, in the form of more extensive, but not fully worked out or polished lecture notes (*"Notes de cours"*).[18] The latter sometimes give the impression of finished texts; at other times, they resemble more "written traces" or telegraphic memory aids used for spontaneous oral elaboration. In the following I shall use both sources; switching back and forth between them, I shall consult the synopses especially in an effort to clarify some of the more cryptic passages in the lecture notes.

The first lecture course offers an overview of conceptions of "nature" in the history of Western philosophy. The course starts out by deploring the neglect of the topic in late modernity, beginning in the nineteenth century. As Merleau-Ponty states (in his synopsis): "Naturalism aside, an ontology which leaves nature in silence shuts itself in the incorporeal and for this reason gives a fantastic image of man, spirit, and history." Even Marxism, despite its dialectical claims, did not manage to tackle the topic properly, but rather juxtaposed a material determinism and a spontaneous revolutionary intervention: "Instead of being mastered or transcended, these two conceptions are simply glued together"; thus, nature in the Marxist philosophy of history remains obscure, by being "everywhere and nowhere, like a visitation." But the problem can no longer be sidelined. If the lecture course takes up the issue of nature, it is from the double conviction "that it cannot by itself solve the ontological problem but that neither is it a subordinate or secondary element in any such solution." In order to make headway in this domain—Merleau-Ponty stresses a familiar point—it is necessary to exit from the traditional dualism of objectivism and idealism. For nature is not simply an external object, an "accessory of consciousness in its tête-à-tête with knowledge." Rather, it is a domain "from which we have arisen, in which our beginnings have been posited little by little until tying themselves to an existence which they continue to sustain and aliment." If we are not resigned to saying that everything outside consciousness or subjectivity is simply a void or blank space, then "we must recognize that primordial being which is not yet the subject-being nor the object-being and which in every respect baffles reflection." From the primordial being to human existence there is not a deductive derivation nor a radical rupture or break: there is "neither the tight construction of a mechanism nor the transparency of a whole which precedes its parts."[19]

The historical overview leads from the Cartesian conception over the stage of "Kantian humanism" to the era of Romanticism, focused on Schelling and Bergson, and concludes with a discussion of recent physics and mechanics. A brief preamble to the course alludes to the ancient Greek and Stoic view of nature, emphasizing the teleological or "finalist" accent, in the sense that "the whole of nature here is divided into qualitatively defined regions or places," each seeking the "more or less successful realization" of its innate telos; but the point is not further pursued. The great break with the classical "chain of being" occurred in early modernity and especially with Descartes. In Merleau-Ponty's words, the Cartesian conception of nature "obliges every being, under pain of being nothing, to exist completely without hiatus and with no hidden possibilities." Once everything hidden or occult is expelled, nature must be seen as a "mechanism," and "one should be able in principle to derive the form of the world from [causal] laws." At this point, a basic dualism emerges: that between *natura naturans* and *natura naturata*. Meaning or significance "finds its refuge in the *naturans*," while *naturata* becomes "product, pure exteriority." Differently put: nature in the sense of *naturata* is "composed of absolutely external parts, completely existent and connected," while everything internal or purposive is "handed over to God's side, the pure *naturans*." To be sure, Descartes was not able to maintain the dualism rigorously intact. This is due to the role of the human body, which seems to participate somehow in both domains. To nature, we read, we have access not only through the causal nexus but also through a "vital relation": namely, our body and the "natural inclination" whose lessons cannot coincide with those of science. Descartes's "hesitations" in his account of the human body are witness to this difficulty.[20]

The section dealing with "Kantian humanism" starts from the *Critique of Pure Reason,* where nature is defined as "the sum of sense data" coordinated under the concepts provided by reason. To this extent, nature for Kant remained the "object" of analysis that Descartes also had in mind. However, in addition to this outlook, Kant also made room for a recessed teleology or "auto-production" that holds all the sense data and causal laws together and works on these materials as "its very own." In a way, this auto-production brings into view a "mode of liaison" of nature as a whole that is "not the connection of external causality," but rather an "interior" unlike the interior of the cogito or consciousness. From this angle, it becomes possible to distinguish two perspectives: on the one hand, that of a "discursive reason with the authority to order our sense experience," and on the other, that of "a 'non-discursive understanding' that would ground simultaneously the possibility of causal explanation and the perception of totality [of nature]." Kant himself did not pursue the path of nondiscursive understanding. For him, nature remained basically a "sum of sense objects" as defined in terms of "the *Naturbegriffe* of Newtonian physics." The point where he allowed teleology to reenter was in the second *Critique,* in the mode of transcendental freedom and purposive practice. In Merleau-Ponty's words, it is in the "concept of freedom" only that an interior purpose is manifest, so that the teleology of nature is a reflection of "noumenal man": "The truth of teleology is the consciousness of freedom. Man is the only goal of nature, not because nature prepares and creates him, but because man retroactively confers upon nature an air of finality by positing its autonomy."[21]

The path of nondiscursive understanding sidelined by Kant was taken up with vigor in Schelling's philosophy of nature. Whereas the former dismissed the path ultimately as the "abyss of reason," Schelling deliberately set out to explore this abyss, defining ultimate reality as what exists "without reason (*grundlos*)," as the "over-being"—the "excess" of Being over the consciousness of Being—which sustains the "grand fact of the world." To be sure, the path for him was never smooth or self-assured. As he admitted, primordial nature (*erste Natur*) is an ambiguous and even a "barbarous" principle that can and needs to be transcended—but a principle or beginning that "will never be as though it had never existed." For Schelling, what was needed to explore this primal grounding was more than rational analysis, namely, a genuine experience elucidated by (what he called) "intellectual intuition," that is, an openness of mind to what grounds and happens to mind. In Merleau-Ponty's words, such intuition is "not an occult faculty, but perception as it is before it has been reduced to ideas"; it grants access to the symbols of "originary knowledge (*Urwissen*) inscribed in nature," a knowledge that is at the same time a mode of unknowing. This means that exploration of nature can never yield an absolute cognition or "gnosis" that would "objectify and absurdly convert nature into a second causality." In terms of the *Course Notes:* "Schelling does not want to appeal to a mystical faculty specialized in this role; rather, what he means is that we rediscover nature in our perceptual experience prior to reflection." By comparison with his idealist predecessors and contemporaries—Fichte and even Hegel— Schelling nurtured "no hatred for nature"; rather, "he recognizes a weight of Being behind freedom, a contingency that is not only an obstacle, but penetrates my freedom which is never constituted as a pure and single negativity: 'Mind is higher nature.'"[22]

In the lecture course, the comments on Schelling's philosophy of nature are directly joined with a discussion of the work of Henri Bergson. For Merleau-Ponty, there is a strong similarity, but also a notable difference between the two thinkers: like Schelling, Bergson seeks to gain access to prereflective, immediately given nature; but unlike the former, he refuses to make any concession to idealism or to a "doubling of reflection" in intellectual intuition. In the terms of *Themes:* with his accent on the élan vital, Bergson "seems to take his stand wholly with the positive [or observable], and if he is dislodged from it in the course of his analysis, it is as though despite himself and in complete unconsciousness of any dialectic." To which the *Course Notes* adds: "There is a positivism in Bergson, as is shown by the critique of the negative ideas of the possible, of negativity, and of disorder." He thus affirms "the contingency of the world in order to be fully positive"; but in doing so, "the idea of nothingness is less chased from than it is incorporated into the idea of Being." Despite this difference, however, Bergson moves beyond the conception of *naturata* as a causal mechanism. Together with Schelling, he conceives nature as "a horizon from which we are already far away, a primordial lost undividedness, a unity which the contradictions of the developed universe negate and express in their own way." Thus, though winding his way through some arguments of Darwin and Herbert Spencer, Bergson ends up with a view not reducible to a naive naturalism. Leaving aside his polemics against reflection and possibility, Merleau-Ponty states, it becomes possible to disentangle "a worthwhile meaning of Bergsonian 'positivism'" that was never held strictly by Bergson himself. Above all, his precept of returning to the evidence of reality might be understood not "as a naïve apology for [scientific] verification, but as an allusion to the pre-existence of natural being, always already there," which is "the proper concern of the philosophy of nature."[23]

From the discussion of Bergson, the lecture course proceeds to the life work of Husserl—presenting the intellectual trajectory of that work again along the lines mentioned before (especially in "The Philosopher and his Shadow").[24] To this presentation, one might usefully add some comments on Alfred North Whitehead offered toward the end of the course. What, for Merleau-Ponty, stands out in Whitehead's approach is the introduction of a radical notion of temporality into experience and thinking. Such an approach, he states, implies a critique of traditional conceptions of matter and substance, as well as space and time: "The traditional idea of space and time as containers 'in which nature is installed' governed the understanding of matter and substance." For Whitehead, however, substance must give way to an accent on "events," that is, happenings that occur in a crosscurrent of temporalities. In Merleau-Ponty's words: "Whitehead no longer wants to define matter and nature by the present and by the instant; he denies that the past is no more and that the future is not yet. Nature is going to be conceived as a spatio-temporal unfurling." Like Heidegger in this respect, the British philosopher distinguishes between calculable "clock time" and a broader "cosmic" time that is inscribed in nature; and to the extent that we participate in the "process" of nature, the latter time is also inscribed in us. In this sense, the traditional dualism is overcome or at least sidelined: "Insofar as we too are nature, subjectivity [or consciousness] is caught up in the system of cosmic time, in a subjectivity of nature." In sum, nature for Whitehead proceeds "by *quanta* of time," and its manifestation is "that of a *Gestalt*."[25]

The subsequent two courses that make up "The Concept of Nature" (1957–1958 and 1959–1960) in part repeat earlier arguments and in part roam over a broad series of topics that resist brief summary in the present context. The main emphasis in the first course is on the notion of "behavior" in modern biology and in the studies of animal behavior (from Jacob von Uexküll to Adolf Portmann and Konrad Lorenz). What one finds in the latter studies, Merleau-Ponty observes, is no longer a focus on self-contained substances or essences, but rather on "dynamic, unstable equilibria" pregnant with latencies and anticipations: "As a result, one cannot conceive the relations between animal species or between these species and human beings in terms of simple hierarchy. What there is rather is a difference of quality, and for this reason living creatures are not superimposed upon each other. The transcendence of one by the other is, so to speak, lateral rather than frontal, and one meets all sorts of anticipations and reminiscences." The chief concern of the final course is with the human body seen as the connecting link and synthesis of nature and consciousness, of the perceived and perception. In contrast to traditional Cartesianism, we read, "we must think of the human body as that which perceives nature which it also inhabits. Hence, that relation of the *Ineinander* which we found can be recovered and confirmed." This insight leads to the demand for a general "aesthesiology," a study of the body as sensing and perceiving animal. As Merleau-Ponty pointedly adds: in the relation between perceiving and the perceived, touching and the touched, "we are not dealing with two natures, one subordinate to the other, but with a double nature." Differently and more boldly phrased: "The body proper embraces a philosophy of the flesh as the visibility of the invisible" (since the touched comprises a dimension not fully accessible to others).[26]

During the period he was presenting these lecture courses, Merleau-Ponty was preparing at the same time a large and multifaceted manuscript—a text that was never completed and that was posthumously published under the title *The Visible and the Invisible, Followed by Working Notes.* In this text, the nexus linking the human body with nature, the perceiving with the perceived, is called the "flesh of the world." "We have to reject," Merleau-Ponty states, "the age-old assumptions that put the body in the world and the seer in the body, or conversely the world and the body in the seer as in a box." What we have to grasp is that the world is not inside my body nor my body inside the world; rather, "as flesh applied to flesh, the world neither surrounds nor is surrounded by it." What is involved here, again, is a generalized sensibility or "aesthesiology." From this angle, the "flesh" is not a bunch of "corpuscles"; it is not a fact or a sum of facts, nor is it a representation for the mind. Being coterminous neither with matter nor mind nor substance, one might designate it best as "an 'element' of Being." The phrase "flesh of the world" implies that "my body is made of the same flesh as the world" and moreover that "this flesh of my body is shared by the world. . . . They are in a relation of transgression or overlapping" (*Ineinander*). As Merleau-Ponty adds, to avoid misunderstanding, the accent on flesh does not eliminate reflection, thoughts, or ideas: "Let us only say that pure ideality is itself not without flesh nor freed from all horizons. . . . It is as though the visibility that animates the sensible world were to emigrate, not outside of every body, but into another less heavy, more transparent body"—or perhaps: "as though it were to change flesh, abandoning the flesh of the body for that of language, and thereby would be emancipated but not freed from every condition."[27]

6

Nature and Being

Heidegger

Among twentieth-century phenomenologists, Merleau-Ponty was not the only one to build a bridge from philosophical reflection to the life-world and ultimately to nature. His endeavor was ably seconded by some of his German contemporaries, especially Max Scheler (1874–1928) and Martin Heidegger (1889–1976). Like the French thinker, both Scheler and Heidegger started out as students of the founder of modern phenomenology: Edmund Husserl; and both moved from an initial transcendental idealism to a more sustained engagement with worldly situatedness, temporality, and human finitude. This was evident in Scheler's elaboration of a phenomenological anthropology; it was even clearer in Heidegger's definition of human existence (*Dasein*) as "being-in-the-world" and "being-toward-death." The move was both a transformation and a continuation of phenomenology's initial impulse. Husserl's famous motto "To the things" (*Zu den Sachen*) could be read, at least incipiently, as an admonition to philosophers to leave dusty ivory towers behind and to turn their attention to concretely experienced phenomena, including the realm of nature. Deliberately and provocatively, Husserl's motto transgressed the Kantian banishment of "things themselves" from human awareness, thereby reestablishing a linkage between experience and the "outer" world. Yet despite this innovation, phenomenology's move beyond Cartesian and Kantian confines was initially quite timid. As formulated by Husserl, cognitive access to the world of phenomena was predicated on the enabling and even "constitutive" role of consciousness or subjectivity; even his later turn to the process of "passive synthesis" left the synthetic competence of consciousness intact. It is at this point that Heidegger launched his new departure. His accent on being-in-the-world aimed to dislodge the metaphysical or ontological primacy of consciousness and subjectivity. Moreover, by shifting the focus from reason, or "reason plus animality" (*animal rationale*), to the existential quality of "care" (*Sorge*), his work inaugurated a basic rethinking of modern Western philosophy as bequeathed by Descartes and Kant.

Even in Heidegger's case, however, Husserl's motto "To the things" was not immediately seen as a call to a serious reconsideration of nature. Still under the influence of his teacher's framework, things—including things in "nature"—tended to be viewed as phenomena accessible to concretely lived experience, as targets either of empirical cognition or of pragmatic utility. With some fluctuations, this approach was clearly manifest in Heidegger's first *magnum opus, Being and Time* (1927). What was not—or only dimly—seen at the time was how nature could itself become a "constitutive" factor of lived experience. A major transformation occurred about a decade later, first in his lectures on Schelling and then in his detailed analysis of Aristotle's concept of nature (*physis*). The actual recuperation of these new insights was disrupted and delayed by the dislocations of World War II and its aftermath. It was only in some of Heidegger's later writings that the new insights on nature came to full fruition or reached a stable maturity. In large measure, this culmination can be attributed to the seasoning effects of Hölderlin's poetry and also of some pre-Socratic fragments. In the following I shall trace the development or maturation of Heidegger's thoughts on nature in three steps: by first examining some salient passages in *Being and Time*, then turning to some of the writings penned during the 1930s, and finally pondering some later texts on Parmenides and on poetic thinking. At no point is there a pretense of exhaustive treatment, something that would conflict with the tentative character of Heidegger's works as part of an ongoing journey.

Being and Time

As indicated before, Heidegger starts his investigations neither from the traditional vantage of *animal rationale* nor from the Cartesian cogito, but from the premise of human "being-in-the-world" seen as an intimately meshed condition. As he writes in *Being and Time:* "The compound expression 'being-in-the-world' indicates in its phrasing that it stands for a unitary phenomenon" that must be "seen as a whole." Hence, "there is no such thing as a mere 'juxtaposition' of one entity called '*Dasein*' [human being] and another entity called 'world.'" What this means is that world or worldiness is not an "attribute" that sometimes belongs and sometimes does not belong to human beings. Differently put: human *Dasein* is not a self-sufficient entity that also maintains occasionally a relation to world: *Dasein* is not a "free-floating" entity that sometimes "enters capriciously into a world-relation. Rather, entering into such world-relation is possible only *because Dasein* is basically being-in-the-world." With this starting point, traditional metaphysics, and especially modern (Western) epistemology with its rigid subject-object bifurcation, are overturned or thrown into disarray. From the perspective of modern epistemology this bifurcation is self-evident. For, says Heidegger, "What is more obvious than that a 'subject' is cognitively related to an 'object' and vice versa?" Yet this seemingly "unimpeachable" assumption turns out to be a "quite disastrous presupposition" as long as "its ontological cogency as well as its ontological meaning" are left in the dark.[1]

In large measure, the subject-object bifurcation endemic to modern epistemology can be traced to Descartes's philosophy, which encapsulated the subject in the "thinking substance" (*res cogitans*) while distancing the world into an "extended matter" (*res extensa*). In Heidegger's words: "Descartes distinguishes the '*ego cogito*' from the '*res corporea.*' This distinction marks subsequently the ontological rift between 'nature' and 'spirit' [or mind]." Although modified and later reformulated in many ways, the Cartesian opposition remains presupposed in Western thought—and "ontologically unclarified." What is completely obscured in this opposition is both the status of "world" and worldliness and the "in-being" of *Dasein* in that world. Based on a traditional (medieval) ontology, Descartes interpreted both human being and world as entities or "substances" (*res*) without questioning the underlying "rei-fication"; thereby he completely missed the meaning of "being" as thematized in Heidegger's text. "Because something ontic-substantive," we read, "is made to underlie the ontological [being], Descartes' expression '*substantia*' functions sometimes in an ontological, sometimes in an ontic, but mostly in a hazily conflated sense. Behind these slights of meaning lies hidden the failure to tackle the basic question of being." Regarding the relation between human thought and the world, the Cartesian framework only made room for a cognitive, epistemological grasp: "The only genuine access to world is cognition, the *intellectio,* and this in the sense of mathematical-physical knowledge. Above all, mathematical knowledge is regarded by Descartes as the one mode of cognition which grants a secure grasp of entities in their being."[2]

By contrast to the Cartesian and modern epistemological paradigm, human *Dasein* in Heidegger's account encounters the world in different ways—though always against the backdrop of its constitutive "in-being" in worldliness. As is well-known, the primordial mode of encounter foregrounded in *Being and Time* is the practical "handling" of things as utensils or "equipment" (*Zeug*). In Heidegger's words: "What we encounter first of all can be phenomenologically elucidated by means of that mode of everyday being-in-the-world which we call our 'dealing' (*Umgang*) with the world." The Greeks had an appropriate term for things with which one is involved in the mode of "concerned dealing" or "*praxis*"; they called them "*pragmata.*" We, Heidegger adds, prefer to call these things "equipment" (*Zeug*); and what makes an item equipment we call "equipmentality" (*Zeughaftigkeit*). What is distinctive about equipment is that it is not merely something to be looked at, but something to be used in a practical or "handy" manner; hence, Heidegger designates the being-character of equipment as "readiness-to-hand" (*Zuhandenheit*). As he adds, this character cannot be grasped by mere observation or from a pure "spectator" perspective. "By only 'theoretically' gaping at such things," he writes, "we fail to understand readiness-to-hand." At the same time, a handy dealing with equipment is "not simply blind"; it exhibits "its own kind of sight which guides our handling and lends to equipment its specific thing-quality." The sight that is exhibited in this context "we call circumspection (*Umsicht*)."[3]

In granting a privileged status to equipment, Heidegger does not deny the possibility of theoretical observation and cognition—provided one remembers that such cognition does not reinstate the subject-object bifurcation, but rather is itself a form (a nonpractical form) of concerned "dealing" with the world. In Heidegger's words: "Cognition itself is grounded in that already-being-with-the-world which is essentially constitutive of *Dasein*'s being." Hence, here too "being-in-the-world is permeated by concern with the cared-for world." To designate beings that are the target of cognition rather than practical handling Heidegger uses the term "presence-at-hand" (*Vorhandenheit*). Such "theoretical" orientation to things, in his presentation, has the character of a certain deficiency of practical involvement. "In order for cognition as observation of 'present-at-hand' things to be possible," we read, "there must first be a deficiency in our concerned handling of beings in the world. By refraining from any kind of producing, handling, and the like, concern retreats into the sole remaining mode of 'in-being,' namely, the mode of simply remaining with (*Verweilen bei*)." Only on the basis of this type of retreat is it possible to reestablish existentially the legitimacy and integrity of theoretical cognition: "On the basis of this mode of world-relation—a mode which allows inner-worldly beings to be encountered solely in their appearance (*Aussehen, eidos*)—an explicitly focused inspection of encountered things becomes possible. This inspection takes its distinct aim in the direction of a grasping of present-at-hand things."[4]

As indicated, both equipment and observed things are encountered in the context of the "worldliness" of world—which demands its own reflective, but nonobjectifying access and elucidation. In Heidegger's words: if phenomena of any kind are to be encountered, then "world itself must be disclosed (*erschlossen*)." Thus, for example, "concerned access to inner-worldly ready-to-hand equipment implies the prior disclosure of world as such." This means that "in any kind of equipment, world is always already 'there.'" Differently put: "Whenever we encounter anything, world is already previously discovered, though not thematically. . . . It is by virtue of world that equipment is found to be ready-to-hand." World or "worldhood" in this context means something like a holistic frame of reference or significance (*Bewandtnis*). This is why one can also say that "the significance of the being of equipment is only discovered on the basis of the prior discovery of a holistic frame of significance. Hence, in the discovered significance of a piece of equipment, there lies pre-discovered the world-character of all equipment." On the basis of these reflections, *Being and Time* delineates three main dimensions of the "question of being": first, the being of "inner-worldly encountered" equipment (readiness-to-hand); second, the being of entities discovered beyond practical use (presence-at-hand); and third, the being of the (ontic) condition of possibility of the discovery of beings at all: "the worldhood or worldliness of world." Heidegger adds: "The last kind of being involves an 'existential' determination of the character of being-in-the-world, that is, of *Dasein*."[5]

This survey of possible modes of being seems to be complete or exhaustive—at least from the vantage point of human being-in-the-world (which is the focus of *Being and Time*). Yet something seems to be missing or neglected in the preceding survey: namely, the status of nature. Can nature be fitted at all into the tripartite scheme? Can it be reduced to a handy equipment or else be distanced as an external object or "*res extensa*"? Or does it perhaps coincide with the holistic frame of worldhood? Heidegger's text remains unclear and halting on this topic—despite a number of suggestive and intriguing comments. In discussing equipment or presence-to-hand, Heidegger notes that, in handling such entities, we also encounter things that in themselves are "not in need of production or handling" (*herstellungsunbedürftig*)—such things as iron, steel, metal, wood. "In the handling of equipment," he adds, "'nature' is co-discovered along with that use—that is, nature as we find it in natural products." Nature here is "co-discovered" and hence not identical with equipment. Does this mean that it coincides with external matter, with a "present-at-hand" object? Heidegger strongly denies this alternative. "Nature," he states, "must not be understood as something merely present-at-hand (*vorhanden*)—not even as the 'force of nature' (*Naturmacht*). For, the wood is also a forest of timber, the mountain a quarry of rock; the river is water-power, the wind is 'wind in the sails.'" Even when its character as equipment is properly discarded, it still remains dubious and illegitimate to define nature simply as presence-at-hand. When the latter is done, what remains hidden is "the 'nature' which 'stirs and strives' (*webt und strebt*), which assails and enthralls us as landscape."[6]

Nature in the proper sense thus remains a hidden and somewhat elusive domain—whose (ontological) character is not explicitly defined or thematized in *Being and Time*. When distinguishing it from equipment and present-at-hand things, Heidegger also is unwilling to conflate nature with worldhood or worldliness. In fact, nature in his treatment seems to hover somewhere at the boundary or outer limit of world. As the text states: "Considered ontologically and categorially, nature constitutes a limit case (*Grenzfall*) of possible inner-worldly encountered beings." In fact, the being of nature can be encountered and discovered by *Dasein* only in a very distinct mode of its being-in-the-world: "This cognitive discovery has the character of a certain 'un-worlding' (*Entweltlichung*) of the world," that is, a certain loss of world as holistic frame of significance. Hence, nature can by no means serve as a synonym or substitute for worldhood: "Understood as the categorial summation of all structures of inner-worldly encountered beings, nature can never render intelligible the meaning of worldhood (*Weltlichkeit*)." Even the phenomenon of "nature" as conceived by Romanticism, Heidegger adds, can ontologically be grasped "only on the basis of the world-concept—that is, the analytic of *Dasein*," and not the other way around.[7] Not being synonymous with nature, however, this world-concept also cannot fully disclose the distinctive meaning of nature—something *Being and Time* leaves basically open.

Schelling and Aristotle

About a decade after completing *Being and Time*, Heidegger presented in Freiburg a lecture course on Schelling's philosophy, more specifically on Schelling's treatise on "human freedom." As one may note, Heidegger at that time was also entering into a "gigantic struggle" (*gigantomachia*) with Nietzsche—in the course of which he came to see the latter basically (and perhaps unfairly) as a defender of an extreme anthropocentrism bent on "super-human" mastery of the world.[8] In approaching the theme of his lecture course, Heidegger did not present Schelling as an antimodernist or opponent of the Enlightenment, but as a proponent of human freedom—the latter seen as the linchpin of modern Western, including German idealist, philosophy. It is precisely in light of his (qualified) endorsement of this centerpiece that Schelling's philosophy becomes startling and thought provoking—mainly because of his simultaneous turn to nature and his endeavor even to link human freedom with a natural substrate. Broadly speaking, this loosely "postmodern" initiative was congruent, or resonated fully, with Heidegger's progressive decentering of human existence, which was a hallmark of his own transformation or "turning" (*Kehre*) during this period. As we read in the "Introductory Remarks" of the course, the basic intent of the investigation was threefold: first, to comprehend the "essence of human freedom" as "the innermost center of philosophy"; second, to gain access from this center to Schelling's own work; and last, through this access to be able to "grasp the philosophy of German idealism as a whole in terms of its moving trajectory." For, Heidegger adds, Schelling was "the truly creative and boldest thinker of this whole age of German philosophy"; in fact, he was it "to *such* an extent that he drives German idealism from within beyond its own fundamental position."[9]

What chiefly attracted Heidegger to Schelling was his (modernist) focus on human freedom coupled with his radical reformulation of the meaning of freedom. As he writes, in the same opening remarks, Schelling raises the question of the "essence" of human freedom—but he does so with a twist: "One knows this question under the customary label 'freedom of the will'; and one proceeds to discuss whether human will is indeed free or unfree and how the one or the other could be properly demonstrated." In this discussion, freedom is taken to be "a faculty or property (*Eigenschaft*) of man"; and one presumes to know sufficiently "what is meant by 'man.'" Heidegger's rejoinder is pointed: "With this question of 'freedom of the will'—a question ultimately wrongly put and thus no question at all—Schelling's treatise has nothing whatever to do." For in that treatise, freedom is seen "not as the property of man, but rather the other way around: man is at best a property of [or owned by] freedom." From this vantage, freedom emerges as "the encompassing and penetrating essence by virtue of which man becomes man [or *Dasein* becomes *Dasein*]." What this means is that "the being of *Dasein* is grounded in freedom. But freedom itself is a name for genuine 'Being' as such, transcending entirely all human being." What happens in Schelling's treatise, thus, is an investigation of human being that moves radically beyond the merely human, in the direction of "something which is more essential and weightier than 'man,' namely, freedom—the latter seen not as a supplement or attribute of human will, but as the essence of genuine Being conceived as the grounding of beings as a whole." But this question regarding Being can easily be shown to be "the broadest, deepest and, thus, most essential question of all."[10]

Given the focus of the present pages, the question arises how the ground of Being—seen as a synonym for freedom—relates to "nature" as viewed in Schelling's treatise. The issue is first taken up in a discussion of "pantheism," a doctrine according to which God (viewed theologically as ground of Being) and the beings found in nature or the world are basically inseparable—with the result that God is potentially confined in worldly "immanence." In one version of this doctrine—partially traceable to Spinoza—all natural-worldly things form a predetermined causal nexus, a nexus incompatible with human freedom. Schelling was vehement in his rejection of this kind of "Spinozism," charging it with being guilty of gross "reification," that is, the reduction of all being(s) to things or entities (in line with the scholastic notion of substances). As he wrote: "The error [of Spinoza or Spinozism] is by no means due to the fact that he locates all things *in God,* but to the fact they are just *things*" and that God "is likewise a thing for him." To this extent, Heidegger comments, Spinozism is "not familiar with what is alive or spiritual as a distinctive and perhaps more primordial mode of being"; even the "will" appears here "as a mere thing (or object)," and necessity "only exists between things in a mechanical manner." If pantheism is taken in this sense, then it is indeed incompatible with freedom (as charged by its opponents). However, the situation changes dramatically if the ground of Being is equated with freedom and human beings are likewise granted freedom (as in Schelling's philosophy). In Heidegger's words: "Pantheism *can* be interpreted fatalistically, that is, as excluding freedom, but it does not have to." This is so little necessary that, on the contrary, "it is precisely 'the liveliest feeling of freedom' which prompts us to interpret beings pantheistically." As he adds: "If the acceptance of human freedom as philosophical anchorage drives us into the arms of pantheism, then the latter cannot possibly amount to a denial of freedom."[11]

In subsequent discussions, Heidegger's lecture course delineates more clearly the peculiar status of "nature" in modern (Western) philosophy from Descartes to Schelling. As indicated before, Descartes erected a dualism between subject and object, thought and nature, while treating both as entities or substances (*res*). In a certain (not uncontested) interpretation of his work, Spinoza sought to overcome this Cartesian dualism, by blending both substances in a reified naturalism or natural determinism. In due course, the conception of nature as a causally linked nexus of "things" became the dominant modern perspective, shaping decisively the character of modern natural science. Heidegger's course presents this perspective as lopsided and even as the basic "mistake" (*Irrtum*) of the modern scientific outlook. For by focusing on the reified nexus of laws, does science really penetrate to the "reality" (*Wirklichkeit*) of nature? It may be entirely true that, by using scientific epistemology, the scientist fastens on something that is fixed as "present-at-hand" (*Vorhandenes*); but presence-at-hand cannot be equated with reality. Undeniably, nature on first inspection displays something like ordered regularity; hence, it is tempting to explain the rule-governed character of natural phenomena by tracing it to "higher-order rules" or laws. But this procedure is circular: "The aim of scientific inquiry only leads to what is already presupposed in its very method, namely, that everything is regular and rule-governed and hence must be scientifically explicable in principle." If this premise or presupposition is buttressed by the further assumption that explanation involves mathematical or quantitative calculation, then the postulate inevitably arises that "all life phenomena must be subject to a completely mechanical explanation" (and prediction).[12]

While critiquing this dominant trend in Western thought, Heidegger also mentions a more recessed countertrend—which later culminates in Schelling's thought. Inspired in part by Giordano Bruno, Leibniz in his *Monadology* attributed to all beings a more dynamic, intrinsically "lively," and spirited character. In this manner, he laid the groundwork for a "higher realism" according to which nature is not something reified or dead, but "something living, a self-sustaining force, and more particularly: a latent, still undeveloped mode of freedom." This insight was later developed by German idealism, an outlook that "transformed the 'I think' of Descartes into the higher conception 'I am free,' that is, into the idealism of freedom." In this conception, Being, and every mode of being, is grasped "not mechanically" or quantitatively, but as an "outgrowth of will" or, in general terms, of "spirit" (*Geist*). To be sure, this transformation was slow and halting. A decisive impulse was provided by Kantian philosophy. In Heidegger's words: "Kant's philosophy accomplishes the transition from the inappropriate [voluntaristic] to the appropriate concept of freedom"—where the latter means "independence as standing within one's own essential being." Kant grasped this independence as self-determination or self-legislation. Yet even in this case, freedom was not yet fully placed in the ground of being as such. Here is a crucial passage:

Freedom here still means mastery over the senses; . . . as autonomy it is located exclusively in man's pure reason. This pure reason is not only distinguished from, but at bottom also separated from, sensuousness, from "nature" as something completely other. The human self is defined exclusively in terms of the ego, of "I think"—an ego-character which is only piled on top of sensuality seen as man's animality, but not really embedded in nature. Basically, nature and what is so designated remains something negative or merely to be overcome; it is not admitted as a constitutive ground of the whole existence of man.[13]

This situation is preserved and even aggravated in the philosophy of Fichte, for whom all modes of being are derived from the "I" or "ego," more specifically from the ego's constitutive act and free activity. For Fichte, Heidegger comments, "the ego as freedom is everything; even the *non*-ego, insofar as it is, is conceived as non-*ego*, that is, ego-like." This formula has consequences especially for nature. In Fichte's "absolute idealism," even nature and especially nature "is seen only as non-ego: it exists only in its ego-reference, namely, as constituting a boundary or limit for the ego. In itself it has no being." To this extent, Heidegger comments, German idealism may have reached "the formal concept of freedom," that is, the general character of freedom as "independence and self-determination"; but it did not, or not yet, grasp the core of human freedom in its concrete "factuality." It is at this point that Schelling rebelled and proceeded to shift the thrust of his philosophy onto a "deeper ground." Against the idealist dissolution of all beings in the centrality of the "I think" as "I constitute," Schelling executed his decisive "countermove." Opposing above all Fichte's "annihilation of nature" and its reduction to a "non-ego," he discovered and demonstrated the "independent being of nature." In his "philosophy of nature," Schelling both continued and transgressed earlier philosophical teachings. His crucial step against Fichte—we read in a central passage—was to reconcile the "higher realism" deriving from Leibniz with important insights of idealism. Hence, "what Schelling calls 'philosophy of nature' does not merely denote inquiry into a special (ontic) area termed 'nature,' but rather means the effort to grasp nature from the guiding principle of idealism, that is, the idea of freedom—but to grasp it in such a way as to grant nature its independent being." This latter independence, one should note, is not merely an "object of experience" in Kant's sense, but must be thought "as sustaining ground of all being(s)."[14]

At this point, the question arises how the free independence of nature relates to human freedom and ultimately to the freedom of the basic ground of beings (or Being as such). Schelling's elaborations on this question, as well as Heidegger's commentary, are extremely complex and nuanced and transcend as such the concern of the present pages. Schelling introduces in this context the distinction between "ground" and "existence," where "ground" means the dark, sheltered enclosure of beings (in their "nature"), whereas "existence" (as eksistence) means the elevation and relevation of beings into the open disclosure of truth. Related to this distinction is also the possible antagonism between particularism and universalism, between the self-enclosure of beings in their particular ground and their releasement into the holistic fulfillment of their being. What distinguishes human freedom from other modes of self-being is the possibility of a radical conflict between particularism and ek-static self-giving and disclosure. In his interpretation, Heidegger uses the terms "jointure (or fugue) of Being" (*Seinsfuge*) and "disjointure," where things are "out of joint." In his reading, the alternatives of jointure and disjunction provide the genuine, ontological underpinning of the distinction between "good" and "evil"—and not an anthropocentric "freedom of will." Undergirding the philosophy of nature and of freedom, he notes, is a notion of being as a simultaneous "becoming," as the progressive unfolding of divine meaning against a darkly yearning nature. Where this yearning and divine meaning are in harmony, the "fugue" of Being is joined. In Schelling's own words: "The process of creation is only an inner transmutation and transfiguration of the original dark principle . . . such that the dark ground [of nature] is the one transfigured into light." In human freedom, however, a major drama unfolds: "In man there exists the whole power of the dark principle, but also the whole force of light. In him, there are both poles—the deepest abyss and the highest heaven."[15]

Although profoundly suggestive, Schelling's view of nature—as interpreted by Heidegger—was still somewhat inchoate and in need of further elucidation (a fact having to do with the lingering effect of absolute idealism).[16] To correct this shortcoming, Heidegger a few years later turned to a still more primordial conception of nature: the conception articulated by the ancient Greeks, especially in Aristotle's metaphysics. As he observes at the very outset: "Since classical times, the term 'nature' has functioned as the key label that designates the basic relations of Western humanity both to human and non-human modes of being." A mere enumeration of customary dichotomies demonstrates this function: "nature and grace, nature and art, nature and history, nature and spirit." At the same time, however, one speaks of "the 'nature' of spirit, the 'nature' of history, and even the 'nature' of human beings." In Christian thought, the "natural state" of humans means their embeddedness in a certain passionate or instinctual nature, which, accordingly, needs to be controlled or "repressed." From another perspective, it is precisely the "unleashing" of drives and passions that constitutes human naturalness; thus, "for Nietzsche, *homo naturae* is someone who makes the 'body' the key to world interpretation." Finally, in the eyes of some poets, nature is something located above or beyond humans and even "beyond gods." In whatever manner the label is used, the term *nature* in Western thought always is invoked in order to pinpoint the basic character of worldly beings and ultimately of Being as such.[17]

In classical Greek thought, a central philosophical strand involved reflection on "nature" or "*physis*," an effort that was termed *metaphysics* because it aimed at the understanding and knowledge of *physis* (*episteme physike*). According to Heidegger, the most sustained reflection of this kind is contained in Aristotle's lectures (*physike akroasis*) found in *Physics*. "Aristotle's *Physics*," he writes, "is the hidden, and therefore never adequately studied, foundational book of Western philosophy." In the opening section of his work, Aristotle right away emphasizes what he considers decisive in the conception of *physis* or nature: namely, "*kinesis* or the state of being in motion"; hence, the key issue in his analysis becomes the proper grasp of "the essence of movement (*Bewegung*)." For Aristotle, Heidegger continues, it was evident that beings are "in motion or at rest"; the basic question remained as to what constitutes the essence of *physis* in the midst of this motion or rest. In the Aristotelian conception, *physis* could not be equated with cause or causation or, above all, with a reified substance (*res*) or object. "Beings," Heidegger comments, "can be experienced as objects only where human beings have become subjects, that is, egos who experience their fundamental relation to beings in terms of the objectification and mastery of what is encountered." This modern way of looking at the world, however, is alien to Greek philosophy: "For the Greeks, human beings are never subjects, and therefore non-human beings can never have the character of ob-jects (things that stand-over against)." Rather, in the Greek and especially the Aristotelian view, *physis* must be seen as something that has a unique independence or quality of "standing-on-its-own" (*Insichstehen von Ständigem*).[18]

To elucidate further the character of *physis,* Aristotle reminds us of its linkage with motion or movement (*kinesis*). Every motion, however, stands under a certain dispensation or guiding orientation (*arche*). At this point, Aristotle introduces a distinction between two types of beings, each governed by a different dispensation: naturally grown beings and man-made beings. In Heidegger's words: "Here, such beings as plants, animals, earth, and air are contrasted with beings such as bedsteads, robes, shields, wagons, ships, and houses. The first group are 'growing things' (*Gewächse*) in the same broad sense that we employ when we speak of a 'field under growth.' The second group are 'artifacts' (*poioumena*, in German *Gemächte*), although this last term must be stripped of deregatory connotations." The guiding dispensation of artifacts is "*techne*"—the term taken not as fabrication or mode of production, but as a mode of knowing or "know-how." Hence, "the essence of *techne* is not movement seen as the activity of manipulation, but rather the know-how required in dealing with things"; and the "*telos*" of the movement is not an instrumental relation, but "end" in the sense of "essential fulfillment." What is crucial in the distinction between "growing things" and artifacts is the source or guiding impulse of the respective dispensation, which in the former case is internal or self-generating, in the latter external. In Heidegger's interpretation: "In the case of artifacts, the *arche* of their motion—and also of the rest once completed—resides not in the artifacts themselves but in something else: the *architekton* or maker, the one who controls the *arche* of the *techne*. With this we have reached a distinction from 'growing things' (*physei onta*) which are called that way because they have the *arche* of their motion *not* in another being, but in the very being which they themselves are."[19]

Following Aristotle, Heidegger does not fail to add that the two kinds of beings to some extent are linked or overlap. Thus, in the case of a wooden bedstead, for example, one can take the completed entity as an artifact, while the wood itself belongs to the "growing things." This linkage, however, does not cancel the basic distinction itself. The linkage as well as the distinction can be illustrated in the case of a convalescent patient whose recovery is assisted by a medical doctor. In this instance, Heidegger notes, two types of motion are curiously "entwined": the medical ministration seen as *techne* and the actual convalescence seen as the work of *physis*. Here, it is not the doctor who is in charge of the dispensation of actual recovery, but rather the patient as an embodied human being. From this example, it is possible to derive important implications. *"Techne,"* Heidegger writes, "can only assist *physis,* can (in this case) only more or less expedite the cure; but, as *techne,* it can never replace *physis* or arrogate to itself the *arche* of health as such. This could only happen if life itself became a 'technically' producible artifact; but at this point, there would no longer be such a thing as health, any more than there would be birth and death." In this connection, Heidegger launches into a broader cultural critique that deserves to be cited in full:

> Sometimes it seems as if modern humanity is rushing head-long toward this goal: where it would *technologically fabricate or produce itself (der Mensch sich selbst technisch herstelle).* If this succeeds, humanity will have exploded itself, that is, its *essence as subjectivity*—exploded itself into thin air, into a region where absolute meaninglessness counts as the only "meaning" and where preserving this meaning takes the form of human "domination" (*Herrschaft*) over the globe. . . . With this we arrive at the extreme counterpoint in regard to *physis* or Being.[20]

In the subsequent discussion, Heidegger is intent on elucidating further the character of *physis*—and also on linking Aristotelian insights with key features of his own philosophy. As previously stated, the distinctive quality of "growing things" (*physei onta*) is that they carry the *arche* of their motion "in themselves"—more specifically: in themselves "inasmuch as they are in and with themselves." Differently formulated: *physei onta* are the perfect emblem of "beingness" (*Seiendheit*), in Greek of *ousia.* Hence, it is possible to say: "*Physis* is *ousia*, beingness—that which characterizes being as such, in a word: Being (*das Sein*)." Now, Being as *ousia* means for the Greeks, and especially for Aristotle, something that is "standing on its own" or that "lies present in openness." Thus, the quality of *ousia* refers to something that allows Being to shine forth or become present: that is, as a mode of "presencing" (*Anwesung*). In Heidegger's words: "The decisive principle that guides Aristotle in his interpretation of *physis* declares that *physis* must be understood as *ousia*, and the latter as a mode of displayed presence." Only when this is understood is it possible to grasp *physis* "as the *original dispensation* guiding the motion of what moves from out of itself and toward itself." The crucial distinction between *ousia* and merely "ontic" things, he insists, is not that between "eternal" and "temporal" beings; decisive is not the mere "duration," but the ability to bring being to presence (*Anwesung*). Such bringing to presence, however, can also be called "unconcealment" (*das Unverborgene*), a synonym for Heidegger's notion of "truth" (*aletheia*). As he adds pointedly, presencing or bringing to presence should not be misunderstood as mere "presence-at-hand" (as discussed in *Being and Time*): "What we mean here is not mere presence-at-hand (*Vorhandenheit*), and certainly not something reducible to mere static stability, but rather *presencing* in the sense of coming forth into the unconcealed, placing itself into openness."[21]

Toward the end of his study, Heidegger returns to the distinction between "*physei onta*" and "*poioumena*," "growing things" and artifacts (*Gewächse* and *Gemächte*). As before, the gist of the distinction is placed in the genesis of these beings, into the respective manner in which they arise or come forth: in the one case self-genesis, in the other case fabrication. For Heidegger, the difference in terms of genesis is crucial. In the case of artifacts, we are faced with "*poiesis*," that is, with "making" (*Machen*) in the sense of fabricating; in the case of "growing things," by contrast, we are not dealing with "making," but with a genesis or generation that allows *physis* on its own to come forth "into the unconcealment of its being, that is, into presencing (*Anwesung*)." Thus, "*physei onta*" do not need the added assistance of a "making" or a maker; if such assistance were necessary, we would be faced with the situation that "an animal could not reproduce itself without mastering the science of its own zoology." In modern times, unfortunately, the distinction has been largely forgotten or sidelined in favor of the pervasive rule of technology. "Modern metaphysics, most impressively formulated by Kant," Heidegger notes, tends to "conceive 'nature' as a 'technique' such that this technique—elevated to the essence of nature—functions as the metaphysical ground for the possibility and even necessity of conquering and mastering nature through machine technology." In light of this modern proclivity, it is all the more important to remember Aristotle's *Physics* and Aristotle's distinction between modes of being and forms of genesis.[22]

Pre-Socratics and Poetic Thinking

With his text on Aristotle's *Physics*, Heidegger's concern with *physis* and the meaning of nature did not come to an end. In many ways, the text only constituted a launching pad for subsequent, still more probing investigations. One possible direction of such investigations was indicated already at the very end of his text. After having delineated the different modes of being, Heidegger indicates that Aristotle's thought actually is dependent on, and only a later accretion to, an earlier stage of Greek thinking—a stage usually designated as that of the "pre-Socratics" (and often devalued as the period of mere "nature philosophy"). "Aristotle's equation of Being (*ousia*) with some kind of *physis*," Heidegger states, "is actually just an *echo* of the great beginning of Greek philosophy and the first glimmers of Western philosophy." In that beginning, "Being was thought as *physis* in such a way that the *physis* conceptualized by Aristotle can only be seen as a late derivative of the originary insight." By way of example, the text cites a fragment of Heraclitus that says: "Being loves to conceal itself." What does this mean? Heidegger asks. Does it merely refer to a particular difficulty, to special tricks required to lure Being from its hiding place? The opposite is the case: "Concealment belongs to the predilection of Being, its manner of safeguarding its essence." But the essence of Being is "to reveal itself, to emerge, to come out into openness or unconcealment—*physis*. [But] only what in its very essence unconceals and must unconceal itself, can love to conceal itself." Hence, the original meaning of *physis*, as seen by Heraclitus, conceives "Being as concealing revealment." At this point, Heidegger brings unconcealment explicitly into connection with "truth" as expressed in the Greek term "*a-letheia*": "Truth as self-revealing belongs to Being itself: *physis* is *aletheia*."[23]

As we know, more than a decade later (during the postwar period), early Greek thought became one of Heidegger's intense and sustained preoccupations. This preoccupation is sometimes dismissed or harshly criticized as a derailment into loose speculation or unphilosophical mysticism. This dismissal, however, is far off the mark. Given Heidegger's persistent trajectory—his relentless inquiry into the meaning of "Being" and the meaning of *physis*—it was in a way inevitable that his inquiry would be drawn to a preepistemological mode of thinking, a mode not yet rigidly separating knower and known, subject and object, in favor of a deeper exploration of their ontological premises. Early Greek thought provides a rich reservoir of insights for such an exploration. (Similar resources might also be found in Indian texts on *brahman* and in East Asian reflections on *tao*). A prominent example of Heidegger's pre-Socratic inquiries is his commentary on a fragment by Parmenides, a text titled "Moira." At issue in the text is the relation between "thinking and being"—a nexus that Parmenides had (seemingly) conceived as a nonrelation or coincidence by stating: "For thinking and being are the same." At the beginning of his exegesis, Heidegger reviews several interpretations, most of which are mistaken. Proceeding on a shallow (merely ontic) level, one interpretation pleads for sameness or identity, on the ground that both sides of the equation are modes of being. "Since thinking, construed as a mode of being," the text states, "is just like every other kind of being, thinking proves to be the same as being." Surely, "one does not need philosophy to draw such a conclusion."[24]

Another reading missing the fragment's meaning is to conceive thinking as the constitutive basis or condition of possibility of being— a conception enjoying prominence and even preeminence in modern Western thought. In Heidegger's words: "The analysis of the relation between thinking and being, thus construed, is one of the chief aims of modern philosophy. With this aim in view, philosophy has even produced a special discipline, called epistemology or theory of knowledge, which today in many respects functions as the chief business of philosophy." Harking back to the terminology of *Being and Time*, modern thought is said to treat Being and beings simply as things "present-at-hand," as objects "standing over against" a subject, objects amenable to "re-presentational" thinking (*Vorstellung*). Prominent illustrations of this outlook are Bishop Berkeley's motto "*esse = percipi*" (being means being perceived), a motto ultimately anchored in the Cartesian cogito. Mediated through Kant's transcendental inquiry, Berkeley's motto surfaces even in Hegel's idealist philosophy—although on an infinitely refined and deepened level. For Hegel, we read, philosophy only comes properly into existence "when the self-thinking of absolute knowledge coincides with reality itself or as such." In his speculative logic, we witness "the complete elevation of Being into the thought of spirit seen as absolute reality." To this extent, Hegel's logic is "not only a proper modern interpretation of Berkeley's motto, but its unconditional realization or fulfillment."[25]

For Heidegger, modern Western thought not only missed the meaning of Parmenides's fragment, but turned it into its opposite. From the pre-Socratic angle, the relation between thinking and being was one neither of coincidence nor of representational constitution, but of responsiveness—a responsiveness respecting their difference, or rather their "unity or mutual belonging in difference" (*Zwiefalt*). Whereas Berkeley, we read, grants priority to thinking (*percipi*) over being, Parmenides "places thinking into the care (*überantwortet*) of being." With the term "Being," Parmenides does not denote the mere sum of possible modes of being; nor does he seek to pinpoint an abstract or transcendental realm set off against beings. Rather, what the term intimates is a differential unity or linked duality (*Zwiefalt*), a relation that is loosely but still inadequately captured in such phrases as the "Being *of* beings" or "beings *in* Being." Although not fully unpacked in pre-Socratic thought, what is implicit in the fragment is a pathbreaking understanding of "thinking," where the latter denotes not a constitutive action, but rather a kind of self-giving or surrender—a surrender to the precognitive call of Being. In Heidegger's words: "Thinking does not belong to Being because, as something present, it somehow merges into the sum of all beings." Rather, thinking is always on the way toward "that *Zwiefalt* to which it corresponds and which calls upon it"—a *Zwiefalt* that is not "a mere cognitive distinction between Being and beings, but rather unfolds by itself as concealing unconcealment."[26] As we know, Heidegger on other occasions—such as his text *Was heisst Denken?*—has linked "thinking" with "thanking" based on the former's anamnesis or recollection of Being (*Andenken*). We might also recall here the ending of his *Letter on Humanism,* where we read: "Thinking gathers language into simple saying; in this way, language is the language of Being as the clouds are the clouds of the sky. With its saying, thinking lays inconspicuous furrows in language—still more inconspicuous than the furrows that the farmer, slow of step, draws through the field."[27]

With these lines, we are brought back to our main theme of "nature." Given the close linkage between Being and self-generating *physis* in Heidegger's thought, it is clear that anamnesis or recollective thinking also narrows the gulf separating humans from nature. Apart from pre-Socratic fragments, another path pursued by the later Heidegger was poetry, especially the poetry of Hölderlin. His turn toward poetry, especially Hölderlin's great hymns, is sometimes denounced as an abandonment of philosophy and an embrace of Romantic mysticism. Like many other accusations, this critique likewise misses the mark—especially in light of the linkage of poetry and recollection. In his *Was heisst Denken?* Heidegger states explicitly: "Memory (*Mnemosyne*), mother of the Muses—the thinking back to what is to be thought—is the source or ground of poetry. . . . Poetry wells up only from thought devoted to thinking back, recollecting." In the same context, he refers to Hölderlin's hymn titled "Mnemosyne," which states: "We are a sign which is not read," and he comments: "Hölderlin's word, just because it is a word of poetry, may summon us with greater urgency and hence greater allure upon a way that tracks in thought what is most thought-provoking."[28] What grants to poetry this urgency is the fact that, among all modes of language, it is the most vulnerable, the most self-giving and receptive—and thus capable of healing the gulf dividing humans from nature and Being. Poetry, in this manner, is closely akin to fairy tales and legends. Like the latter, genuine poetry guides us into a realm where the languages of animals and humans are not yet rigidly separated, thus making room for a cosmic communion of understanding. In approaching this realm, to be sure, poets have to cultivate an unstudied simplicity and childlike innocence that alone reveals the wonder of the world. In the words of Emerson: "The lover of nature is he . . . who has retained the spirit of infancy even into the era of adulthood."[29]

As we know, the preeminent poet for the later Heidegger was

Hölderlin—although he frequently also interpreted the work of other poets, like Rilke, Trakl, and Stefan George. An important text highlighting the role of poets is an essay penned during the postwar period titled "What Are Poets For?" ("Wozu Dichter?"). The essay refers to one of Hölderlin's elegies that contains the line: "and what are poets for in a destitute time" ("in dürftiger Zeit")? In Heidegger's reading, the time invoked in the elegy is our modern age, a time marked by the lack of basic sustenance, the widespread lack of anamnesis and of the recollection of Being and *physis,* in favor of the wholesale embrace of fabricated artifacts (termed *Gemächte* in the essay on Aristotle). In Hölderlin's language, the lack of grounding is also equated with the complete erasure of the divine or the absence or "default of God" ("Fehl Gottes"). What renders our age particularly destitute is the fact that such absence or default is no longer even noticed. "The night time engulfing our world," Heidegger comments, "is the destitute time because its destitution constantly grows. It has already grown so destitute that it can no longer discern the absence of God as a lack." What is needed in the "world's night" is that somehow the yawning abyss be experienced and endured; but for this, the world needs people able "to reach into the abyss"—an endurance preeminently shouldered by poets. "Poets," we read, "are mortals who . . . sense the trace of the absent or fugitive gods, stay on their tracks and thus pave the way for other humans toward a turning (*Wende*)." Couched in Hölderlin's own idiom, to be a poet in a destitute time means "to attend singing to the trace of the fugitive gods. In this manner, the poet during the world's night guards the 'holy,' and the world's night for Hölderlin is 'holy night.'"[30]

A large part of the cited essay is devoted to the exegesis of some poems by Rainer Maria Rilke, seen as another, more recent poet in a destitute time. What is particularly relevant in the present context is Heidegger's rearticulation and sharpening of the contrast between *physis* and artifacts (familiar from the Aristotle essay); going beyond his earlier analysis, he now links fabrication or artifacts with "willing" or the "will to will," while portraying the trajectory of artifacts under the summary heading of technique or technology (*Technik*). As Heidegger states: in Rilke's notion of nature, "we still find resonances of the earlier term '*physis*' which can be equated with '*zoe*' (translated a 'life')." Hence, nature here designates "the ground of all beings," the

"*Urgrund*" that "since ancient times is called Being." By contrast to this natural self-genesis, modern civilization aims at the reduction of all beings to "present-at-hand" objects—a reduction that, propelled by the will to will, allows for unlimited technical mastery of things. "Willing," we read, "here means fabrication in the sense of objectification through deliberate self-assertion." Moreover, willing has the character of a "command" (*Befehl*) by virtue of which all things and beings are pressed into "unified sameness." In portraying this process, Heidegger's language is stark and bitter, testifying to a profound agony: "Progressively, the earth and its atmosphere are turned into raw material; man likewise becomes a material utilized for preordained purposes. The sway of unconditional self-assertion leading to the refashioning of the world through human commands reveals the hidden character of technology." What alone can bring relief from this process is a willingness that goes beyond willing, a willingness transcending the pull of self-assertion or egomania. Such transcending transformation, however, leads to a condition of self-exposure, vulnerability, and nonpossession—a condition that is precisely the lot of poets. Toward the end of his essay, Heidegger returns to the legacy of Hölderlin, who—more than anyone—exposed himself to the abyss of despair, thereby remaining "on the track" of a healing grace: "Hölderin is the preeminent precursor of poets in a destitute time. For this reason, no poet in this age can overtake him."[31]

Poets, seen in this light, are guideposts, mentors, path markers; but they are meant to guide not only themselves but their fellow human beings. For this reason, poetry is not just the poet's private "business," but the concern of humanity. In another postwar essay, Heidegger refers to one of Hölderlin's late poems that contains this phrase: "poetically man dwells." What, he asks, can be the possible meaning of this phrase? Is poetry not some empty daydreaming or flight from reality? And how can such flight possibly be linked with human "dwelling"? Here it becomes necessary to look more closely at the full phrasing of the poem, which reads: "Full of merit, yet poetically man dwells on this earth." With its emphasis on "this earth," the poem completely denies any kind of escapism. The poem even makes room for human "merit" accumulated through building, production, and construction. Yet can the simple construction of habitats by the modern housing industry fully capture the meaning of "dwelling"? In order to grasp the latter's meaning, one has to pay attention—with Hölderlin—to the peculiar location of human beings: their "ek-static" position between earth and heaven, between perishable things and immortals (or the divine). This in-between dimension—although the shared habitat of all humans—is preeminently plumbed and explored by poets. Hence, Heidegger notes, one can say that the proper human "dwelling place" is illuminated by poetry and that humans essentially "dwell poetically." In his words: the phrase "poetically man dwells on this earth" means that poetry "allows habitation to become a genuine dwelling"; hence, it enables humans "to dwell in the proper sense." The same phrase also guards against a shallow sentimentalism or a cult of belles lettres. In Hölderlin's understanding, poetry "does not surmount and transcend the earth in order to escape and hover above it." Rather, "poetry properly situates humans on this earth [and under heaven] and thus makes possible a genuine dwelling."[32]

7

Nature and the Way

Asian Thought

In the opening chapter, reference was made to a certain "counterhistory" accompanying the more official or dominant history of Western thought. Subsequent chapters explored prominent stages of this alternative trajectory—stages that, in different ways, sought to recuperate the intrinsic integrity of nature and to heal the widening gulf between nature and reason. With the relentless advance of modern science and technology, the need for such a recuperation became steadily more urgent. As it happens, in promoting the process of globalization and intercivilizational encounters, modern culture also brings into view helpful allies in the search for recuperation: namely, Asian thought, or rather the various traditions of Asian thought. In many ways, without being reducible to the recuperative task, Asian traditions provide important philosophical and practical resources that are compatible with, or congenial to, the alternative history sketched in these pages. This congenial resonance has been noted several times before. Thus, in discussing Spinoza's work, Hegel compared his piously holistic system with aspects of "Eastern (or Asian) thought." As has also been shown, leaders of the Romantic movement—above all Emerson and Thoreau—were deeply immersed in the study of Indian and Far Eastern texts. These examples can be rounded out and further deepened by reference to a central feature of Heidegger's work: his persistent emphasis on journeying and wayfaring (rather than apodictic knowledge)—which resonates strongly with the Asian accent on *tao*, interpreted as "way."

What is important and distinctive about the Asian notion of the "way" is that it does not denote a set of abstract rational principles or maxims, but rather a "way of life": a life conduct enacted in accordance with a holistic, ethical, and/or religious frame of reference. Seen in this light, the *tao* is not simply the construction or willful fabrication of a Cartesian cogito; nor is it a passive submission to externally operating causal forces. Rather, what is involved is the balanced, passive-active participation in the cultivation of the "good life"—where goodness means careful attentiveness to the demands of "heaven, earth, and the myriad things" (as one famous formulation says). To be sure, such cultivation takes different forms at different times and in different traditions of Asian thought. In classical Indian thought—especially Advaita Vendata—holism is expressed in the notion of *brahman,* seen as the all-pervasive and all-sustaining ground of all beings. As one should note, however, far from coinciding with an abstract concept, this grounding at the same time offers guideposts for *dharma,* that is, proper ethical conduct in given circumstances. In the Buddhist tradition, the notion of plenary being is replaced or supplemented by the accent on "nonbeing" (*sunyata*), preventing the rigid solidity of things—but an accent giving rise again to proper conduct in accordance with the "noble eightfold path." Chinese Confucianism, in turn, presents human life as embedded in a complex network of relationships, all of which require cultivation and responsiveness— outside of any rigid dogmatism or inflexibility. Spontaneous following of the "way," finally, is the hallmark of Taoism, with its emphasis on harmonious uncoerced right conduct. In the following, I shall discuss some central Indian, Buddhist, and Chinese teachings, taking a few leading Asian experts as my guides or mentors along the "way."

Classical Indian Thought

Searching for the core of classical Indian thought, one inevitably turns to the ancient Vedas and Upanishads. What is remarkable about the Vedas is that they do not offer a simple creation story (juxtaposing God and world) or a facile tale of natural evolution, but start out by recollecting an intrinsic wholeness, a groundless grounding. In the words of the *Rig-Veda:* "There was neither death nor immortality then; no signs were there of night or day. Only oneness was—and nothing beyond. . . . And in oneness arose love: the first seed of the soul. The truth of this the sages found in their hearts: seeking for wisdom in their hearts, they found that bond of union between Being and non-being." Comparing these lines distantly with the poems of St. Francis, Sanskrit scholar Juan Mascaró comments: "In the songs of the Vedas, we find the wonder of humanity before nature: fire and water, the winds and the storms, the sun and the rising of the sun are sung with adoration." As one needs to add, however, the insights of the Vedic sages are not simply wisdom passively to be contemplated, but admonitions and inducements to right living. In the words of the same *Rig-Veda:* "May the stream of my life flow into the river of righteousness. Loosen the bonds of sin that bind me! Let not the thread of my song be cut while I sing, and let not my work end before its fulfillment."[1]

The emphasis on oneness or wholeness, on the intimate union of humanity and the cosmos, is further accentuated in the Upanishads, the great teaching poems of the post-Vedic age, especially through their celebration of *brahman* as the present-absent bond sustaining everything. To quote Mascaró again: "The spirit of the Upanishads is the spirit of the universe; *brahman* is the underlying soul." This spirit or soul is not an external force or compulsion, but ultimately coincides with the inner spirit of humanity, with the genuine human "self" defined as *atman:* "Thus the momentous statement is made in the Upanishads that God must not be sought as something far away, separate from us, but rather as the very inmost of us, as the 'higher self' in us above the limitations of our little self."[2] The most stirring and eloquent formulations of the linkage of humanity with *brahman* are found in the so-called *Brihadaranyaka* and *Chandogya Upanishads.* The former contains the famous exchange between the sage Yajñavalkya and Maitreyi, where the sage compares *brahman* with a lump of salt, saying: "When thrown into water, the salt becomes dissolved in it and could not be taken out again; and yet, wherever we taste the water, it is salty." In the same manner, "this great being [*brahman*], endless, unlimited, consisting of nothing but insight, rises from out of all elements and vanishes in them again." In the same text, Yajñavalkya in a discussion with Gargi describes *brahman* as "neither coarse nor fine, neither short nor long, without darkness, without light, having no within and no without"—and yet as something "unseen, but seeing, unheard but hearing, unknown but knowing," by virtue of which "sun and moon stand apart." The *Chandogya Upanishad,* in turn, offers the equally famous dialogue between the sage Uddalaka and his son Shvetaketu, where the former instructs his son about the coincidence of *brahman* and *atman:* "Now that which is this subtle essence, the root of all, has in all that exists its being. It is the true (*sat*), it is the self (*atman*), and thou, O Shvetaketu, are it."[3]

Again, bypassing any theory-practice split, the Upanishads should not be read as detached mental exercises, but as marking pathways for proper human conduct. "One of the messages of these texts," Mascaró states, "is that spirit can only be known through union with [or participation in] *brahman,* and not through mere abstract learning." Participation here means the cultivation of the proper "self" through the overcoming of divisive selfishness, that is, the sustained training for the vision of the *atman-brahman* union—a training that is called *yoga.* The pathways of *yoga* are delineated in many classical texts, including the *Patanjali Yoga*—but also in the somewhat later *Bhagavad Gita,* which famously discusses the modalities of meditation, feeling, and action as suitable pathways for reaching wholeness or blessedness. It is particularly the pathway of action (*karma yoga*)—of which the Mahatma Gandhi was a sublime practitioner—that is celebrated in the *Gita.* As we read there: "Do your work (*karma*) in the peace of *yoga* and, free from selfish desires, be not moved in success or failure. For yoga is evenness of mind, a peace that does not waver." To these lines, the text adds a bit later: "Great is the person who, free from selfish attachments and with a mind ruling its powers in harmony, travels on the path of *karma yoga,* the path of consecrated action." A human being who journeys along this path or "way" cannot fail in the end to reach "sagehood" (*shtitaprajña*) and experience the union of his deeper being with the ocean of *brahman* or the divine spirit: "This is the eternal essence in humans (*brahmasthiti*); reaching it, all delusion is gone. Even in the last hour of life upon earth, a human being can reach the bliss (*nirvana*) of *brahman* and thus find peace in the peace of God."[4]

Following in the tradition of the Vedas and Upanishads, the emphasis on the wholeness of the cosmos was maintained especially in the philosophical school of "nondualism," or Advaita Vedanta, represented chiefly by the philosopher-teacher Adi Shankara (ca. 800). In his writings and commentaries, Shankara insisted on the ultimate unity of *brahman*—while relegating the status of separate entities to the level of illusion (which may involve a somewhat one-sided privi-

leging of sameness over difference). In the words of Sanskrit scholar
T. Mahadevan: "Vedanta seeks to discover the real nature of all beings
constituting the world." In their search, Vedanta philosophers seek
to overcome the subject-object division and to view the world from
the vantage of neither private consciousness nor objective data, but
from the dimension of being (or truth) undergirding both. "Vedan-
tic metaphysics," he adds, "would say that being is the real subject
in all judgments; it is being that appears as 'pot' or 'table.' And ultimately, being is the (true) self." From the angle of this metaphysics,
truth (*satya*) is disclosed when one follows the subjective or objective
path—in Upanishadic language, the path of *adhyatma* or *adhidaiva*
(where *adhyatma* means what relates to one's own self, and *adhidaiva*
what relates to the cosmos): "By coordinated inquiry, the discovery
is made that the reality of oneself is the reality of the cosmos too:
atman is *brahman*." Mahadevan cites a passage from the *Ishavasya
Upanishad,* which declares: "He who uniformly sees all beings even in
his self and his own self in all beings does not ever feel repelled from
them. To the one who knows [the sage], all beings are truly identical
with one's own self. Hence, what delusion or what sorrow can befall
someone who has seen this union?"[5]

In his book *Advaita Vedanta,* philosopher and Indologist Eliot
Deutsch strongly underscores this holistic perspective of classical Indian thought. As he writes, *brahman* in classical texts is seen as "pure
unqualified being," as something that "alone truly exists"—though not
in the manner of the existence of (ontic or finite) beings, but rather
as their (ontological) premise. The same might be said of *atman* or
paramatman, the highest self—which is described as "pure, undifferentiated awareness, timeless, spaceless, and non-different from *brahman.*" Taken in this sense, *atman* is distinguished from cognition or
cognitive reasoning. For while the latter is directional, the former is "a
state of being"; while cognitive thought objectifies its target, *atman* is
the pure ground "that underlies all subject/object distinctions." This is
why the famous saying of the Upanishads "tat tvam asi" (you are that)
can assert the coincidence or nondualism of self and *brahman.* Apart
from these metaphysical presuppositions, Deutsch also alerts readers
to the practical-ethical implications of Vedanta, that is, their manner
of guiding us on the "way." The teaching of the sages, he states, is not
mere empty speculation, but is grounded in real-life "experience" (*an-*

ubhava), the experience of journeying toward releasement. Although Vedanta is not a moral theory narrowly conceived, it does implicitly endorse and privilege an ethical way of life: namely, a path that leads practitioners toward releasement from selfishness and a continuously deepened bonding with "being." "The most basic criterion for moral judgment recommended by Advaita," Deutsch states, "is that those acts, desires, and thoughts that lead the moral agent to the highest good of 'self-realization' are 'good' and that those that lead toward the fulfillment of egoistic desire . . . are 'bad.'" Thus, the end here does justify the means—"provided that the end is the highest virtue, the *summum bonum*, self-realization" (or union of *atman* and *brahman*).[6]

Buddhist Thought

In many ways, Buddhism arose as an insurgence or rebellion against classical Hindu thought, which was suspected of harboring an ontological "positivism" and a reification of phenomena. Once the accent is placed entirely on plenary fullness of being, it was felt, the hidden, recessed, or "negative" aspects of *brahman* are necessarily sidelined or neglected. The suspicion was probably overdrawn. As Deutsch points out in *Advaita Vedanta,* classical Indian thought was quite capable of resisting positivism, namely, by distinguishing between the *saguna* and *nirguna* dimensions of *brahman*—where the former refers to its manifest presence, the latter to its hiddenness or absence. Whereas *nirguna brahman,* he says, is *brahman* "without qualities," an indeterminate state of being "about which ultimately nothing can be affirmed," *saguna brahman,* or *brahman* "with qualities," is a state of being "about which something can be said." Although differentiated, the two dimensions are not strictly opposed or antithetical; for, considered as "oneness" or wholeness, no wholly true positive or else negative statements can be made about *brahman*. Moreover, the two sides are ultimately connected on the level of experience: *Saguna brahman* is "the 'content' of a loving experience of unity," while *nirguna brahman* is the core of the experience of selflessness, self-transcendence, or self-loss in *brahman*.[7]

Whatever the nuances of classical Hindu metaphysics may have been, Buddhism from the beginning considered it preferable or prudent to shift the accent to "nonbeing" or "emptiness" (*sunyata*) and "nonselfhood" (*anatman*)—which does not in any way involve a slide into nihilism or an abandonment of the search for wholeness. On the contrary: precisely because there is brokenness, fragmentation, and rupture in the world, the search for wholeness or healing is crucial, and its path has to be diligently pursued. In the words of Buddhologist Robert Thurman: "Too often the fact of suffering (*dukkha*), the un-compromising starting point of the experiential *dharma,* is mistaken for the whole of Buddhist teaching"—an interpretation that robs Bud-dhism of its liberating and transformative thrust. To correct this mis-reading, Thurman presents a four-stage sequence of Buddhist views of nature as experienced—a kind of pilgrim's progress along the way to releasement. In the first stage, the accent is entirely on the brokenness of the world, on inner and outer suffering; every aspect of the natural life cycle is seen as miserable: "birth, sickness, aging, death, parting from the agreeable, meeting with the disagreeable." In large measure, the misery is induced by selfishness or selfish desire, by the "egocen-tric delusion of being a real self, an 'I am'" (separate from the rest). Awareness of this condition leads to the ascetic demand—prominent especially in Hinayana Buddhism—that desire be repressed and ego-centrism be abandoned. However, repression and negation are not the final word, but only gateways to a new and higher awareness: the awareness of the intrinsic relatedness of all things in lieu of their sep-aration or disjointedness. This is the second stage of the mentioned progression, a stage articulated especially by Mahayana Buddhism un-der the influence of the great philosopher Nagarjuna (ca. 100). At this point, all things or beings in the world are seen not as fixed, plenary entities, but as empty (*sunya*) and amenable to transformation, just as human individuals are seen as malleable and selfless (*anatman*). In lieu of a one-sided causal relation—between self and other, God and nature—the accent is on correlations or (what Buddhists call) "de-pendent co-arising" (*pratitya samutpada*). With this shift, Thurman comments, Buddhism brings "a relative living nature back into central prominence: as relativity, a universally relational nature."[8]

The third stage along the path builds upon the first and sec-ond stages, but with a quasi-dialectical twist (inspired again largely by Nagarjuna). What is realized at this point is that emptiness itself cannot be a plenary affirmation, but has to be transcended. In Thur-man's words: "Crucial here is that no absolute realm of emptiness is objectively absolute. Emptiness itself is not objectively discovered, because emptiness is empty of itself. The absolute is found to be just relationality." This insight triggers a shift from abstract metaphysics to praxis, to what is sometimes called the "stage of the path of magnificent ethics." One way of expressing this shift, Thurman notes, is to say that "wisdom (*prajña*) is the womb (*garbha*) of, and is indivisible from, the practice of compassion (*karuna*)." With regard to nature, a new attitude comes into view that regards nature as neither disjointed nor merely empty, but "as wholly excellent, as a perfect vessel of the evolution of beings from selfish suffering to selfless bliss." This is a view of the world "as an infinite panorama of Buddha-lands." Persevering in this view requires the steady cultivation of virtues along the "noble eightfold path"—a path that ultimately, at the fourth stage, prompts the practitioner to return to the world of brokenness, shouldering the task of the *bodhisattva* to bring healing to human suffering. It is at this point, Thurman notes, that the full radiance of Buddhist teaching becomes manifest, by urging the overcoming of aggressive egocentrism through "generosity, moral sensitivity, and patience." He quotes in this context a poem of the Mongolian Lama Jangkya Rolway Dorje that says: "The mutual interdependence of mother emptiness in whom nothing has real status, and father relationality in whom everything appears—this is exactly what needs to be understood."[9]

Thurman's observations are amply supported by the Japanese Buddhist scholar Masao Abe, a member of the famous Kyoto School. As Abe points out, Asian Buddhism does not share the anthropocentric bias nor the focus on individual separateness that characterizes much of Western philosophy and politics; rather, human life is seen as embedded in a holistic context, more specifically the context of "naturalness" or *jinen*. Human being, he states, is taken "as a member of the class of 'sentient beings' or 'living beings' and further (as clearly seen by Dogen) even as belonging among 'beings' living and non-living." From the perspective of "naturalness," the problem of "birth and death" (*shoji*) is regarded in Buddhism as the basic starting point, and its solution is the primary concern of the Buddhist path of releasement. However, even this issue is not constructed in an anthropocentric manner, but as part and parcel of the "generation-extinction" problem of all beings (and ultimately of the being-nonbeing or being-emptiness nexus). Thus, it is in a nonanthropocentric perspective "that the Buddhist conceptions of both 'birth-death' (*samsara*) and emancipation from 'birth-death' (*nirvana*) are to be grasped." In this context, *samsara* refers to the condition of transience and brokenness that needs to be overcome through self-transcendence along the eightfold path. When transience is thus transcended "in the depths of one's existence," Abe observes, "then the boundless dimension of '*jinen*' or 'naturalness,' in which both man and nature are equally enlightened and respectively disclose themselves in their original nature, is opened up for all." This is the meaning of such familiar Buddhist phrases as: "All trees and plants and lands attain Buddhahood" and "Mountains and rivers and all the earth disclose their *dharma-kaya,* or essential Buddhahood."[10]

Together with Thurman, Abe stresses the difference between Buddhist thought and the subject-object or cause-effect polarities endemic to much of Western philosophy. From a Buddhist perspective, he writes, "to attain 'reality' one should transcend not only the duality of life-death, but also the wider dualities: that is, those involving generation-extinction, appearance-disappearance, and being-non-being." The requisite step for overcoming dualisms is the taming of ego attachments and the abandoning of selfish desires. The practitioner journeying along this path of releasement ultimately will reach the "boundless dimension of being-non-being," a dimension that also discloses the basic noncausal connectedness of all things and beings, that is, their mutually "dependent co-arising" (*pratitya samutpada*). In Abe's words: "Dependent co-origination, a basic idea in Buddhism, indicates that there is no irreversible [or unidirectional] relation between 'man' and 'God,' nature and the supernatural." This codependence is stressed eloquently in Mahayana Buddhism, especially in the familiar phrasing: "*Samsara* as it is *nirvana.*" Once this stage comes into view, the path of liberated and liberating praxis opens up for practitioners, who are now fully able "to live and work creatively in the world." Differently put: the so-called Buddha-nature, which is said to be inherent in everyone and everything as well, is simply another term for the realization of universal transitoriness, naturalness or *jinen* in which every thing discloses itself as it truly is. "It is from this realization of *jinen* that the Buddhist life of wisdom and compassion begins."[11]

Chinese Thought

With some modifications, similar themes and arguments can also be found in Chinese thought, especially in its two major intellectual traditions: Confucianism and Taoism (or Daoism). The most prominent parallel is the emphasis on wholeness or holism and the preference for continuity over discontinuity, coherence over fragmentation. Western students of Chinese thought have been quick to notice and highlight this feature. In the words of Sinologist Frederick Mote: "The genuine Chinese cosmogony is that of an organismic process, meaning that all parts of the entire cosmos belong to one organic whole and that all interact as participants in one spontaneously self-generating life process." This aspect implies the rejection of all rigid dualisms or oppositions: the dualisms of creator God and world, of *natura naturans* and *naturata,* of transcendence and immanence. Without taking recourse in an explicit "creation myth," Mote adds, Chinese philosophical and religious traditions "have regarded the world and man as uncreated," though continuously self-generating. Since Chinese thinkers perceived the cosmos as the unfolding of continuous creativity, they could not entertain "conceptions of creation *ex nihilo* by the hand of God, or through the will of God, and all other such mechanistic, teleological, and theistic cosmologies." The thrust of Mote's argument is seconded by China scholar Joseph Needham when he describes the Chinese worldview as that of "an ordered harmony of wills without an ordainer."[12]

The rejection of the creator/world dualism does not mean a simple lapse into a crude naturalism devoid of spiritual energies. On the contrary: the idea of the world or nature as "self-generating" is predicated on the working of a dynamic energy that in the Chinese tradition is called *ch'i,* translated usually as "vital power" or "vital force." Again, it is important here not to lapse into dualism by assigning this force one-sidedly either to matter or to spirit. This point is eloquently made by Chinese American scholar Tu Weiming. "The most basic stuff that generates the cosmos," he writes, "is neither solely spiritual nor material but both. It is a vital force," a force that "must not be conceived of either as disembodied spirit or as pure matter." Tu Weiming in this context refers to the historian of Chinese philosophy Wing-tsit Chan, who observed that *ch'i* originally denoted a "psychophysiological power" and not simply a material force. He also appeals to two great Confucian thinkers—Chang Tsai (1020–1077) and Wang Fu-chih (1619–1692)—who, while rejecting an abstract spiritualism or intellectualism, defined *ch'i* as "not simply matter but a vital force endowed with all-pervasive spirituality." With a side glance to the Western tradition of thought, Tu states that *ch'i* is obviously "different from the Cartesian dichotomy between spirit and matter." Yet, he adds, it would be misleading to depict Chinese thought as a sort of "pre-Cartesian naïveté lacking any differentiation between mind and body." Analytically, Chinese thinkers were clearly able to make this distinction; but they did not stop there, moving from analysis backward or forward to synthesis, thereby recollecting the union of distinguished elements. In this manner, "the loss of analytical clarity is compensated by the reward of imaginative richness."[13]

In the notion of a spontaneously self-generating life, Tu Weiming detects three main motifs or themes: those of continuity, wholeness, and dynamism. Under the rubric of the first motif, all modes of being, "from a rook to heaven," are integral parts of a continuum that is often referred to as the "great transformation" (*ta-hua*). This means that the psycho-physiological energy of *ch'i* is present everywhere; in a gesture to a quasi-Buddhist conception, he adds that this presence even "suffuses the 'great void' (*t'ai-hsü*)," which is the source of all being-nonbeing. Continuity is directly related to the theme of wholeness or holism. For if genuine creativity is "not the creation of something out of nothing, but a continuous transformation of what is already there," then the unfolding world represents "the authentic manifestation of the cosmic process in its all-embracing fullness." Unfolding and self-generating point immediately to the third motif of dynamism—a motif, however, which should not be equated with unilinear progress or development or with the circular movement of cyclic repetition. "The Chinese world view," Tu comments, "is neither cyclical nor spiral; it is transformational." For this reason, Chinese cosmogony should be seen not as a fixed or static pattern, but as an "open system" whose transformation in unceasing or constantly under way.[14]

Apart from allusions to quasi-Buddhist perspectives, Tu Weiming's text also refers to some Taoist teachings, especially their notions of the "way" (*tao*) and of "nature" (*tzu-jan*). As Tu explains: "The Taoist idea of *tzu-jan* ('self-so')—used in modern Chinese to translate the English 'nature'—[points to] a nondiscriminatory and non-judgmental position which allows all modalities of being to display themselves as they are." This position can be reached only when subject-object polarities are left behind and when "competitiveness, domination, and aggression are thoroughly transformed" or discarded. This does not mean, he adds, that Taoist thinkers were completely ignorant of the struggle occurring in nature and of the ruptures or dislocations caused by natural catastrophes and/or humanly induced calamities; they were quite aware that history is littered with "internecine warfare, oppression, and injustice." However, they preferred to draw attention to a deeper layer where things display themselves in their "suchness" or as "self-so." In the midst of conflict and tension, which are "like waves of the ocean," they celebrated a deeper structure that is tranquil and serene. Such attentiveness for them was also the core of the "way" (tao) seen as a journey to releasement. The same insight or disposition, one needs to add, was shared by many non-Taoist, especially Confucian, thinkers. Tu here invokes again the legacy of the great Confucian sage Chang Tsai, who described the cosmos as the "great harmony" and defined the latter as the tao: "The Great Harmony is called the Tao. It embraces the nature which underlies all counter processes of floating and sinking, rising and falling, motion and rest. It is the origin of the process of fusion and intermingling, of overcoming and being overcome, of expansion and contraction."[15]

An important point stressed in Tu's essay—and in accord with our discussion of Indian and Buddhist perspectives—is that Chinese thought, on the whole, is not purely contemplative or abstractly metaphysical, but intimately related to concrete life experience. Although not narrowly anthropocentric, Chinese cosmology is not inhuman or antihuman. Although we know, Tu writes, that the cosmos is, by and large, indifferent to "our private thoughts and whims," we are yet an integral part of it: "Like mountains and rivers, we are legitimate beings in this great transformation." Chang Tsai again is a powerful witness: "Heaven is my father and earth is my mother, and such a small being as I finds an intimate place in their midst. Therefore, that which fills the universe I regard as my body and that which directs the universe I regard as my nature. All people are my brothers and sisters, and all things are my companions." To be part of the cosmos, from this angle, means for human beings to respect its processes and to participate in the ongoing "great transformation." This, in turn, requires steady self-cultivation on the level of both intelligence and moral sensitivity. Importantly, following the "way" does not just involve "doing what comes naturally." Tu's text cites again Wang Fu-chih: "The profound person acts naturally as if nothing happens, but . . . he acts so as to make the best choices and remain firm in holding to the 'mean.'" Paraphrasing this statement, Tu writes: "To act naturally without letting things take their own course means, in Neo-Confucian terminology, to follow the 'heavenly principle' (*t'ien-li*) without being overcome by 'selfish desires' (*ssu-yü*)." Summing up his entire review of Chinese visions of nature, Tu Weiming offers by way of conclusion this inspiring formulation: "It is true that we are consanguineous with nature. But as humans, we must make ourselves worthy of such a relationship."[16]

This statement can also serve as an appropriate conclusion or capstone of the present book.

Appendix A

Ecological Crisis and Human Renewal

A Tribute to Thomas Berry

One of the most urgent problems in our time is the issue of climate change or (what is called) the looming "ecological crisis." If unchecked and progressively more severe, this crisis can lead to the destruction of our natural habitat, that is, of nature as the sustaining matrix of human life. Taken by itself, climate change is a natural process that can be scientifically measured and traced back to empirical processes in nature, such as the effect of greenhouse gases or carbon dioxide emissions. In the view of many, the ecological crisis of our time is the result of faulty technology; hence, its solution or overcoming requires mainly the resources of better science and more advanced technology. Without disputing the role of science and technology, I want to focus here on another, deeper dimension of the ecological crisis: its character as a human crisis or a crisis of humanity. The latter crisis, in my view, is the result not of scientific deficiencies, but of a faulty relation between modern (chiefly Western) humanity and nature or the cosmos. If this is so, then the basic relationship between nature and humanity needs to be recast, in the direction of replacing the model of human mastery over nature with the model of mutual dependence and ecological responsibility. To a considerable extent, this change requires a dramatic new learning process: where the modern West is willing to learn both from countercurrents in Western thought and from older ethical and cosmological traditions of the non-West.

In large measure, the model of mastery over nature can be traced to the onset of modern Western philosophy, when the human "mind" was separated rigidly from "extended matter," that is, from the whole realm of inner and outer "nature." With this innovation, human mind became the lord and master of the world, and anthropocentrism replaced older visions of cosmological interdependence. To some extent, this division from nature can also be traced to aspects of "Abrahamic" religions—especially a certain accent on radical divine "transcendence"—although the implications of this accent only surfaced in modern times. In our period, the effects of the ecological crisis have driven home the untenability of the Cartesian paradigm. The question is how to proceed. Can we simply give up human autonomy and the acquisitions of modern freedom? Should we replace dualism with a slide into biological naturalism and determinism? Many great minds have wrestled with this problem during the past century—from Alfred North Whitehead and William James to Martin Heidegger and Merleau-Ponty. In my talk, I want to pay a special, memorial tribute to Thomas Berry, who passed away a few months ago, on June 1, 2009, at the age of ninety-four. Berry has rightly been acclaimed as one of the leading ecologists, cosmologists, and even "eco-theologians" of our age. In the following I shall first give a brief overview of his life. Next, I shall discuss some of his major writings and seminal ideas, in order finally to draw parallels between his work and that of other contemporary proponents of ecological and spiritual renewal around the world.

Thomas Berry's Life

I did not have the good fortune of knowing Thomas Berry well. I knew him only distantly through our joint membership in the Forum on Religion and Ecology, in which he participated intensively and ceaselessly—and I only intermittently, time permitting. I wish particularly that I had been able to attend the memorial service held in his honor on September 26 in New York. On that day, about one thousand people from all around the globe gathered at the Cathedral of St. John the Divine in Manhattan to celebrate the memory and the rich life of Thomas Berry. The event began with the presentation of the Thomas Berry Award to Martin Kaplan, a lifetime supporter of Berry's work in the fields of ecology, religion, and intercultural dialogue. In his lecture, Kaplan invoked the global vision of Berry and issued a strong appeal to political and religious leaders to implement the findings of the international reports on climate change for the sake of present and future generations. Following the award ceremony was the memorial service for Berry—which, entirely transcending the somber occasion, culminated in a surge of interreligious and cross-cultural celebration (including the Omega Dance Company, the Mettawee River Company, Paul Winter's soprano saxophone solo, as well as cello and organ recitals). As one participant observed: "It was a summit meeting of wisdom-keepers—all Thomas's children. . . . The community that emerged from this event was itself a Cathedral." And in the words of another participant: the service "afforded a glimpse of what Thomas called the Grand Liturgy of the Universe."[1]

Thomas Berry was born on November 9, 1914, in Greensboro, North Carolina. This was the beginning of the First World War; but his childhood was remarkably untouched by the gloomy effects of the war and the Great Depression. In his own recollection, he spent his childhood roaming the woods and meadows around his hometown. He was, it seems, an ecologist by birth. At the age of eleven, he reports that a sense of "natural wonder and numinous presence" overcame him in one of his outdoor activities. "The field," he says, "was covered with white lilies rising above the meadow. A magic moment, this experience gave to my life something that seems to explain my being at a more profound level than almost any other experience I can remember. . . . It was a wonder world," he added, "that I have carried in my unconscious and that has deeply governed my thinking."[2]

In 1934, at the age of twenty, Berry entered the novitiate of the Passionate Order, taking the name of Thomas after Thomas Aquinas (his original name was William Nathaniel). In 1942, he was ordained as a Passionate priest. He next studied intellectual history at the Catholic University of America and received his doctorate in 1949 with a thesis on Giambattista Vico—that great Italian intellectual who placed himself deliberately at the outskirts of European modernity. Following his doctorate, Berry spent several years studying the cultural and intellectual traditions of Asia. He lived in China, studied Chinese at a language school in Beijing, and also traveled to other parts of Asia (such as India and Japan). During this time, he authored two books on Asian religions: *Buddhism* and *Religions of India*.

Following these global excursions, Berry took up in earnest his academic career. From 1956 to 1960 he taught the cultural history of India and China at the Institute for Asian Studies at Seton Hall University and then taught for six years at the Center for Asian Studies at St. John's University in New York. From 1966 on, he served as professor of the history of religions and also as director of the history and religion program in the Theology Department of Fordham (until 1979). In 1970 he also founded the Riverdale Center of Religious Research along the Hudson River and served as its director until 1987.[3] It was during this period that he began to lecture widely on the intersection of cultural, spiritual, and ecological issues; his lectures and writings came to reflect increasingly the influence of Pierre Teilhard de Chardin (1881–1955), the great evolutionary and cosmological thinker. Among his publications during this period let me mention *The Dream of the Earth* (published by Sierra Club Books in 1988) and *Befriending the Earth* (published by Twenty-Third Publications in 1990). These were followed by a joint effort with physicist Brian Swimme, *The Universe Story: A Celebration of the Unfolding of the Cosmos* (published in 1992), and also by one of his key books, *The Great Work: Our Way into the Future* (published in 1999). More recently, a number of books have appeared that admirably pinpoint the gist of Berry's thought: *Evening Thoughts: Reflections on Earth as Sacred Community* (published by the Sierra Club and the University of California Press in 2006) and still more recently *Christian Future and the Fate of Earth* (Orbis Books, 2009) and *The Sacred Universe: Earth, Spirituality, and Religion in the Twenty-first Century* (Columbia University Press, 2009). In the words of Father Diarmuid O'Murchu, author of *Quantum Theology* and *Reclaiming Spirituality:* "For me, Thomas Berry was the single greatest disciple of Teilhard de Chardin who awakened in me a profound sense of the sacredness of God's creation. In his writings, one almost feels the sense of an evolving spirituality, capturing its innovative élan on the one hand, but also the birth pangs which beget the evolutionary process at every stage."[4]

Nature as Sacred Liturgy

Thomas Berry's writings are sprawling and multifaceted; but there is also a developmental line. Unsurprisingly for an evolutionary thinker, his work also reflects a process of evolution and maturation, leading to steadily more nuanced formulations. Basically, in his writings, Berry moves from the history of European ideas toward steadily expanding ecological, cosmological, and even "eco-theological" frameworks. His rootedness in European intellectual history is particularly evident in his earliest publication: *The Historical Theory of Giambattista Vico,* an outgrowth of his doctoral dissertation of 1949. In his study, Berry places Vico into the thick intellectual context of his time; but he also discusses Vico's relevance for modern and contemporary scholarship. It is in the latter context that he takes up Vico's well-known distinction between "philosophy" and "philology"—where the former designates a rationalist Cartesian enterprise, while the latter (far from being narrowly limited to linguistics) denotes something close to (what we call) "human studies" or the "humanities." In Berry's words: philology is "much closer to the German word *Geisteswissenschaften.* It included [for Vico] the study, not only of languages and literature, but also of the history of every aspect of human social life. It embraced equally the social and historical views of religion, ideas, customs, laws, ethics, and, in general, all the arts and the sciences."[5]

It is in Berry's discussion of the historical dimension of philology that one discovers first, embryonic glimmers of his later evolutionary theory. As he points out, history for Vico was not simply governed by a rationalist teleology (inspired by Platonic or Cartesian ideas) or else by a transcendent religious eschatology; nor was he willing to abandon history and its *"corsi e ricorsi"* to naturalistic and/or pagan assumptions of a physical determinism. Rather, Vico's approach was more subtle and mediated. In his *Scienza nuova,* Berry observes, Vico "neither denied nor embraced the view of history presented in the Christian religious tradition. Instead [without rejecting that tradition], the transcendent in his view gave way to the immanent, the supernatural to the natural, and in a most impressive way, simplicity gave way to multiplicity. This increase in the various influences entering history gives to the work of Vico its substance and its richness as well as its difficulty and obscurity." In other words: what Vico tried to accomplish was to correlate and reconcile sacred history with natural or immanent history, or—in Berry's words—"the resplendent eternal order with the historical order immersed in the obscure depths of time."[6] To be sure, these comments offer only some glimpses of evolution; and there was still a long way to traverse to reach Berry's later vision of the "Grand Liturgy of the Universe."

As mentioned before, following his university studies, Berry visited Asia and sought to absorb some of the great religious traditions of that Eastern world. In his study titled *Buddhism* (1967), Berry offered an erudite overview of the development and major doctrines of that Asian religion; but he also reflected on the relevance and importance of that tradition for contemporary life in the West and elsewhere. As he wrote: "To be ignorant of Buddhism is to be ignorant of a large part of man's spiritual, intellectual, and cultural formation. . . . All the basic spiritual traditions of man are open, clear, direct expressions of the manner in which human beings have structured their personal and social life in order to give it some higher, transcendent significance. . . . What Buddhism has contributed belongs among the highest moral, spiritual, intellectual achievements ever attained by humanity." Recognition of this accomplishment was important and even crucial also from a Christian point of view. Reflecting on the present emergence of truly global horizons, Berry compared this emergence with the encounter of the early church fathers with the Hellenic world: "A new patristic age is in process of formation, an age vaster in its scope than the earlier patristic age. We can expect it to be equally more fruitful in its consequences, for it is leading toward a new world culture in which all the world traditions will have their finest and fullest expression."[7]

The same ecumenical spirit is abundantly evident in Berry's next major book, *Religions of India: Hinduism, Yoga, Buddhism.* As he wrote in his introduction to the first edition (of 1973), Indian traditions offer a rich panoply of teachings that steer a course between abstract rationalist philosophy and dogmatic theology and that might broadly be called "spiritual": "They belong in the realm of spirituality, the realm in which much of St. Augustine's work was done, the realm of Dionysius [the Areopagite], of Bonaventure, Meister Eckhart, John of the Cross, and more recently of Nietzsche and to some extent Heidegger." They are concerned not just with rational enlightenment, but with the spiritual or existential improvement of humanity. Moreover, Indian spirituality is not static, but exhibits constant dynamic movement, by creating ever new forms "as is seen in such moderns as Ramakrishna and Vivekananda, in Tagore and Gandhi." A peculiar feature of Indian traditions is their espousal of "contradictory" positions that are ultimately reconciled: "There is insistence on extreme immanence and extreme transcendence at the same time. The two, it is felt, implicate each other and finally identify with each other. Absolute immanence and absolute transcendence must eventually be the same." (Forebodings or echoes of a "sacred liturgy of the world"?) And in the conclusion we read: "Hinduism, Yoga, and Buddhism are no longer merely Indian traditions; they are world traditions. India has lost forever its exclusive claim on these traditions. Now they are part of the universal human heritage. . . . Humankind is now an integral part of the Indian spiritual process."[8]

Let me briefly draw your attention to the foreword to the second edition (of 1992), which brings out more clearly the ecological and eco-spiritual implications of Indian traditions. Since the first publication of the book, Berry writes there, "the human situation has become even more critical. We are moving from a period of industrial plundering of the planet [hopefully] into a more intimate way of relating to the planet. We can no longer violate the integrity of the Earth without becoming a destructive force for both the surrounding world and for ourselves." In seeking to move in the required new direction, Indian traditions can help us find our way. This way, to be sure, is steep and difficult, because we have largely gone astray. "We have shaped for ourselves," Berry says, "a mechanistic wonder world that we seem determined to build even when we are obviously reducing the entire planet to a condition of waste and ruin. In a kind of mental fixation we have become autistic in relation to the natural world. We have closed it out as an unacceptable world." In this situation, our senses have to be opened up to a world that speaks to us in a nonmechanistic and unobjectifiable way: "We need to hear the voices of the natural world, the voices of the ocean and the sky and the wind and all natural phenomena. The traditions of India can assist in teaching us this, if only we first enter into its deepest experience of the divine as expressed in its great spiritual heritage."[9]

In some of his subsequent writings, Berry sought to offer a more philosophical or reflective account of what the encounter between Western modernity and Eastern spirituality means in terms of the larger story of human development or evolution. It is at this point that the work of Teilhard de Chardin exerted its profound influence. In a paper published in 1978, in a monograph series entitled "Teilhard

Studies," Berry tried to delineate (what he called) "The New Story" of evolution as an alternative both to traditional biblical salvation history and to secular biological evolutionism. In Berry's account, the older biblical story can no longer function today as "*the* story of the Earth" nor as "the integral story of mankind"; it has become a "sectarian story." At the same time, scientific evolutionism has reduced nature to an externally objectified process, thus eliminating the role of human freedom and spirituality. What is dawning today on the horizon, however, is a "new story" where humankind is not merely "a detached [scientific] observer," but is "integral to the entire process." That story becomes "the latest expression of the cosmic-earth process," as a movement in which "the cosmic-earth-human process becomes conscious of itself." In a way, Berry's new story can be seen as a step integrating or reconciling the earlier biblical and scientific accounts. Although novel and unfamiliar to both the scientist and the believer, the story (he says) amounts to "a new revelatory experience. . . . A new paradigm of what it means to be human emerges."[10]

The paper just discussed resonates in many ways with the teachings of Teilhard de Chardin; it should be noted, however, that Berry was by no means an uncritical disciple. A follow-up monograph published a few years later (in 1982) and titled "Teilhard in the Ecological Age" articulated quite clearly his critical reservations. The essay placed Teilhard's work at the intersection or confluence of diverse evolutionary perspectives: the mechanistic worldview, the "natural history" concept, and the mystical and arcadian traditions. "All of these traditions," Berry notes, "were absorbed into the vast perspective of Teilhard's vision." Yet there was a problem with this integral vision—a problem that resulted from Teilhard's unabashed endorsement of modern (Western) technological "progress" or advancement. In Berry's words: "While he rejected the mechanistic worldview in favor of a more organic-spiritual worldview, [Teilhard] fully accepted the industrial and technological exploitation of the planet as a desirable human activity." Thus, Teilhard's vision ultimately amounted to an effort to "spiritualize" or sugarcoat modern technological progress, thereby rendering the latter immune from transformation. The subordination of the natural world to human domination and exploitation, Berry states bluntly, in effect became the position of Teilhard. It fitted into his view of the human as advancing over new thresholds of the evolutionary process. . . . In this context, Teilhard became the heir to the imperial tradition in human-earth relations, the tradition of human control over the natural world. The sublime mission of scientific research and technological innovation was to support this advance into the ultra-human. . . . In this manner, we might consider that Teilhard is a faithful follower of Francis Bacon, in his assertion that human intelligence should subordinate the natural world to human needs.[11]

What emerges from this critique is a salient deficit marking Teilhard's work—a deficit resulting from his relative neglect of ecological imperatives. Now, Berry says, "the challenge of the ecological disturbance of the planetary functioning consequent on modern scientific technologies is forcing Teilhard's thought to a more profound level of self-criticism and this in confrontation with problems never fully envisaged by Teilhard." The challenge at this point is not to go in search of an "ultra-human" superprogress, but rather to teach a chastened humanity the needs of our ecological habitat. What neither Teilhard nor his followers (and opponents) could see was "that the glory of the human was becoming the desolation of the earth or that the desolation of the earth was becoming the destiny of the human."[12] To escape this desolation a more thorough-going "turning" or transformation was needed. To explore the implications of this turning became the central theme of Berry's later works. A text of the mid-1980s sketched a vision of a "new cosmology"—a cosmology distinctly *not* anthropocentric in character and where humanity's role is seen as deeply embedded in nature and the revelatory sparks of the universe. As Berry stated at the time: "Neither humans as a species, nor any of our activities, can be understood in any significant manner except in our role in the functioning of the earth and of the universe itself. . . . [For] the universe in every phase is numinous in its depths, is revelatory in its functioning, and in it human life finds its fulfillment in celebratory self-awareness" (not self-centeredness).[13]

In his following writings from the early 1990s, Berry made the important move from cosmology to "cosmogenesis," that is, from a static to a "becoming" universe—which implies a new conception of evolution. In Berry's formulation, cosmogenesis in our time involves the progression from an earlier "Cenozoic" period—witnessing the rise and rapid evolution of a multitude of species—to a new "Ecozoic" period initiating new forms of human-earth relationships. As one should note, the latter period for him was only a possibility, one strongly contested by a "Technozoic" alternative future in which the condition of the planet is entirely dominated by technology. I do not wish to dwell on Berry's somewhat peculiar terminology. More interesting is the evolutionary scheme implicit in his account. At one point, he compares cosmogenesis with the Christian doctrine of the trinity, speculating that God the Father signifies the original unity of creation, Christ as Son the inner awareness and articulation of the cosmogenetic process, and the Holy Spirit the "bonding force" of all beings. Stated in more general, secular-sociological language, cosmogenesis for Berry means a movement from an initial holistic cosmos to a stage of progressive differentiation, particularistic self-assertion, and identity formation to the final emergence of a new "bonding" and possible "community" formation—where the latter bonding is the result not of top-down imposition, but of a free lateral engagement and shared practice. In his words: "I propose that there is a new and in some ways better model" of cosmogenesis: "That is the model of differentiation, inner articulation, and communion which emerges from our scientific understanding of the universe."[14]

In recent times, especially in the Western world, he finds an excessive emphasis on differentiation and particularistic identity formation, especially on the differentiation of humans from nature. The results are palpable. "The devastation of the planet," Berry writes, "is attributable to this exaggerated understanding of particularity in election in the biblical, Western tradition. In this case, it is the feeling that only the human—and not the natural world—is elected." For Berry, this kind of antropocentrism has led to a widespread condition of "autism" or human self-enclosure: "That, I think, is what has happened to the human condition in our time. We are talking [only] to ourselves. We are not talking to the river, we are not listening to the river. We have broken the great conversation." As an antidote to this "autistic" condition, Berry points to the experience of "primal peoples" as expressed in the book *Black Elk Speaks* and also to a series of paintings by Margaret Mee titled *In Search of Flowers of the Amazon Forest*.

Being attentive to such voices and experiences involves for humans a profound "turning" and chastening. "There is no such thing," Berry states unequivocally, "as a *'human* community' without the earth and the soil and the air and the water and all the living forms. Without these, humans do not exist. . . . Humans are woven into this longer community. The large community is the sacred community."[15]

The details of Berry's cosmogenetic conception were developed more fully in texts of the late 1980s and 1990s, such as *Dream of the Earth* (1988), *The Universe Story* (with physicist Brian Swimme, 1994), and *The Great Work: Our Way into the Future* (1999–2000). The theme of the "sacred community" resurfaces especially in two still more recent texts: *Evening Thoughts: Reflections on the Earth as Sacred Community* (2006) and *The Sacred Universe: Earth, Spirituality, and Religion in the Twenty-first Century* (2009). I cannot possibly do full justice to these later writings; I limit myself to a few comments. *Evening Thoughts* inserts the current ecological crisis into the broader framework of cosmogenesis and modern cultural history. Offering a dramatic narrative of creation, diversification, and human-earth community, the book seeks to reconcile modern evolutionary thinking with cross-cultural traditions of spirituality and also with aspects of traditional biblical teachings. *The Sacred Universe* brings together a series of essays written over several decades, all dealing with our ecological crisis, the ongoing destruction of ecosystems, and the need for interreligious and cross-cultural dialogues as a way of rekindling awareness of the sacred quality of the world. Far from surrendering to a fashionable "gloom and doom" mentality, the book issues a clarion call for the cultivation of ecological responsibility and for the creation of a true partnership between humans and the earth.[16]

For present purposes I want to round out my overview of Berry's writings by drawing attention briefly to his posthumously published book: *Christian Future and the Fate of the Earth*. The book deserves special attention, in my view, because it illustrates how a Christian—in fact, any religious believer—comes to terms with the ecological problem without entirely discarding his or her faith commitment. In his book, Berry discusses three kinds of relationships or what he calls "mediations." The first mediation is that "between the divine and the human." This relation was first powerfully articulated in ancient Israel and then continued by the other "Abrahamic" religions. The second mediation involves "inter-human" relations, the "reconciliation of different human groups"—an issue that became predominant in Western modernity. That period, Berry notes, "saw the rise of the great nation-states, each so absolute in its demands that it could not tolerate opposition or injury from any other state." A similar exclusiveness came to prevail among religious, ethnic, and socioeconomic groups. The third mediation not only seeks to overcome these modern fissures but introduces a new imperative: the reconciliation "between the human community and the Earth, the planet that surrounds and supports us." In our time, the three mediations overlap and interpenetrate; but the third also puts strong pressure on the earlier relationships and especially on the "human-divine" relation. As Berry as a priest admits frankly: "So far Christians have not distinguished themselves by their concern for the destiny of the Earth." The problem is that Christianity, as well as many other great religions, has been "excessively oriented toward transcendence," that is, toward the distance between God and humans. Moreover, not only has divine transcendence been an overwhelming preoccupation, but "human transcendence over the natural world has also been emphasized," with the result that, in modernity, the natural world has been ruthlessly reduced to a target of human domination.[17]

What is needed in our time is a correction of the lop-sided emphases of the past—a correction that will be a challenge especially for Christian believers. As Berry notes candidly: a viable future will depend above all "on the ability of Christians to assume their responsibility for the fate of the Earth. The present disruption of all the basic life systems of Earth has come about within a culture that emerged from a biblical Christian matrix." The disruption, he adds, "did *not* arise out of the Buddhist world or the Hindu or Chinese or Japanese worlds or [even] the Islamic world. It emerged from within our Western Christian–derived civilization." Hence, until Christians accept the fact that some of their beliefs "carry with them a vulnerable aspect," the dilemma cannot be overcome. There are powerful obstacles or resistances standing in the way of such acceptance. Most important, Christians are highly apprehensive about what they tend to call "naturalism, paganism, or even pantheism." Thus, a genuine "sense of Earth" and the "pull toward an intimacy with Earth" does not come easily for them; in fact, "the more intense the Christian commitment, the more difficult such a sense, such a pull is." In this context, Berry sees the need for a new spiritual religiosity, which operates "not by domination but by invocation." "What is needed now," he writes, "is not exactly a new religion but new religious sensitivities in relation to planet Earth that would arise in all our religious traditions." The new sensitivities would remedy not only the distance between faith and ecology but also the lateral distance between faith communities in our world. Here is an admirable statement that summaries Berry's spiritual-ecological or eco-theological convictions:

> If, as Christians, we assert the Christian dimension of the en-
> tire world, we must not refuse to be a dimension of the Hindu
> world, of the Buddhist world, of the Islamic world. Upon this
> intercommunication on a planetary scale depends the future
> development of the human community. This is the creative
> task of our times, to foster the global meeting of the nations
> and of the world's spiritual traditions.[18]

Some Parallel Initiatives

Berry has not been alone in perceiving and articulating the "creative task" of our time. As it happens, his call for a spiritual reorientation has been ably seconded in recent times by an impressive number of like-minded intellectuals and thinkers. A prominent exemplar is the Spanish-Indian philosopher Raimon Panikkar. What Panikkar has called the "cosmotheandric" or else the "anthropocosmic" experience corresponds in large measure to the three "mediations" and their nec-essary interrelation mentioned by Berry. As he writes at one point, there is a "nondualist" (*advaitic*) connection among the divine, the human, and the natural cosmos: "Each of us is a nondualist unity be-tween spirit and body, and each of us exists in the corporeality proper to natural-material things. The 'three' (the 'divine,' the 'human,' and the 'natural material') go together with neither confusion nor separa-tion." His cosmotheandric perspective has also led Panikkar to deep insight into the contemporary ecological crisis—a crisis he perceives as requiring both a new approach to nature and the cultivation of a new spirituality. This combined requirement is articulated with par-ticular cogency in his book *Ecosofia: La nuova saggezza per una spiri-*

tualità della terra (1993)—which might be translated as "Ecosophy: A New Wisdom Regarding Earth Spirituality." As he writes in that context: we need to restore our harmony with nature "by something other than simple ecological cosmetics. *Ecosophy* is a contemporary global imperative of human consciousness (adumbrating a cosmic brotherhood/sisterhood)."[19]

Other notable figures wrestling with the ecological crisis are the ecophilosopher Henryk Skolimowski and the ecoethicist Tomonobu Imamichi. The idea of an ecophilosophy was first launched by Skolimowski in 1974, when he served as a professor of the humanities at the University of Michigan. In that year he published a seminal article titled "Ecological Humanism" that laid out all the key elements of the new philosophy. A few years later, in 1981, an "Eco-Philosophy Center" was established in Ann Arbor, its purpose "to further ecological awareness, ecological values, and all other means which are necessary to heal the Earth." Skolimowski has authored a number of books, all seeking to promote the same goal, among them *Eco-Philosophy: Designing New Tactics for Living* (1981), *Technology and Human Destiny* (1983), *Eco-Theology* (1985), and more recently *Philosophy for a New Civilization* (2005).[20] The idea of an "ecoethics" (or *Eco-Ethica*) was inaugurated by Professor Tomonobu Imamachi at an international symposium in 1981. For the next twenty years, similar symposia were held near Kyoto, Japan, always attended by leading ecologists around the world. In 2003, on the occasion of the twenty-first World Congress of Philosophy in Istanbul, the first volume of an *Introduction to Eco-Ethica* was published. A few years later, in 2005, a self-governing body, the Tomonubu Imamachi Institute for Eco-Ethica, was created with headquarters in Copenhagen, where annual symposia on the topic are now being conducted.[21]

All of these initiatives, of course, are only the tip of the iceberg. There is by now a burgeoning literature on ecological problems, and many additional institutions, associations, and research groups have been established in many parts of the world. Among recent publications, let me just mention as more or less representative these: *Ecology at the Heart of Faith,* by Denis Edwards (2006); *Radical Ecology: The Search for a Livable World,* by Carolyn Merchant (2005); and *Deep Ecology and the World's Religions,* edited by David L. Barnhill and Roger S. Gottlieb (2001).[22] Among institutions and societies, I have already mentioned—in addition to the Imamachi Institute—the Forum on Religion and Ecology, in which Thomas Berry was active and which is headquartered at Yale University. Quite well-known in this field are also the Earth Policy Institute in Washington, D.C., and the California Institute of Integral Studies, which, among other things, serves as umbrella for the "Gaía Center for Subtle Activism." The Department of Philosophy and Religion Studies at the University of North Texas has recently emerged as the country's leading department in the area of environmental philosophy, with a focus on the linkage between religion and ecology. It is home to the journal *Environmental Ethics* and the Center for Environmental Philosophy. Another journal with a similar focus is titled *Worldviews: Global Religions, Culture, and Ecology.* It is edited at Loyola Marymount College and published by Brill in Holland.

Rather than prolonging this recital of initiatives, however, I would like to return by way of conclusion to Thomas Berry. On the eve of the global conference on climate change to be held in Copenhagen next month (December 2009), it is good to remember the close connection between ecological crisis and the need for "human renewal" (the title of my talk). Nobody, in my view, has placed greater emphasis on such renewal in our crisis than Thomas Berry. In his preface to one of Berry's latest works, distinguished theologian John Cobb Jr. has this to say:

> Berry believed that the changes we need will not occur at the many levels until they occur at the basic one—the way we understand ourselves and our world. He refused to be distracted from the fundamental task. . . . Thousands of people, perhaps tens or even hundreds of thousands, have been led to give real primacy to the task of living into the Ecozoic Age. No other writer in the ecological movement has had analogous effectiveness. In the decades ahead, more and more people, tens of millions at least, will fully recognize that the ecological crisis has the ultimacy that Berry has insisted on throughout his career. Others will come up with new formulations and make different proposals. But Berry's formulation has pride of place, and it may prove the most durable of all.[23]

Appendix B

The Return of Philosophical Anthropology
Some Personal Reflections

The issue of "human nature" has been a perennial concern of both philosophical and social-political inquiry. In the well-known classical formulation, "man" was defined as a "rational animal," a definition that left obscure or fuzzy the relation of human beings both to nature at large and to the "divine." During the nineteenth century, with the development of modern social science, the issue became the central preoccupation of what came to be known as "philosophical anthropology." The concern continued unabated into the next century. For a number of reasons, however (especially certain antihumanist tendencies), the topic fell out of favor in recent decades—to the point that it virtually ceased to occupy the attention of both philosophers and professional anthropologists. This neglect stands in stark contrast to the situation prevailing in Europe during the early and mid-twentieth century—which can be described as the heyday of philosophical anthropology.[1] The basic aim of the present pages is to rescue the topic from oblivion and more specifically to recover the older European legacy while also transforming it in the light of more recent experiences and intellectual developments.

Traditional Humanism and Philosophical Anthropology

It so happens that my own youth and early intellectual development stood strongly under the influence of the cited European legacy. A major intellectual figure shaping my early years was that of Max Scheler (1874–1928)—certainly a leading mentor of philosophical anthropology at the time. It was Scheler's central ambition to overcome the dualisms marking modern Western thought, including the bifurcation between a shallow empiricism and an abstract (Cartesian/Kantian) rationalism—an aim that brought him into the proximity of the early Heidegger. Through his study *Die Stellung des Menschen im Kosmos* (*The Human Place in the Cosmos,* of 1927), Scheler established himself as the leading protagonist of a perspective in which the more elusive-universalist accents of Enlightenment philosophy were fruitfully combined with the more concrete concerns of anthropology and human biology. Above all, his notion of the human "person" or "personhood"—a notion opposed both to the Cartesian cogito and to all forms of empirical reductionism—allowed Scheler to emerge as protagonist of a spiritual, yet concretely situated "humanism," a humanism able to serve as an ethical benchmark during the darker years of European history. In correlating philosophy and human life, his thought did not subscribe to an indiscriminate amalgam, but rather envisaged a complex texture of dimensions corresponding to different levels of human experience. One aspect of this texture was the triadic structure of human knowledge, where Scheler differentiated among empirical-instrumental knowledge (*Leistungswissen*), humanistic understanding (*Bildungswissen*), and reflective-speculative insight (*Erlösungwissen*), a structure departing in important ways from the traditional dichotomy of natural and human sciences.[2]

To be sure, Scheler was not alone in inaugurating and solidifying philosophical anthropology. His efforts were ably supported, and also modified, by a number of other European intellectuals. Foremost among the latter were Arnold Gehlen (1904–1976) and Helmuth Plessner (1892–1985).[3] The differences between the two were striking, testifying to the broad range of possible conceptions of philosophical anthropology. Basically, Gehlen's conception was more restrictive and closed, while Plessner's view was flexible and dynamic, pointing toward open-ended horizons and possibilities. Both thinkers accepted the thesis of the "premature birth" of humans and their resulting instinctual deficiency and vulnerability; however, their conclusions were radically divergent. For Gehlen, instinctual deficiency was something to be overcome or domesticated, and the latter could be achieved only through the resolute institutionalization of social and cultural patterns and the routinization or standardization of role expectations; from this vantage point, human frailty urgently needs to be compensated through social and political stability. By contrast to this "conservative" outlook, Plessner favored a more "liberal" or emancipatory perspective, viewing human beings as precariously located between nature and culture, a position requiring constant creative adjustments in light of deeper aspirations for "meaning." One of Plessner's central notions was that of the "eccentricity" or "eccentric positionality" of human existence, a notion not far removed from Heidegger's thesis of the "ek-static" quality of human being-in-the-world.[4]

Among the various protagonists, my own distinct preference at the time was for Plessner—even to the point of trumping my admiration for Scheler's work. As I pointed out in an essay of 1974—meant as a contribution to celebrate his eightieth birthday—Plessner's writings signaled for me a resolute stride beyond the Cartesian mind/matter or spirit/nature dualisms, a paradigm that still lingered in recessed form in Scheler's "spiritualism." What attracted me particularly to Plessner's approach was his ability to correlate (without total fusion) the natural-biological situatedness of human beings with their capacity for creative interpretation and transformation. This aspect was clearly illustrated in *The Unity of the Senses* (of 1923)—a study that, as I came to see later, anticipated in many ways Maurice Merleau-Ponty's *Phenomenology of Perception.* How was it possible, the book argued, for phenomena to have an impact on human sensory organs unless the latter are seen as interpretive and sense-finding organs (and not simply as passive instruments)? Rather than being viewed as mute receptacles, sensory organs had to be seen as sensible media in the distillation of meaning out of the multitude of opaque stimuli. In some of his later writings—especially *The Stages of the Organic World and Man* and *Conditio Humana*—Plessner articulated the concept of human "eccentricity," a quality partially attributable to the "erect position" of humans. Seen in this light, the human condition for Plessner was "doubly mediated and 'reflexive' by virtue of man's 'ex-centric' status in regard both to himself and his environment. . . . Rather than being safely enmeshed in a life-cycle or the stimulus-response nexus, man has to 'lead' his life by designing a web of cultural and symbolic meanings—patterns which provide him at best with a fragile habitat."[5]

The "End of Man"?

As mentioned before, philosophical anthropology fell on bad days in the later part of the last century. Several factors account for this development. Not aiming to be exhaustive, I want to single out two main factors: the first of a chiefly philosophical nature, the second of a more political or geopolitical character. The first is related to the rise of (what is loosely called) "postmodernism" after 1968, with its pronounced antihumanist bias. During its early phase, the postmodern agenda resounded with such catchphrases as "the death of the subject" and "the end of man"—slogans coined as countermottos to the earlier reign of existential "humanism" and that clearly implied also the end of philosophical anthropology. No one was more eloquent and zestful in proclaiming this agenda than Jacques Derrida. In an essay of 1968 provocatively titled "The Ends of Man," Derrida took aim at two possible meanings of the phrase: one accentuating "end" in the sense of goal or *telos,* the other accentuating "man" as a finite creature. Under the first rubric, the essay "deconstructed" the idea of a philosophical or historical teleology of the human species; under the second rubric, the accent was shifted from *telos* to finitude, ending, or termination. Despite a complex interlacing of meanings, it was the second aspect that finally overshadowed and dominated the essay's argument. Taking his lead from Nietzsche's *Zarathustra,* especially the distinction between the "higher man" and the "overman," Derrida affirmed that the latter "overcomes" the human itself and thus is no longer "humanist" in any sense. Rather than cultivating past memories, the overman "burns his text and erases the traces of his steps; his laughter then will burst out, directed toward a return which no longer will have the form of a metaphysical repetition of humanism."[6]

Referring to the events of 1968 and their aftermath, Derrida at the time noted a radical rupture of philosophical dispositions. Prior to these events, he wrote, it was "the tide of humanism and anthropologism that covered French philosophy." During that earlier period, it was humanism and anthropologism that served as "the common ground of Christian or atheist existentialisms, of the philosophy of values (spiritualist or not), of the 'personalisms' of the right and left, and [even] of Marxism in the classical style." Using a broad brush, he asserted that humanist anthropologism was "the unperceived and uncontested common ground of Marxism and of Social Democratic or Christian-

Democratic discourse." Since 1968, however, things have changed. What followed were an "anti-humanist and anti-anthropologist ebb" and an intense "questioning of humanism." In fact, the critique of humanism and anthropologism became "one of the dominant and guiding motifs of current French thought" (at the time of Derrida's writing). Inspired by the "new" Nietzscheanism, what Derrida complained about was not this critique itself, but rather its half-hearted character and the lingering persistence of humanist traces in current discourse. What particularly chagrined him was the continued humanist reading of such thinkers as Hegel, Husserl, and even Heidegger, a reading tending to "amalgamate" these thinkers with "the old metaphysical humanism." As he pointedly observed: "Among those who do practice this amalgamation, the schemas of the anthropologistic misinterpretation from Sartre's time are still at work, and occasionally it is these very schemas which govern the banishment of Hegel, Husserl, and Heidegger into the shadows of humanist metaphysics."[7]

The second main factor accounting for the "ebb" of humanism and philosophical anthropology was the accelerating pace of globalization. Although incipiently heralded by two "World Wars," globalization in the second part of the last century took the form of an increasingly relentless pursuit of global economic, cultural, and political-military agendas. Under the impact of steadily expanding markets and communications networks, national and cultural traditions or frames of reference were inevitably placed under siege; the same developments also put pressure on older conceptions of humanism and of philosophical anthropology. Given the growing awareness of cultural and religious differences (fomenting a possible "clash of civilizations"), how was it possible to discern something like a shared humanity or humaneness—beyond the level of a technological *homo faber* and the global uniformity of consumerism? Were all assertions of a universal "human nature" not inevitably tainted by an ethnocentric, perhaps Eurocentric, bias? Under these circumstances, how was it possible to renew a conception of philosophical anthropology that does not elope into an abstract transcendentalism (or spiritualism), while at the same time resisting the lure of biological or ethnological reductionism? As it appears, humanism as well as philosophical anthropology was bound to be stranded on the proverbial "horns" of the dilemma between universalism and reductive particularism—unless an alternative path were found, a path that cannot invoke any "top-down" formula, but must rely on the experiential process of "globalization from below."[8]

Resurgence of a Chastened Humanism

In the meantime, the "ebb" of antihumanism and antianthropologism (diagnosed by Derrida) is itself beginning to ebb. What we are experiencing today is not, to be sure, a high tide of old-style humanism, but the tentative resurgence of a subdued, self-critical and non-Eurocentric (that is, nonhegemonic) view of the "human" on the far side of absolute affirmation and absolute negation. Several factors again account for this resurgence. One is the danger of antihumanism to slide into in-humanity and the denial of human rights—a slide that is utterly unacceptable given the upsurge of new forms of imperialism, of state-sponsored and privately sponsored forms of "terrorism," and of the widespread violation of elementary standards of human rights in many parts of the world. Another factor is the immense pressure placed by advances in the biological sciences on acceptable conceptions of the "human" or "humaneness"—a pressure evident in the programs of genetic engineering, cloning, and stem-cell research. What also needs to be taken into account is the rediscovery and revitalization of such resources of philosophical anthropology as social phenomenology, hermeneutics, and various modes of social psychology.

All these factors combined have inspired a number of writers to pay renewed attention to this domain of inquiry neglected for some time. A prominent example is Jürgen Habermas, a participant in the earlier vogue of philosophical anthropology. In a series of essays on "the future of human nature," Habermas has directly confronted the challenge posed by certain ambitions of genetic engineering. As he observes, in the face of these ambitions, it is "an urgent matter" to initiate "a public discourse on the right understanding of cultural forms of life. And philosophers no longer have any good reasons for leaving such a dispute to biologists or engineers intoxicated by science fiction." Without explicitly invoking the label, Habermas's intervention clearly gives a boost to the resurgence of philosophical anthropology at this new stage of development. In his view, what philosophy can contribute in this context is its capacity for reflective judgment, its ability to illuminate the "ethical self-understanding of the species"—certainly no small matter. In the assessment of Nikolas Kompridis, Habermas's intervention has in a way corrected his own leanings toward a rationalist universalism: "By speaking in the name of the human future, Habermas has helpfully (if unintentionally) exposed the cost of adhering to a merely proceduralist conception of philosophy." In doing so, it has exposed the "limitations of a sharp distinction between morality and ethics, between justice and the good life," by showing that the morality of reason is itself sustained "by a prior *ethical self-understanding of the species* shared by all moral persons."[9]

In the field of political theory, William Connolly recently has launched an initiative whose parameters mesh with philosophical anthropology broadly conceived. In his study entitled *Neuropolitics: Thinking, Culture, Speed* (of 2002), Connolly endeavored to reconnect and mutually interpolate "nature"—traditionally the domain of exact science—with "culture," the central domain of the humanities and philosophy. As he writes there: "Every theory of culture bears an implicit relation to biology and biological theory"—a relation that has tended to be sidelined by both hard scientists and cultural "idealists," giving rise to various kinds of one-sided reductionism. "In their laudable attempt to ward off one [biologistic] type of reductionism," he adds, "too many cultural theorists fall into another: they lapse into a reductionism that ignores how biology is mixed into thinking and culture and how other aspects of nature are folded into both." Among philosophers, Connolly invokes chiefly the legacies of Henri Bergson, William James, Merleau-Ponty, and Gilles Deleuze, while in the field of neuroscience his chief mentors are such practitioners as Antonio Damasio, Joseph LeDoux, and V. S. Ramachandran. The reconnection that his text envisages is not so much a harmonious symbiosis, as rather a fragile and tension-ridden bond where insights garnered from different fields rub against each other and thereby release new energies and horizons. In its emphasis on openness, contingency, and shifting horizons, the text in a way harkens back to earlier philosophical anthropology, especially to Plessner's notion of the "eccentric positionality" of human existence.[10]

Of late, my own thinking has also returned to the issues raised by Scheler, Plessner, and other protagonists of half a century ago. In my case, the return was mainly prompted by the debilitating effects of a radical antihumanism celebrating the "death of the subject," effects evident especially in the areas of public life and political agency. Another motivating factor was a resurgent interest in the legacy of Merleau-Ponty, a legacy sidelined for several decades by the "postmodern" vogue.[11] These and related motives led me back to perhaps the central concern of philosophical anthropology: that of "human nature" and the meaning of humanism. Chastened by the experiences of intervening decades, my endeavor was to renew some older teachings without, however, validating their frequent derailment into a compact, self-possessed, and hegemonic (perhaps Eurocentric) humanism. In an essay titled "Who Are We Now? For an 'Other' Humanism," I have sought to clear a path beyond anthropocentrism and antihumanism, a path that also avoids derailment into (biological or idealistic) modes of reductionism.[12]

As it seems to me, the interlude of antihumanism may actually have served the salutary purpose of cleansing humanism of some of its traditional arrogance. Seen from this angle, the presumed "end of man" is in effect "nothing else but the continuous and ever renewed beginning of a journey"—a journey in search of the "human." What the deflation of anthropocentrism makes possible above all is "a released openness to others, to nature, and the recessed ground of being(s)." I invoke at this point Heidegger's famous *Letter on Humanism,* where we read: "If we do keep the label, the term 'humanism' signifies that human nature is indeed crucial for the truth of 'being'—but crucial precisely in a way where everything does not depend on 'man' alone or as such." In lieu of this dependence, what comes into view here is a complex mode of interdependence among humans, nature, and the world—perhaps in the direction of the "cosmotheandric" perspective articulated by Raimon Panikkar and the different "mediations" thematized by Thomas Berry.

Notes

Introduction

1. See in this regard Helen Thornton, *State of Nature or Eden? Thomas Hobbes and His Contemporaries on the Natural Condition of Human Beings* (Rochester, N.Y.: University of Rochester Press, 2005); and Perez Zagorin, *Hobbes and the Law of Nature* (Princeton: Princeton University Press, 2009).

2. The invocation of spiritual resources is at the heart of perspectives variously called "ecopiety," "deep ecology," or "radical ecology." For some fine examples of this genre, see Hwa Yol Jung, *The Way of Ecopiety: Essays in Transversal Geophilosophy* (New York: Global Scholarly Publications, 2009); Roger S. Gottlieb, *This Sacred Earth: Religion, Nature, Environment* (New York: Routledge, 2004); Gary T. Gardner, *Invoking the Spirit: Religion and Spirituality in the Quest for a Sustainable World* (Washington, D.C.: Worldwatch Institute, 2002); David L. Barnhill and Roger S. Gottlieb, eds., *Deep Ecology and World Religions* (Albany: State University of New York Press, 2001); and Carolyn Merchant, *Radical Ecology: The Search for a Livable World* (Albany: State University of New York Press, 2005). For the work of Thomas Berry, see appendix A, below.

3. Gilles Deleuze and Claire Parnet, *Dialogues*, trans. Hugh Tomlinson and Barbara Habberjam (London: Athlone Press, 1987), 14–15.

4. For some recent (and conflicting) interpretations, see Warren Montag and Ted Stolze, eds., *The New Spinoza* (Minneapolis: University of Minnesota Press, 1997); Steven Nadler, *Spinoza: A Life* (Cambridge: Cambridge University Press, 1999); Etienne Balibar, *Spinoza and Politics*, trans. Peter Snowdon (London: Verso, 1998); Michael Hardt and Antonio Negri, *Empire* (Cambridge: Harvard University Press, 2000); and Antonio Negri, *Subversive Spinoza: (Un)Contemporary Variations*, trans. Timothy S. Murphy (Manchester, U.K.: Manchester University Press, 2004). While Hardt and Negri find a "populist" strand in Spinoza, Jonathan Havercroft by contrast aligns him more closely with Thomas Hobbes; see his "The Fickle Multitude: Spinoza and the Problem of Global Democracy," *Constellations* 17 (Mar. 2010): 120–136.

5. Genevieve Lloyd, *Part of Nature: Self-Knowledge in Spinoza's Ethics* (Ithaca: Cornell University Press, 1994), 1–3. Cf. also Edwin Curley, *Behind the Geometrical Method* (Princeton: Princeton University Press, 1988);

Gilles Deleuze, *Spinoza: Practical Philosophy*, trans. Robert Hurley (San Francisco: City Light Books, 1988); and Eccy de Jonge, *Spinoza and Deep Ecology* (Burlington, Vt.: Ashgate, 2004).

6. See Lloyd, *Part of Nature*, 6–7. Hegel's critique is even further accentuated by Roger Scruton in his book *Spinoza* (Oxford: Oxford University Press, 1986). Without fully sharing Hegel's or Scruton's criticism, Lloyd agrees at least with Pierre Macherey's point that, from a contemporary perspective, "Hegel stands between Spinoza and ourselves, and we cannot read Spinoza today without thinking of Hegel" (*Part of Nature*, 7). See also Pierre Macherey, *Hegel on Spinoza* (Paris: Francois Masperó, 1979).

7. Cf., e.g., Jason M. Wirth, ed., *Schelling Now: Contemporary Readings* (Bloomington: Indiana University Press, 2005); and Judith Norman and Alistair Welchman, eds., *The New Schelling* (New York: Continuum, 2004).

8. I should make it clear that, in this chapter, I do not aim to present a detailed overview of all modes of "Asian" thought, but only to lift up certain strands helpful for contemporary ecological thought. For some relevant literature, see, e.g., Mark Hathaway and Leonardo Boff, *The Tao of Liberation: Exploring the Ecology of Transformation* (Maryknoll, N.Y.: Orbis Books, 2009); David R. Kingsley, *Ecology and Religion: Ecological Spirituality in a Cross-Cultural Perspective* (Englewood Cliffs, N.J.: Prentice Hall, 1995); Richard Sylvan, *Out of Utopias: Tao and Deep Ecology* (Canberra: Australian National University, 1990); Rajdeva Narayan and Janardan Kumar, eds., *Ecology and Religion: Ecological Concepts in Hinduism, Buddhism, Jainism, Islam, Christianity, and Sikhism* (New Delhi: Deep and Deep Publications, 2003); Lauren Kearns and Catherine Keller, eds., *Ecospirit: Religions and Philosophies of the Earth* (New York: Fordham University Press, 2007); Irene Bloom, "Human Nature and Biological Nature in Mencius," *Philosophy East and West* 47 (1997): 21–32; Mary Evelyn Tucker, *Worldly Wonder: Religions Enter Their Ecological Phase* (Chicago: Open Court, 2003).

9. In the latter context, see especially Antonio Damasio, *Looking for Spinoza: Joy, Sorrow, and the Feeling Brain* (Orlando, Fla.: Harvest Books, 2003); Antonio Damasio, *Descartes' Error: Emotion, Reason, and the Human Brain* (New York: Harper-Collins, 1995); Jaak Panksepp, *Affective Neuroscience: The Foundations of Human Emotions* (New York: Oxford University Press, 1998); Jean-Pierre Changeux, *Neuronal Man: The Biology of Mind* (New York: Pantheon, 1985); and Karl Pribram, *Languages of the Brain: Experimental Paradoxes and Principles in Neuropsychology* (Englewood Cliffs, N.J.: Prentice-Hall, 1971).

1. Nature and Divine Substance

1. Maurice Merleau-Ponty, "Everywhere and Nowhere," in *Signs*, trans. Richard C. McCleary (Evanston, Ill.: Northwestern University Press,

1964), 147. He adds, "The seventeenth century is that privileged moment when natural science and metaphysics believed they had discovered a common foundation. It created a science of nature and yet did not make the object of science the rule of ontology. . . . Being is not completely reduced to or flattened out upon the level of external being. There is also the being of the subject or soul, the being of its ideas, and the interrelations of these ideas, the inner relation of truth. And the latter universe is as extensive as the former, or rather it encompasses it" (148).

2. Lewis S. Feuer, *Spinoza and the Rise of Liberalism* (Boston: Beacon Press, 1964), ix, 5, 21, 39–40. Feuer admirably sums up Spinoza's general position at the cusp of two ages. He writes that the young Spinoza "gave to the pantheist mysticism of the revolutionary movements its noblest expression; he was also, however, stirred by the marvels which were being opened by the new technology of science, the telescope and microscope. He tried with immense power to identify the God of his mystic vision with the mathematical God of science" (ix).

3. Ibid., 41, 45. He adds that among the so-called Collegiant-Mennonites in Rijnsburg, "periodic meetings took place which were known as the Assembly of the Free-minded. . . . There were no ordained ministers. They chose their ministers by a vote of the majority, and those selected had no special authority. They believed that the word of God was internal. . . . The Collegiants were Mennonite adherents who met in so-called *collegia* rather than churches in order to evade the government's religious restrictions. The Rijnsburg Collegiants had been much influenced by Cartesian philosophy, and employed its language in stating their religious standpoint" (41, 45).

4. Baruch Spinoza, *On the Improvement of Understanding*, trans. and with an introduction by Joseph Katz (New York: Liberal Arts Press, 1958), 3 (translation slightly altered for the sake of clarity). As Feuer correctly states, this is not just an epistemic tract, but belongs to the genre of "pilgrim's progress" (*Spinoza and the Rise of Liberalism*, 44).

5. Spinoza, *On the Improvement of Understanding*, 3–5.

6. Ibid., 6. "Above all," he continues, "a way must be found to improve the intellect and purify it as much as is possible right at the start, so that it will not be encumbered with errors and will understand things properly. It is clear that I wish to direct all sciences to one basic end or purpose: the achievement of the highest human perfection" (6–7).

7. Ibid., 7–8, 10–13, 16, 28. A bit later, around 1663, Spinoza wrote his succinct analysis of the Cartesian system: *Principles of Cartesian Philosophy* (*Principia philosophiae cartesianae*), trans. Samuel Shirley (Indianapolis: Bobbs-Merrill, 1998).

8. Spinoza, *The Book of God*, ed. and with an introduction by Dagobert D. Runes (New York: Philosophical Library, 1958), 7. With this formulation, Spinoza adopts and vindicates another, very traditional bifurcation: that be-

tween a realm of permanent or eternal essences and a realm of changing and perishable phenomena.

9. Ibid., 10–12. What needs to be noted here is that the term *cause* must be taken not in the sense of an external, mechanical causation, but in that of an internal motivation. As Spinoza says: "There is no external cause outside Him" (but also no "external cause" inside Him) (12). A little later, he uses a better term than *cause* to express his thought, namely, *providence*—of which he distinguishes two kinds: "*General providence* is that through which all things are produced and sustained insofar as they are parts of the whole of nature. *Special providence* is the striving of each thing separately to preserve its existence, considered not as part of nature, but as a whole by itself" (13).

10. Ibid., 17, 19, 23.

11. Ibid., 24, 34–35, 38–39, 41.

12. Ibid., 107–108.

13. Spinoza, *The Ethics*, in *The Chief Works of Benedict de Spinoza*, trans. R. H. M. Elves, vol. 2 (New York: Dover Publications, 1951), 45.

14. Ibid., 54–55, 62, 68–69, 82–84.

15. Ibid., 130, 136, 138, 149. Since, in seeking to persist, particular beings precisely strive to preserve the essence of God/nature, self-preservation for Spinoza means nearly the opposite of what it means for Hobbes (for whom it involves radical separateness). Hence, the so-called state of nature (to the extent that there is such a thing) for Spinoza means not a relentless "war of all against all," but rather a condition of complementarity and possible solidarity.

16. Ibid., 195, 202, 204–205. If one substitutes for *pleasure* the term *happiness* (in the sense of *eudaimonia*), then Spinoza's conception is not far removed from that of Aristotle—although his employment of the term *useful* is misleading and has in fact misled many later philosophers.

17. Ibid., 205–209. These statements throw into relief the difference between Spinoza and the Hobbesian conception of the "state of nature" (as a war of all against all). As he adds, in a distinctly Aristotelian vein: human beings "are scarcely able to lead a solitary life, so that the definition of man as a social animal has met with general assent; in fact, men do derive from social life much more convenience than injury" (210). The difference between the two thinkers ultimately derives from their different conceptions of self-being and self-preservation: whereas for Hobbes "self-being" means the preservation of the individual self, for Spinoza the term means the grounding of the self in God-nature.

18. Ibid., 211, 216–219. Admittedly, the flow of Spinoza's presentation is somewhat marred by apparent concessions to the Hobbesian conception, especially comments referring to everyone's "sovereign natural right" and the establishment of the "state" by power (213–214). On the other hand, there can be no doubt about Spinoza's own preference for joyfulness or happiness.

As he writes, "I reason and have convinced myself as follows: no deity nor anyone else, save the envious, takes pleasure in my infirmity and discomfort, nor sets down to my virtue the tears, sobs, fears and the like, which are signs of infirmity of spirit; on the contrary, the greater the pleasure wherewith we are affected, the greater the perfection to which we reach—in other words, the more must we necessarily partake of the divine nature. Therefore, to make use of what comes in our way and to enjoy it as much as possible . . . is the part of a wise man" (219).

19. Micah 6:8; see also Spinoza, *Ethics*, 212.

20. Steven Nadler, *Spinoza's Ethics: An Introduction* (Cambridge: Cambridge University Press, 2006), 22–23. The reference is to Pierre Bayle's *Dictionnaire historique et critique* (of 1695–1697). According to Joseph Katz, in Spinoza's philosophy, theoretical knowledge "often seems to be a means toward 'doing well and rejoicing,' toward action." See Katz's introduction to Spinoza, *On the Improvement of Understanding*, xvi. In this connection one might also recall Martin Heidegger's description: "All who knew Spinoza, even his enemies, appreciated his character which was marked by simple clarity and serenity. One never saw him laughing or mourning; always friendly, he was ready to offer help and advice, in a manner free from hypocrisy and pride, and devoid of ostentation." See Heidegger, *Geschichte der Philosophie von Thomas von Aquin bis Kant*, ed. Helmuth Vetter (*Gesamtausgabe*, vol. 23; Frankfurt: Klostermann, 2006), 146 (lecture course of 1926–1927), (my translation).

21. Spinoza, *Ethics*, 126–127.

22. See Nicholas Rescher, *G. W. Leibniz's Monadology: An Edition for Students* (Pittsburgh: University of Pittsburgh Press, 1991), 17–19 (nos. 1, 3, 7, 8, 9, 10, 11, 15, 18). In his text, Leibniz frequently draws on some of his earlier writings, especially his *Theodicy* of 1710.

23. See Lloyd, *Part of Nature*, 13. For an excellent introduction to Leibniz's entire system see Heidegger, *Geschichte der Philosophie von Thomas von Aquin bis Kant*, 167–189. For a shorter version, see Heidegger, *Die metaphysischen Grundstellungen des abendländischen Denkens* (*Gesamtausgabe*, vol. 88; Frankfurt: Klostermann, 2008), 99–115 (seminar of 1937–1938).

24. Rescher, *Leibniz's Monadology*, 22–24 (nos. 38, 40, 47, 56, 58).

25. Heidegger, *Geschichte der Philosophie von Thomas von Aquin bis Kant*, 187. The complexity of this Leibnizian kind of holism is more fully developed in Heidegger's text from 1928 titled "Aus der letzten Marburger Vorlesung," in *Wegmarken* (Frankfurt: Klostermann, 1967), 375–398; trans. as "From the Last Marburg Lecture" in *Pathways*, ed. William McNeill (Cambridge: Cambridge University Press, 1998), 63–81.

26. Rescher, *Leibniz's Monadology*, 23 (no. 52), 26 (nos. 67, 68, 69).

27. Ibid., 28 (nos. 83, 84, 85, 86). The last passages should be compared

with the concluding section in Leibniz's "Principles of Nature and of Grace" (of 1714), which articulates an intriguing relation between happiness and unceasing striving (pointing to some extent beyond Spinoza): "One can say that loving God offers us already now a foretaste of the future happiness or blessedness. . . . This aspect gives rise to a genuine peace of mind, not as with the Stoics (through forced control), but a present serenity assuring us of a future happiness. Yet, no matter how closely associated with a happy contemplation and knowledge of God, this highest blessedness can never be complete, because God is infinite and can never be completely known. Thus, our happiness cannot coincide with full possession . . . but can only consist in a persistent movement to new happiness and new levels of perfection." See Leibniz, *Principes de la nature et de la grace fondé en raison*, ed. André Robinet (Paris: Presses Universitaires de France, 1986), 61–65 (my translation).

28. *Hegel's Lectures on the History of Philosophy*, trans. E. S. Haldane and Frances H. Limson, 3 vols. (New York: Humanities Press, 1955), 3: 252, 257–258, 260–261. In Spinoza's substance-metaphysics, Hegel also detected a dismissal of negativity: "Because negation was conceived by Spinoza only in a one-sided fashion [as lack], there is . . . in his system an utter blocking out of the principle of subjectivity, individuality, personality, the moment of self-consciousness in Being" (3: 287). Cf. also Macherey, *Hegel on Spinoza;* and the section "Hegel and Spinoza," in Lloyd, *Part of Nature*, 141–147.

29. See *Hegel's Lectures on the History of Philosophy*, 3: 325, 330, 347.

30. To be sure, Hegel also wrote on the philosophy of nature, but more as a subordinate theme. See *Hegel's Philosophy of Nature*, ed. and trans. M. J. Petry (New York: Humanities Press, 1970).

2. Nature and Spirit

1. See Friedrich Wilhelm Joseph Schelling, *Ideas for a Philosophy of Nature*, trans. Errol E. Harris and Peter Heath (Cambridge: Cambridge University Press, 1988), 54–55 (translation slightly altered for the sake of clarity in the above and subsequent quotations).

2. The endorsement of Spinoza was initially halting and circumspect. Some of his early writings seem to share the critical reservations of Kant and Fichte vis-à-vis nature philosophy. Thus, in a text of 1795, Spinoza was placed in the company of uncritical "enthusiasts" (*Schwärmer*) because of his willingness to surrender his critical consciousness to the absolute or the divine. See Schelling, "Philosophische Briefe über Dogmatismus und Kritizismus," in *Schriften von 1794–1798* (Darmstadt: Wissenschaftliche Buchhandlung, 1995), 161–221, especially 199: "He believed himself to be identical with the absolute object and thus lost in its infinity. He was mistaken in this belief."

3. As we read in the same "Philosophische Briefe": in opposition to a lazy dogmatism, critical philosophy means "striving for imperishable self-

hood, unconditional freedom, unrestrained activity. . . . In this lies the last hope for the salvation of a humankind which—having long languished in the chains of superstition—at last finds the answer *in itself* . . . by discovering the freedom of will" (215, 219).

4. Schelling, "Abhandlungen zur Erläuterung des Idealismus der Wissenschaftslehre," in *Schriften von 1794–1798,* 246–247.

5. Ibid., 237–238, 247–249.

6. Schelling, *Ideas for a Philosophy of Nature,* ix, 9–11. Cf. also Joseph L. Esposito, *Schelling's Idealism and Philosophy of Nature* (Lewisburg, Pa.: Bucknell University Press, 1977); and Thomas Bach and Olaf Breidlach, eds., *Naturphilosophie nach Schelling* (Stuttgart: Frommann-Holzboog, 2005).

7. Schelling, *Ideas for a Philosophy of Nature,* 11–15. Schelling adds that the basic maxim from which Leibniz started was "that the ideas of external things arise in the soul by virtue of her own laws as in a distinct world, as if nothing existed but God (the infinite) and the soul (the intuition of the infinite)" (16). In subsequent passages, the text mentions some of the shortcomings of Spinoza's outline of a system. Thus, we read: "Spinoza, as it seems, was worried early on about the connection of our ideas and things outside us, and could not tolerate the separation set up between them. He saw that the ideal and the real (thought and object) are most intimately united in our nature. . . . However, instead of descending into the depths of his self-consciousness and from that vantage observing the rise of two worlds (the idea and the real), he overleaped himself; instead of explaining from our nature how the finite and the infinite (originally united in us) proceed reciprocally from each other, he lost himself in the idea of an infinite outside of us" (27).

8. Ibid., 12–13.

9. Ibid., 14, 23–25, 27–28. Schelling at this point returns to Leibniz: "By the (so-called) preestablished harmony Leibniz could not have meant what one usually means by it. For he asserts explicitly that no spirit could have been generated, since the concepts of cause and effect are inapplicable to it. Spirit is the ground of its own being and knowing and by its very existence it is what it is: namely, a being to whose nature belongs that system of ideas about external things. Hence, philosophy is nothing other than *a natural history of our spirit*" (29–30).

10. Ibid., 30–31, 35, 38–40, 42. In a "Supplement" to his introduction, Schelling forcefully emphasizes the union and even coincidence of real and ideal dimensions: "The first step of philosophy and its condition of possibility is the insight that the absolute ideal is also the absolute real, and that without this there is only sensible and conditioned but no unconditioned reality. . . . The first idea of philosophy already rests on the tacit assumption of a possible indifference between absolute knowing and the absolute itself, and hence on the fact that the absolute-ideal is the absolute-real" (44). In the same context,

he differentiates his "higher" idealism from a merely empirical realism and a subjective idealism (50).

11. Schelling, "Von der Weltseele," in *Schriften von 1794–1798*, 414–416.

12. Ibid., 421–423, 428, 430–432. This insight is reaffirmed at the very end of the study: "Since the principle [of basic connectedness] supports the continuity of inorganic and organic beings and links all of nature in a universal organism, we are able to perceive in it again that spirit which the most ancient philosophy saluted as the *common soul of nature*" (623).

13. Keith R. Peterson, introduction to Schelling, *First Outline of a System of the Philosophy of Nature*, trans. Keith R. Peterson (Albany: State University of New York Press, 2004), xiii, xxiii.

14. Schelling, *First Outline of a System*, 13, 15, 24.

15. Ibid., 56, 194–195.

16. Ibid., 202–203. In the above, I have substituted "creativity" for the translator's choice of "productivity," mainly because in modern times productivity has become too closely linked with fabrication or instrumental action.

17. Ibid., xxxiii, 187, 232.

18. Schelling, *System of Transcendental Idealism*, trans. Peter Heath, with introduction by Michael Vater (Charlottesville: University of Virginia Press, 1978), xxii, 1–2.

19. Schelling, *System of Transcendental Idealism*, xxii, 5–7 (translation slightly altered for the sake of clarity in the above and subsequent citations).

20. Ibid., 217–221. As Vater explains: "In this context, intellectual intuition is not the *immediate* intuition, . . . not the immediate ascent to the Absolute which it will be in the 'Identity-System,' the holistic grasp of the totality. Here, in the *System*, intellectual intuition is the mode of being of the self, of the unity of the known and knowing. . . . [It is] an unconscious principle of consciousness" (introduction to Schelling, *System of Transcendental Idealism*, xxiii).

21. Schelling, *System of Transcendental Idealism*, 225, 229–232. In the same concluding remarks, Schelling envisages a dialectical relation where poetry appears as the original mother of philosophy and science, which, having reached completion, return to their mother on a new and higher level: "Philosophy was born and nourished by poetry in the infancy of knowledge, and with it all those sciences it has guided toward perfection. We may thus expect them on completion to flow back, like so many different streams, into the universal ocean of poetry from which they took their source" (232).

22. Manfred Durner, introduction to Schelling, *Bruno oder über des göttliche und natürliche Prinzip der Dinge* (Hamburg: Felix Meiner Verlag, 2005), xv. See also Schelling, "Darstellung meines Systems der Philosophie," in *Schriften von 1801–1804* (Dramstadt: Wissenschaftliche Buchgesellschaft, 1976), 1–108.

23. Durner, introduction to Schelling, *Bruno*, xxi–xxii. The letter to the parents was dated July 8, 1802 (cited by Durner, introduction, ix–x). Cf. also Schelling, *Timaeus* (1794), ed. Hartmut Buchner (Stuttgart: Fromman-Holzboog, 1994).

24. Schelling, *Bruno*, 74. See also Schelling, *Bruno; or, On the Natural and the Divine Principle of Things*, ed. and trans. Michael J. Vater (Albany: State University of New York Press, 1984), 178 (translation slightly altered for the sake of clarity and accuracy in the above and subsequent citations).

25. Schelling, *Bruno* (German), 123–124; Schelling, *Bruno* (English), 221–222.

26. Schelling, *Bruno* (German), 17; Schelling, *Bruno* (English), 128.

27. Schelling, *Philosophie der Kunst* (Darmstadt: Wissenschaftliche Buchgesellschaft, 1976), 17, 21–24; *The Philosophy of Art*, ed. and trans. Douglas W. Scott (Minneapolis: University of Minnesota Press, 1989), 23, 26–28 (translation slightly altered for the sake of clarity in the above and subsequent citations).

28. Schelling, *Philosophy der Kunst*, 26, 29; Schelling, *Philosophy of Art*, 29, 31.

3. Nature and Sentiment

1. "Miscellaneous Observations," in Novalis, *Philosophical Writings*, ed. and trans. Margaret M. Stoljar (Albany: State University of New York Press, 1997), 23.

2. In his wide-ranging study of the period, Manfred Frank uses the apt phrase "infinite approximation or rapprochement" to capture this crucial feature. See Frank, *Unendliche Annäherung: Die Anfänge der philosophischen Frühromantik* (Frankfurt: Suhrkamp, 1997).

3. In recent decades, considerable scholarly attention has been devoted to the task of excavating the "philosophy" undergirding Romanticism and also the philosophical relevance of the movement in our time. Some of these efforts have led to slightly odd conclusions—as, for example, the linkage of Romanticism with postmodern "antifoundationalism" and deconstruction or else with Western "analytical" philosophy. Historical evidence seems to point to the close affinity of early Romanticism and idealist philosophy, especially the work of Schelling (particularly his *Bruno* and *Philosophy of Art*). For some of the recent literature, see, e.g., Manfred Frank, *The Philosophical Foundations of Early German Romanticism*, trans. Elizabeth Millán-Zaibert (Albany: State University of New York Press, 2004); Frederick Beiser, *The Romantic Imperative: The Concept of Early German Romanticism* (Cambridge: Harvard University Press, 2003); Elizabeth Millán-Zaibert, *Friedrich Schlegel and the Emergence of Romantic Philosophy* (Albany: State University of New York Press, 2007); and Robert Richards, *The Romantic Conception*

of Life (Chicago: University of Chicago Press, 2002). Curiously, in view of Frank's emphasis on "infinite approximation," his *The Philosophical Foundations* links early German Romanticism with "ontological and epistemological realism" (28), while Beiser's *Romantic Imperative* stresses (perhaps excessively) its roots in "absolute" idealism.

4. In her book *Friedrich Schlegel and the Emergence of Romantic Philosophy*, Millán-Zaibert distinguishes three phases of German Romanticism: the early phase mentioned above; the phase of Middle or High Romanticism (1808–1815), including such figures as Achim von Arnim and Clemens Brentano; and that of Late Romanticism (1815–1830), including E. T. A. Hoffmann, Johann von Eichendorff, and the later Friedrich Schlegel (2–3). The inclusion of Hölderlin here in the early phase may be problematical. In the words of Michael Hamburger, Hölderlin was "a poet who produced essentially classical work in a Romantic age." See his introduction to *Friedrich Hölderlin: Selected Poems and Fragments*, trans. M. Hamburger, ed. Jeremy Adler (New York: Penguin Books, 1998), 22.

5. As Oskar Walzel writes (with some hyperbole): "During the seventies [1770s], men of culture, with Hamann and Herder at their head, were wont to mock at reason; the early Romanticists, along with the critic Kant, sponsored its use." See his *German Romanticism*, trans. Alina E. Lussky (New York: Capricorn Books, 1966), 9.

6. In the words of Hans Eichner: "Caught between Herder and Kant, Schlegel took from each what best suited his purposes and evolved his own theory, according to which there were two types of civilization, each subject to its own law of development: the 'natural' civilization which obeys the laws of Herder's philosophy of history, and the 'artificial' civilization which embodies Kant's notion of infinite progress." See his *Friedrich Schlegel* (New York: Twayne Publishers, 1970), 21. The most pertinent writings of Schlegel during this period were his studies on classical antiquity and especially his "History of the Poetry of the Greeks and Romans."

7. See "Critical Fragments" (1797), in Friedrich Schlegel, *Philosophical Fragments*, trans. Peter Firchow (Minneapolis: University of Minnesota Press, 1991), 1–2, 6–8, 10 (fragments 7, 9, 14, 21, 47, 54, 69, 82).

8. See "Athenaeum Fragments," in Schlegel, *Philosophical Fragments*, 23–24, 27, 31–32, 35 (fragments 43, 54, 76, 116, 131).

9. Ibid., 19, 30, 47, 56, 58, 82, 93 (fragments 10, 105, 220, 274, 285, 406, 450, 451). For Schlegel, Leibniz was not spirited enough: "Leibniz was such a passionate moderate that he even wanted to fuse the I and the not-I. . . . [He] viewed existence as an office in court that one has to hold in fee. . . . To steal from the divine privy chancellory a title of nobility for a slumbering monad is a fruitful affair." See 56, 73 (fragments 276, 361). For the passage from the novel *Lucinde* (1799), see Ernst Behler, *Friedrich Schlegel: Schriften und Fragmente* (Stuttgart: Kröner Verlag, 1956), 129.

10. See Margaret M. Stoljar, introduction to *Novalis: Philosophical Writings*, trans. and ed. Margaret M. Stoljar (Albany: State University of New York Press, 1997), 4. Manfred Frank speaks of Novalis's "pivotal role in early German Romanticism"; see his *Philosophical Foundations of Early German Romanticism*, 151.

11. See "General Draft" and "Last Fragments," in *Novalis: Philosophical Writings*, 124, 159–160, 162. At the same time, Novalis seemed to find some limitations in Spinoza. Thus, he wrote: "It is all *one* whether I posit the universe in myself or myself in the universe. Spinoza posited everything outside—Fichte everything inside. So it is with freedom" (131). Occasionally, he even expresses reservations regarding Schlegel: "What Schlegel so sharply characterizes as irony is to my way of thinking nothing other than . . . the true presence of spirit" (29).

12. *Novalis: Philosophical Writings*, 76, 122–123, 156–157.

13. See Thomas Pfau, "Critical Introduction," in *Friedrich Hölderlin: Essays and Letters on Theory*, trans. and ed. Thomas Pfau (Albany: State University of New York Press, 1988), 18, 21. While detecting a certain affinity between Schelling and Hölderlin with regard to "intellectual intuition," Pfau also notes a difference resulting from Schelling's greater stress on intellectual synthesis: For Hölderlin, "the aesthetic does not serve as the 'objective' manifestation between the subjective and objective (Schelling), but only affords an 'accidental' glimpse into a past that was never quite present. For Hölderlin, then, the aesthetic manifestation of an intellectual intuition cannot occur systematically, mainly because it is the essential characteristic of such an intuition that it recognizes the impossibility of an absolute system" (26). (The parallels with Martin Heidegger's thought on this point are obvious.)

14. "Judgment and Being," in *Friedrich Hölderlin*, 37–38. This may be one reason why Martin Heidegger has presented Hölderlin as an "impending" poet-thinker anticipating the future; cf., e.g., his *Erläuterungen zu Hölderlins Dichtung* (*Gesamtausgabe*, vol. 4; Frankfurt: Klostermann, 1981). Hölderlin's comments above are clearly at odds with Schelling's quest for "identity-philosophy." For comments on Hölderlin's essay, see also Frank, *Philosophical Foundations of Early German Romanticism*, 97–111; Manfred Frank, "Hölderlins Philosophische Grundlagen," in *Hölderlin und die Moderne: Eine Bestandsaufnahme*, ed. G. Kurz et al. (Tübingen: Attempto, 1995), 174–194; and Dieter Henrich, *Der Grund im Bewusstsein: Untersuchungen zu Hölderlins Denken (1794–1795)* (Stuttgart: Klett-Cotta, 1992). In his essay "Hölderlin and Novalis," Charles Larmore links the two writers together—probably too closely—with regard to the descent into "Being"; see his article in *The Cambridge Companion to German Idealism*, ed. Karl Ameriks (Cambridge: Cambridge University Press, 2000), 141–160.

15. "The Ground for 'Empedocles,'" in *Friedrich Hölderlin*, 53, 57. The

text also contains the famous line: "So at this moment, at this birth of the *highest hostility,* the *highest reconciliation* appears to be the case" (54).

16. William Wordsworth, "Preface to *Lyrical Ballads,* with Pastoral and Other Poems," in *Wordsworth: The Major Works,* ed. Stephen Gill (New York: Oxford University Press, 2000), 595–597. The "Preface" was first written in 1800 and revised in 1802. The basic aim of the volume was already indicated in an "Advertisement" of 1798 that states: "The majority of the following poems are to be considered as experiments. They were written chiefly with a view to ascertain how far the language of conversation in the middle and lower classes of society is adapted to the purposes of poetic pleasure" ("Preface to *Lyrical Ballads,*" 591). Coleridge was basically in agreement with Wordsworth's views, stating in a letter of 1802 that "Wordsworth's Preface is half a child of my own brain" (qtd. in *Wordsworth,* 739).

17. Wordsworth, "Preface to *Lyrical Ballads,*" 603, 605–606, 611. To these lines should be added the breathtaking statement countering all the diremptions of modernity: "The poet binds together by passion and knowledge the vast empire of human society, as it is spread over the whole earth, and over all time" (606).

18. *The Collected Works of Samuel Taylor Coleridge: Biographia Literaria,* ed. James Engel and W. Jackson Bate, 2 vols. (Princeton: Princeton University Press, 1983), 2: 5–6. As Coleridge writes explicitly: "My own differences from certain supposed parts of Mr. Wordsworth's theory ground themselves on the assumption that his words had been rightly interpreted as purporting that the proper diction for poetry in general consists altogether in a language taken, with due exceptions, from the mouths of men in real life, a language which actually constitutes the natural conversation of men under the influence of 'natural' feelings. My objection is, first, that in any sense this rule is applicable only to *certain* classes of poetry; secondly, that even to these classes it is not applicable except in such a sense as has never by anyone . . . been denied or doubted; and lastly, that as far as and in that degree in which it is practicable, yet as a *rule* it is useless, if not injurious, and therefore either need not or ought not be practiced" (2: 42) Another distinguishing feature that Coleridge stresses in his relation to Wordsworth is his much stronger reliance on "imagination"; see especially 1: 304.

19. Ibid., 1: 129–130, 144, 152–153, 166. Rejecting the suggestion of dependence or direct borrowing, Coleridge attributes the "congenial coincidence" to similar life experiences: "We had studied in the same school; been disciplined by the same preparatory philosophy, namely, the writings of Kant; we had both equal obligations to the polar logic and dynamic philosophy of Giordano Bruno; and Schelling has lately, and as of recent acquisition, avowed that same affectionate reverence for the labors of [Böhme] and other mystics which I had formed at a much earlier period" (instead of "Böhme," Coleridge writes "Behmen") (1: 161).

20. Ibid., 1: 252, 254–255, 270, 272–273, 282. Stressing this point, Coleridge notes that "for us the self-consciousness is not a kind of *being*, but a kind of *knowing*, and that to the highest and farthest that exists for *us*"—adding somewhat confusingly or ambivalently: "Even as natural philosophers we must arrive at the same principle from which as transcendental philosophers we set out: that is, in self-consciousness in which the *principium essendi* does not stand to the *principium cognoscendi* in the relation of cause to effect. . . . Thus the true system of natural philosophy places the sole reality of things in an *absolute* which is at once *causa sui et effectus*—in the absolute identity of subject and object, which it calls 'nature' and which in its highest power is nothing else but self-conscious will or intelligence" (1: 285). Thus, while clearly moving beyond Wordsworth's reduction of nature to the level of simple, rustic experience, Coleridge's conception is in danger of allowing nature to evaporate in rational speculation.

21. Already in 1829, James Marsh published an American edition of Coleridge's text *Aids to Reflection* that introduced readers to the important idealist distinction between common-sense "understanding" (*Verstand*) and higher "reason" or intellect (*Vernunft*). Soon afterward, Frederick Henry Hedge, a minister closely familiar with German and English thought, wrote a laudatory article on Coleridge's works. Greatly impressed by the article, Emerson called it "a living leaping *Logos*." See http://www.age-of-the-sage .org/transcendentalism.

22. Ralph Waldo Emerson, *Nature* (New York: Penguin Books, 2008), 1–2.

23. Ibid., 2–5. The passage is reminiscent of Hindu scripture (with which Emerson was familiar), where the self or *atman* is finally merged with the ground of all being or *brahman*.

24. Ibid., 5–6, 19, 21–23. The passage evokes the teaching of Giambattista Vico that the origin of human language and culture is poetic.

25. Ibid., 23, 28–29, 44. "It is the organ," the text continues, "through which the universal spirit speaks to the individual, and strives to lead back the individual to it" (44). In these passages, it is not difficult to discern echoes of Spinoza's *deus sive natura*.

26. Ibid., 12, 41–42, 44–45, 54.

27. See *The Essential Writings of Ralph Waldo Emerson*, ed. Brooks Atkinson (New York: Modern Library, 2000), 83, 86–87, 133, 153, 237, 250. The notion of the "over-soul" seems to have been borrowed from Schelling. One may wish to ponder at this point the affinity between Emerson's "over-soul" and Nietzsche's "over-man." In many ways, the latter's writings also oscillate between self-transcendence and absolute self-assertion.

28. See http://www.age-of-the-sage.org/transcendentalism/henry-david-thoreau, 2.

29. Henry David Thoreau, "Walden (1854)," in *The Portable Thoreau*,

rev. ed., ed. Carl Bode (New York: Penguin Books, 1982), 258–259, 323, 336, 390. Apart from the aspect of self-cultivation, the text also emphasizes the need for individual difference: "I desire that there may be as many different persons in the world as possible; but I would have each one be very careful to find out and pursue *his own way,* and not his father's or his mother's or his neighbor's instead" (325).

30. Ibid., 380–381, 383, 386. He adds pointedly: "Society is commonly too cheap" (387).

31. "Civil Disobedience," in *Portable Thoreau,* 109, 136. As he adds: "A state which bore this kind of fruit, and suffered it to drop off as fast as it ripened, would prepare the way for a still more perfect and glorious state which also I have imagined, but not yet anywhere seen" (137).

32. "The Last Days of John Brown" (1860), in *Portable Thoreau,* 676–682.

4. Nature and Experience

1. Cf. in this context J. David Greenstone, "Dorothea Dix and Jane Addams: From Transcendentalism to Pragmatism in American Social Reform," *Social Science Review* 53 (1979): 527–559.

2. John Dewey, "From Absolutism to Experimentalism," in *The Essential Dewey,* 2 vols., ed. Larry A. Hickman and Thomas M. Alexander (Bloomington: Indiana University Press, 1998), 1: 14–15.

3. Ibid., 15–17.

4. Ibid., 17.

5. Ibid., 18. This attachment to Plato, however, is immediately qualified in a telling fashion: "Nothing could be more helpful for present philosophizing than a 'Back to Plato' movement; but it would have to be back to the dramatic, restless, cooperatively inquiring Plato of the *Dialogues . . .* whose highest flight of metaphysics always terminated with a social and practical turn" (18).

6. Dewey, "The Development of American Pragmatism" (1925), in *Essential Dewey,* 1: 5, 8.

7. Ibid., 6, 8–10. In the same context, Dewey links atomistic empiricism deriving from Locke with an atomistic individualism neglectful of social obligations: "One-sided and egoistic individualism in American life has left its imprint on our practices; . . . it penetrates even our current individualism which is unreflective and brutal." To this "brutal" individualism Dewey opposes the conception of an individual "who evolves and develops in a natural and human environment, an individual who can be educated" (12).

8. See Martin Heidegger, "Hegels Beriff der Erfahrung," in *Holzwege* (Frankfurt-Main: Klostermann, 1950), 105–192; translated by J. Glenn Gray and Fred D. Wieck as *Hegel's Concept of Experience* (New York: Harper and Row, 1970).

9. Dewey, "The Postulate of Immediate Empiricism" (1905), in *Essential Dewey*, 1: 115–118.

10. Dewey, "The Need for a Recovery of Philosophy" (1917), in *Essential Dewey*, 1: 47–49, 51. As he adds: "Just as there is no assertive action, no aggressive attack upon things as they are, which is all action, so there is no undergoing which is not on our part also a going on and a going through" (49). In Continental philosophy, this kind of conduct is sometimes called acting "in the middle voice."

11. Dewey, "The Pragmatic Acquiescence" (1927), in *Essential Dewey*, 1: 36.

12. Dewey, *The Influence of Darwin on Philosophy, and Other Essays in Contemporary Thought*, ed. Larry A. Hickman (Carbondale: Southern Illinois University, 2007), 5. Dewey added somewhat provocatively: "Intellectually, religious emotions are not creative but conservative. They attach themselves readily to the current view of the world and consecrate it" (5).

13. Ibid., 6–8.

14. Ibid., 8–11. Dewey adds pointedly: "In having modesty forced upon it, philosophy also acquires responsibility" (11).

15. Ibid., 16, 22–23, 32. "Absolute goods," the chapter continues, "will fall into the background, but the question of making more sure and extensive the share of all men in natural and social goods will be urgent, a problem not to be escaped or evaded" (33). One may wonder, of course, to which extent Dewey's comments here go beyond "Darwinism" as commonly understood.

16. Ibid., 43, 105, 125. The volume also contains the essay "The Postulate of Immediate Empiricism," which was discussed previously. In offering the above summary, I have to some extent followed the lead provided by Douglas Browning in his excellent introduction to Dewey, *Influence of Darwin*, ix–xxxii.

17. Dewey, *Experience and Nature* (New York: Dover Publications, 1958), ix–x, 37. As he adds: "The serious matter is that [past] philosophies have denied that common experience is capable of developing from within itself methods which will secure direction for itself and will create inherent standards of judgment and value" (38).

18. Ibid., 40–41, 54, 59, 65, 72. As the text adds: "Apart from the materialistic and spiritualistic schools, there is the Spinozistic division into attributes and modes; the old division of essence and existence, and its modern counterpart of subsistence and existence" (57). Although stressing the aspect of change, Dewey does not endorse absolute change, because where everything changes nothing does; moreover, absolute randomness does not allow for the emergence of meaning. As he says, somewhat harshly: "Romanticism is an evangel in the garb of metaphysics. It sidesteps the painful, toilsome labor of understanding and of control which change sets us, by glorifying it for its own sake. Flux is made something to revere, something profoundly akin

to what is best within us, will and creative energy. It is not, as it is in experience, a call to effort" (51).

19. Ibid., xi–xii, 105–106. The turn from a fixed teleology to storytelling and narratives is also a prominent feature of recent hermeneutics. Cf., e.g., Paul Ricoeur, *Time and Narrative*, 3 vols., trans. Kathleen McLaughlin and David Pellauer (Chicago: University of Chicago Press, 1984–1988).

20. Dewey, *Experience and Nature*, xiii, 242–244. Although critical of a self-contained individualism, Dewey by no means questions the significance of individual courage and creativity in shaping events: "Those who do not fare forth and take the risks attendant upon the formation of new objects and the growth of a new self, are subjected perforce to inevitable change of the settled and closed world they have made their own" (246). On the other hand, he is critical of the cult of private, antisocial solitude, singling out again the Romanticist example: "Romanticism has made the best and the worst of the discovery of the private and incommunicable. It has converted a pervasive and inevitable color and temper of experience into its substance. In conceiving that this inexpugnable uniqueness, this ultimate singularity, exhausts the self, it has created a vast and somnambulic egotism out of the fact of subjectivity" (243). These comments also seem applicable to some extreme forms of recent "postmodernism."

21. Ibid., 248–252.

22. Ibid., 260–262, 265–266, 272. As Dewey adds: "Viewed from this standpoint, the traditional 'mechanical' and 'teleological' theories both suffer from a common fallacy, which may be suggested by saying that they purport to be explanatory in the old, non-historical sense of causality. One theory makes matter account for the existence of mind; the other regards happenings that precede the appearance of mind as preparations made for the sake of mind" (273).

23. Ibid., xv, 355, 392–393.

24. Dewey, "Nature and Experience," in *Essential Dewey*, 1: 155–158, 160. This lecture was followed three years later by an essay titled "Anti-Naturalism in Extremis," which takes aim at certain extreme "transcendentalist" attacks on pragmatism; see *Essential Dewey*, 1: 162–171. As he writes there: "Democracy cannot obtain either adequate recognition of its own meaning or coherent practical realization as long as anti-naturalism operates to delay and frustrate the use of methods by which alone understanding of, and consequent ability to guide, social relationships can be attained" (163–164).

5. Nature and Life-World

1. See John Wild, "Foreword," in Maurice Merleau-Ponty, *The Structure of Behavior*, trans. Alden L. Fisher (Boston: Beacon Press, 1963), xvii;

and Alphonse de Waelhens, "A Philosophy of the Ambiguous" (foreword to the 2nd ed.), in ibid., xxiv.

2. Wild, "Foreword," xii–xvi.

3. Merleau-Ponty, *Structure of Behavior*, 3–4.

4. Ibid., 103–104, 125, 127.

5. Compare, e.g., Max Scheler, *The Human Place in the Cosmos* (1928), trans. Manfred S. Frings (Evanston, Ill.: Northwestern University Press, 2009). As is well-known, Scheler was very fond of American pragmatism, especially the work of William James.

6. Merleau-Ponty, *Structure of Behavior*, 137, 186–187.

7. Ibid., 196–197, 201, 206–210. As Merleau-Ponty adds, "We are not returning to the distinction of matter and form. . . . The distinction which we are introducing is rather that of the lived and the known. The problem of the relations of the soul and body is thus transformed instead of disappearing: now it will be the problem of the relations of consciousness as flux of individual events, of concrete and resistant structures, and that of consciousness as a tissue of ideal significations" (215).

8. Merleau-Ponty, *Phenomenology of Perception*, trans. Colin Smith (London: Routledge and Kegan Paul, 1962), ix, xiii–xiv, xvi. In this context, another passage pays tribute to Heidegger: "Far from being, as has been thought, a procedure of idealistic philosophy, phenomenological reduction belongs to existential philosophy: Heidegger's 'being-in-the-world' appears only against the background of the phenomenological reduction" (xiv).

9. Ibid., 24, 47–49.

10. Ibid., 71–72, 346–347. The issue of conscious and natural time forms the topic of a separate chapter entitled "Temporality," where we read: "We found beneath intentionality related to acts, or thetic intentionality, another kind which is the condition of the former's possibility: namely, an operative intentionality already at work before any positing or any judgment, a '*Logos* of the aesthetic world,' an 'art hidden in the depths of the human soul,' one which, like any art, is known only in its results" (429).

11. Ibid., 363–365.

12. Hubert L. Dreyfus and Patricia A. Dreyfus, "Introduction," in Merleau-Ponty, *Sense and Non-Sense*, trans. Herbert L. Dreyfus and Patricia A. Dreyfus (Evanston, Ill.: Northwestern University Press, 1964), x–xi, xvii–xviii. As they add, however: "In Merleau-Ponty's view, Hegel failed to take seriously the contingency of experience evident in the perspectivity and incompletability of perception" (xvii).

13. "Hegel's Existentialism," in Merleau-Ponty, *Sense and Non-Sense*, 63–64, 69–70.

14. "Marxism and Philosophy," in Merleau-Ponty, *Sense and Non-Sense*, 134–135.

15. Merleau-Ponty, "The Philosopher and His Shadow," in *Signs*, 172–173.

16. Merleau-Ponty, "Everywhere and Nowhere," 147–148. He adds, "Leibniz will wonder why there is 'something rather than nothing,' at a certain moment positing nothingness in respect to Being. . . . Finally, Spinoza's determination which is 'negation,' although subsequently understood in the sense of a determining power of the negative, can only be for him a way of underlining the immanence of determinate things in a substance which is positive and equal to itself" (147–148).

17. Ibid., 156–158.

18. See Merleau-Ponty, *Themes from the Lectures at the Collegè de France, 1952–1960*, trans. John O'Neill (Evanston, Ill.: Northwestern University Press, 1970); and Merleau-Ponty, *Nature: Course Notes from the Collegè de France*, compiled with notes by Dominique Seglard, trans. Robert Vallier (Evanston, Ill.: Northwestern University Press, 2003).

19. Merleau-Ponty, *Themes from the Lectures*, 62–66.

20. Ibid., 69–71; Merleau-Ponty, *Nature: Course Notes*, 7, 9–10, 19 ("The body is destined to serve as an instrument of the soul"). The *Course Notes* also makes brief reference to Spinoza, where *naturans* and *naturata* are made to coincide: "The idea is that essence is posited by itself. . . . This thought that installs itself in positive reality and sees only an absence in negativity, will fulfill itself in Spinozism" (13). There is also a brief mention of Leibniz, who "no more than Descartes, does not absolutely succeed in separating God and matter" (11).

21. Merleau-Ponty, *Themes from the Lectures*, 71–73; Merleau-Ponty, *Nature: Course Notes*, 21–26. The *Course Notes* adds comments on Léon Brunschvicg, which I bypass (27–35).

22. Merleau-Ponty, *Themes from the Lectures*, 74–76; Merleau-Ponty, *Nature: Course Notes*, 38–39, 47–48. The *Course Notes* in this context returns to Leibniz and implicitly to Spinoza: "What Schelling discovers here is what Leibniz had already suggested: perception teaches us an ontology that it alone can reveal to us. . . . Thus, between the *naturans* and the *naturata* there is something other than a relation of derivation: *naturata* is one, unevenly perfect expression of the ground plan" (40). Regarding Schelling's notion of a natural stage sequence, the text states: "The development of nature consists in that the higher is lifted up to a higher potency—not by suppression, but by elevation. We pass from physical to living being by an internal development and not by rupture" (41).

23. Merleau-Ponty, *Themes from the Lectures*, 77–79; Merleau-Ponty, *Nature: Course Notes*, 51–52. As the *Course Notes* adds: Bergson "seems to oscillate between a spiritualism which would see analogues of souls in all things, and a materialism which would make the awareness of extrinsic relations of matter come to the fore. . . . [He] thus posits consciously a paradox inherent to perception: Being is anterior to perception, and this primordial Being is conceivable only in relation to perception" (55). There is also a com-

parison with Spinoza: "It thus seems that Bergson oriented himself to the Spinozist conception of a Being without fault. Yet, Bergson himself criticizes this comparison. The Spinozist idea of Being as equal [or identical] with itself seems to him still to imply nothingness as a contradictory idea in relation to Being" (68).

24. In Merleau-Ponty's crisp formulation: "Thus, a philosophy which seemed, more than any other, bent on understanding natural being as the object and pure correlate of consciousness [or the *cogito*] rediscovers through the very exercise of reflective rigor a natural stratum in which spirit is virtually buried in the concordant functioning of bodies within brute being" (*Themes from the Lectures*, 93). Cf. also "Husserl's Concept of Nature," in Merleau-Ponty, *Texts and Dialogues: On Philosophy, Politics, and Culture*, ed. Hugh J. Silverman and James Barr Jr., trans. Michael B. Smith et al. (Amherst, N.Y.: Humanity Books, 1992), 162–168.

25. Merleau-Ponty, *Nature: Course Notes*, 116, 119. As the *Course Notes* adds: "If we want to understand the process of nature in itself, we might say that nature is the memory of the world" (120).

26. Merleau-Ponty, *Themes from the Lectures*, 97, 128–129. Cf. also these comments in *Nature: Course Notes:* "The theme of nature is not a numerically distinct theme. There is a unique theme of philosophy: the nexus, the *vinculum* 'nature-man-God.' Nature as a 'leaf' of Being and the problems of philosophy are concentric. . . . Nature in us must have some relation to nature outside of us; moreover, nature outside of us must be unveiled to us by the nature that we are. . . . The human [must] be taken in the *Ineinander* with animality and nature. . . . From this follows that the relation of the human and animality is not a hierarchical relation, but lateral, an overcoming that does not abolish kinship. . . . It is starting from the visible that we can understand the invisible. Starting from the sensible that we can understand Being, the latency and its unveiling. And reflection as the coming-to-itself of Being, as the *Selbstung* of Being, without a notion of the subject" (204, 206, 208, 268). Cf. in this context also Merleau-Ponty, *The Incarnate Subject: Malebranche, Biran, and Bergson on the Union of Body and Soul* (lecture course of 1947–1948), trans. P. Burke, A. Bjelland, and P. Milan (New York: Humanities Press, 2002).

27. Merleau-Ponty, *The Visible and the Invisible, Followed by Working Notes*, ed. Claude Lefort, trans. Alphonso Lingis (Evanston, Ill.: Northwestern University Press, 1968), 138–139, 153, 248.

6. Nature and Being

1. Martin Heidegger, *Being and Time*, ed. John Macquarrie and Edward Robinson (New York: Harper and Row, 1962), 78, 81, 84, 86 (translation slightly altered for the sake of clarity in the above and subsequent quotations).

2. Ibid., 123, 127–128.

3. Ibid., 95–98.

4. Ibid., 88.

5. Ibid., 106, 114, 118, 120.

6. Ibid., 100.

7. Ibid., 93–94.

8. The reference is to Heidegger, *Nietzsche*, 2 vols., 2nd ed. (Neske: Pfullingen, 1961); for an English translation see Heidegger, *Nietzsche*, ed. David F. Krell, trans. Frank A. Capuzzi, 4 vols. (San Francisco: Harper and Row, 1979–1982).

9. Heidegger, *Schelling's Treatise on the Essence of Human Freedom*, trans. Jean Stambaugh (Athens: Ohio University Press, 1985), 4. (Stambaugh's translation is based on the 1971 edition of Heidegger's lecture course by Hildegard Feick, not on the more comprehensive and much better-organized 1988 edition by Ingrid Schüssler in the *Gesamtausgabe*, vol. 42.) As Heidegger adds, Schelling's initiative in his view did not quite reach its intended goal or fulfillment: "If one may say so, Schelling had to get stranded in his work because his inquiry could not find a stable resonance in the condition of philosophy at the time. The only essential thinker after Schelling, Nietzsche, also suffered shipwreck in his central work, *The Will to Power*, and for the same reason. But this double shipwreck of great thinkers is not a failure and nothing negative at all—on the contrary. It is the sign of the advent of something completely different, the weather lightning of a new beginning" (3) (translation slightly altered for the sake of clarity in the above and subsequent quotations).

10. Ibid., 9–10. As one should note, Heidegger's comments focus on Schelling's treatise of 1809 and not on his earlier "philosophy of nature" (as developed between 1796 and 1802).

11. Ibid., 68, 89. The charge against pantheism not only as fatalism but as a form of atheism and nihilism was raised especially by F. H. Jacobi, with whom Schelling was involved in a lively polemic (in which, by general consent, Schelling prevailed).

12. Ibid., 138.

13. Ibid., 84, 89, 93–94.

14. Ibid., 91–94.

15. Ibid., 134–135, 139–140. For a fuller discussion of Heidegger's comments on Schelling's treatise, see "Heidegger on Ethics and Justice," in my *The Other Heidegger* (Ithaca: Cornell University Press, 1993), 106–131; also "Heidegger's Ontology of Freedom," in my *Polis and Praxis* (Cambridge: MIT Press, 1984), 121–127. Regarding the linkage of "being" and "becoming," cf. especially Heidegger's comment: "Schelling wants to accomplish precisely this: namely, to conceive God's self-development, that is, how God—not as an abstract concept but as living life—unfolds toward himself.

A *becoming* God, then? Indeed. If God is the most real of all beings, then He must undergo the greatest and most difficult becoming; and this development must exhibit the farthest tension between its 'where-from' and its 'where-to.'" See Heidegger, *Schelling's Treatise*, 109.

16. As Heidegger repeatedly states, Schelling's underlying idealist premises frequently prompted him to treat the elements of *"Seinsfuge"* in a dichotomous fashion. See, e.g., *Schelling's Treatise*, 161–162.

17. Heidegger, "On the Essence and Concept of *Physis* in Aristotle's *Physics* B, 1," trans. Thomas Sheehan, in *Martin Heidegger, Pathmarks*, ed. William McNeill (Cambridge: Cambridge University Press, 1998), 183–184.

18. Heidegger, "On the Essence and Concept," 186–189 (translation slightly altered for the sake of intelligibility in the above and subsequent citations).

19. Ibid., 189, 191–193.

20. Ibid., 194, 196–197. From the above citation it becomes clear how an extreme emphasis on artifacts (*Gemächte*) paves the way to what Heidegger comes to call "machination" (*Machenschaft*) and later *"Gestell."* Regarding the discussion of health and recovery, see Hans-Georg Gadamer, *The Enigma of Health: The Art of Healing in a Scientific Age*, trans. Jason Gaiger and Nicholas Walker (Stanford: Stanford University Press, 1996); also my "Nature and Artifact: Gadamer on Human Health," in *Small Wonder: Global Power and Its Discontents* (Lanham, Md.: Rowman and Littlefield, 2005), 156–175. Regarding *"Gemächte"* and machination, see my "Resisting Totalizing Uniformity: Martin Heidegger on *Macht* and *Machenschaft*," in *Achieving Our World: Toward a Global and Plural Democracy* (Lanham, Md.: Rowman and Littlefield, 2001), 189–209.

21. Heidegger, "On the Essence and Concept," 198–200, 205–206, 208. At this juncture, Heidegger brings the notion of *physis* in connection with the Greek distinction between *hyle* (matter) and *morphe* (form)—a discussion that I omit. Likewise, I bypass passages dealing with *telos*, entelechy, and *energeia*.

22. Ibid., 220–222.

23. Ibid., 229–230.

24. Heidegger "Moira (Parmenides VIII, 34–41)," in Heidegger, *Early Greek Thinking*, trans. David F. Krell and Frank A. Capuzzi (San Francisco: Harper and Row, 1984), 79–80 (translation slightly altered for the sake of clarity in the above and subsequent citations).

25. Ibid., 81–83.

26. Ibid., 83, 86, 95–96.

27. Heidegger, "Letter on Humanism," in *Martin Heidegger: Basic Writings*, ed. David F. Krell (New York: Harper and Row, 1977), 242. See also Heidegger, *Was heisst Denken?* (Tübingen: Max Niemeyer Verlag, 1954). The text was translated by Fred D. Wieck and J. Glenn Gray under

the somewhat misleading title *What Is Called Thinking?* (New York: Harper and Row, 1968). For an excerpt of the text under the more appropriate title "What Calls for Thinking?" see *Heidegger: Basic Writings*, 345–367. There we read: "Memory is the gathering of thought upon what everywhere demands to be thought first of all. Memory is the gathering of recollection, thinking back" (352).

28. Heidegger, "What Calls for Thinking?" 352–353. Cf. in this context Jennifer A. Gosetti-Ferencei, *Heidegger, Hölderlin, and the Subject of Poetic Language: Toward a New Poetics of Dasein* (New York: Fordham University Press, 2004); Gerald L. Bruns, *Heidegger's Estrangements: Language, Truth, Poetry in the Later Writings* (New Haven: Yale University Press, 1989).

29. Emerson, *Nature*, 4.

30. Heidegger, "What Are Poets For?" in Heidegger, *Poetry, Language, Thought*, trans. Albert Hofstadter (New York: Harper and Row, 1971), 91–92, 94 (translation slightly altered for the sake of clarity in the above and subsequent citations).

31. Ibid., 101, 110–111, 141–142. Heidegger adds that such poets "will" nothing in the sense of self-assertion: "If willing means self-assertion, their willing wills nothing. They will nothing precisely because they are more willing" (or self-giving) (140–141). Regarding his harsh statements on technology, cf. these: "Modern science and the total state are necessary consequences of technology and its companions. The same holds true for the means and forms of public opinion formation. . . . Basically, life itself is supposed to yield to technical fabrication. . . . Technological domination spreads over the world ever more quickly, ruthlessly, and completely. Not only does it harness all things in the process of production, it also delivers its products by means of the [global] market. . . . What is deadly is not the much-discussed atom bomb as this particular death machine. What has long since been threatening humans with death, and indeed with the death of their very being, is unconditional willing in the sense of deliberate self-assertion in everything" (112, 114, 116). For similar comments, see Heidegger, "The Question Concerning Technology," in *Heidegger: Basic Writings*, 283–317, especially 296–298.

32. Heidegger, ". . . Poetically Man Dwells . . . ," in Heidegger, *Poetry, Language, Thought*, 213–215, 218. As one may note, the essay makes room for both building and poetic dwelling and thus for a balanced interplay of artifacts and natural self-genesis. This balanced interplay is more fully developed in Heidegger's *Hebel—Der Hausfreund*, 5th ed. (Pfullingen: Neske, 1985). See in this regard "Heidegger as Friend of the World," in my *The Other Heidegger* (Ithaca and London: Cornell University Press, 1993), 181–199. As I note there, according to this text, "the basic dilemma of our time is the division between (calculating) reason and (lived) experience, between science and ordinary understanding; hence the house-friend's sympathy today must extend to science and technology as well as to the life-world, to 'calcu-

lable' nature as well as to nature's primordial 'naturalness'" (197). Cf. in this context also Heidegger, "Building Dwelling Thinking," in Heidegger, *Poetry Language Thought*, 143–161, a text that thematizes the in-between dimension of humans under the rubric of the "fourfold" (*Geviert*) comprising earth and heaven, mortals and immortals.

7. Nature and the Way

1. See *The Upanishads*, trans. from Sanskrit with an introduction by Juan Mascaró (New York: Penguin Books, 1965), 8–10; also Rig-Veda 2:28, 10:129.

2. *Upanishads*, 11–12.

3. *Brihadaranyaka Upanishad*, 2:4, 3:8; *Chandogya Upanishad*, 9th Khanda.

4. *The Bhagavad Gita*, trans. from Sanskrit with an introduction by Juan Mascaró (New York: Penguin Books, 1962), 52 (2:48), 55 (2:72), 56 (3:56).

5. T. M. P. Mahadevan, "Nature, Real and Unreal," in *Man and Nature*, ed. George F. McLean (Oxford: Oxford University Press, 1978), 182, 184–186. The union of *atman* and *brahman* was somewhat relaxed in the school of "qualified non-dualism" (*Vishist-Advaita*), associated with Ramanuja, in favor of an infinite rapprochement or approximation.

6. Eliot Deutsch, *Advaita Vedanta: A Philosophical Reconstruction* (Honolulu: East-West Center Press, 1969), 10, 48–49, 100–101. As Deutsch adds: "The individual human person, the *jiva*, is a combination of reality and appearance. It is 'reality' so far as *atman* is its ground; it is 'appearance' so far as it is identified as finite, conditioned, relative" (51).

7. Ibid., 12–14.

8. Robert A. F. Thurman, "Buddhist Views of Nature: Variations on the Theme of Mother-Father Harmony," in *On Nature*, ed. Leroy S. Rouner (Notre Dame: University of Notre Dame Press, 1984), 97, 101–103.

9. Ibid., 104–107, 109–110.

10. Masao Abe, "Man and Nature in Christianity and Buddhism," in McLean, *Man and Nature*, 165–167. Abe's reference is to the Soto-Zen master Eihei Dogen (1200–1253).

11. Ibid., 168–169, 171. Cf. also Masao Abe, *Zen and Western Thought*, ed. William R. LaFleur (Honolulu: University of Hawaii Press, 1985).

12. See Joseph Needham and Wang Ling, *Science and Civilization in China*, 2 vols. (Cambridge: Cambridge University Press, 1969), 2: 287; also Frederick W. Mote, *Intellectual Foundations of China* (New York: Alfred A. Knopf, 1971), 17–18, 20.

13. Tu Weiming, "The Continuity of Being: Chinese Visions of Nature," in Rouner, *On Nature*, 113–116. Cf. also Wing-tsit Chan, trans. and comp., *A Source Book of Chinese Philosophy* (Princeton: Princeton University Press, 1969), 784.

14. Tu, "Continuity of Being," 116–118.

15. Ibid., 116–119. Chang Tsai is from Wing-tsit Chan, *A Source Book of Chinese Philosophy*, 500–501.

16. Tu, "Continuity of Being," 118–119, 121, 125–127. Chang Tsai's lines are taken from the "Western Inscription," in Wing-tsit Chan, *Source Book of Chinese Philosophy*, 496. Wang Fu-chih's lines are from Wing-tsit Chang, *Source Book of Chinese Philosophy*, 699–700. Tu Weiming notes some differences of accent among Chinese traditions. Thus, Confucian "humanism" contrasts with "the Taoist idea of noninterference, on the one hand, and the Buddhist concept of detachment, on the other" ("Continuity of Being," 121–122). As he would agree, these are matters of relative emphasis, rather than stark opposition. For a more detailed discussion of the Taoist view of "action by non-action" or "letting-be" (*wu wei*), see Chang Chung-yuan, "The Nature of Man as Tao," in McLean, *Man and Nature*, 143–153. Cf. also Chang Chung-yuan, *Tao: A New Way of Thinking* (New York: Harper and Row, 1975).

Appendix A

This paper was first presented at the conference "Responsibility across Borders: Climate Change as a Challenge for Intercultural Inquiry on Values," held at the University of Aarhus, Denmark, Nov. 3–6, 2009.

1. For this event, see Tara C. Maquire, "Overview of the Thomas Berry Award and Memorial Service," in *Forum on Religion and Ecology Newsletter* 3, no. 10 (2009): 2–4. For memorial tributes, see http://www.thomasberry.org/tributes_and_photos/index.html.

2. See Rich Heffern, "Thomas Berry, Environmentalist-Priest, Dies," *National Catholic Reporter*, June 1, 2009.

3. For an overview of Berry's life, see Anne Lonergan, "Introduction: The Challenge of Thomas Berry," in *Thomas Berry and the New Cosmology*, ed. Anne Lonergan and Caroline Richards (Mystic, Conn.: Twenty-third Publications, 1987), 1–4; also http://www.thomasberry.org.

4. Quoted in Heffern, "Thomas Berry."

5. Thomas Berry, *The Historical Theory of Giambattista Vico* (Washington, D.C.: Catholic University of America Press, 1949), 50.

6. Ibid., 109, 111.

7. Berry, *Buddhism* (New York: Hawthorn Books, 1967), 183–184 (above quotations corrected for gender bias).

8. Berry, "Introduction to the First Edition" and "Conclusion," in *Religions of India: Hinduism, Yoga, Buddhism*, 2nd ed. (Chambersburg, Pa.: Anima Publications, 1992), n.p. and 193 (respectively).

9. Berry, "Foreword," in *Religions of India*, n.p. As one should note, Berry does not just ignore the threatening and possibly destructive aspects of

nature. However, he does not allow the need to guard against such dangers to overwhelm or cancel an indebtedness to nature's bounty.

10. Berry, "The New Story," *Teilhard Studies,* no. 1 (1978): 3, 5, 9.

11. Berry, "Teilhard in the Ecological Age," *Teilhard Studies,* no. 7 (1982): 15–16.

12. Ibid., 32–33.

13. Berry, "Economics: Its Effect on the Life Systems of the World," in Lonergan and Richards, *Thomas Berry and the New Cosmology,* 24.

14. Stephen Dunn and Anne Lonergan, eds., *Befriending the Earth: A Theology of Reconciliation between Humans and the Earth (Thomas Berry in Dialogue with Thomas Clarke, S.J.)* (Mystic, Conn.: Twenty-third Publications, 1991), 15. I have presented a similar developmental scheme in my book *Integral Pluralism: Beyond Culture Wars* (Lexington: University Press of Kentucky, 2010).

15. *Befriending the Earth,* 18, 20, 43. As one should note, Berry does not simply reject differentiation or the pluralism of particular beings. His account, he writes, does not "do away with differentiation, because differentiation is the grandeur of the totality of things. With this primary election, *everything* is elected, each in its own modality" (17).

16. See Berry, *Evening Thoughts: Reflections on the Earth as Sacred Community* (Berkeley: University of California Press, 2006); and *The Sacred Universe: Earth, Spirituality, and Religion in the Twenty-first Century* (New York: Columbia University Press, 2009).

17. Berry, *The Christian Future and the Fate of the Earth,* ed. Mary Evelyn Tucker and John Grim (Maryknoll, N.Y.: Orbis Books, 2009), 8–11. As he adds pointedly: "Our church authorities, universities, theologians, and Catholic media seem to be showing no significant interest in the fate of the Earth as it is being devastated by a plundering industrial system. As Christians, the question of human-Earth relations seems outside our concern" (27).

18. Ibid., 5, 12, 35, 38–39, 45.

19. Cf. Raimon Panikkar, *The Cosmotheandric Experience: Emerging Religious Consciousness* (Maryknoll, N.Y.: Orbis Books, 1993); *Ecosofia: La nuova saggezza per una spiritualità della terra* (Assisi: Citadella, 1993); *The Rhythm of Being: The Gifford Lectures* (Maryknoll, N.Y.: Orbis Books, 2010); and *Christophany: The Fullness of Man,* trans. Alfred DiLasia (Maryknoll, N.Y.: Orbis Books, 2004), 6, 183.

20. Cf. Henryk Skolimowski, *Eco-philosophy: Designing New Tactics for Living* (Boston: Boyers, 1981); *The Participatory Mind* (New York: Penguin Books, 1994); *Philosophy for a New Civilization* (New Delhi: Sage India, 2005); also Anthony Weston, *The Incompleat Eco-Philosopher* (Albany: State University of New York Press, 2009).

21. For some of this information, see Peter Kemp, preface to "Introduction to Eco-Ethics II," *Revue Internationale de Philosophie Moderne* (special

issue for the twenty-second World Congress of Philosophy, Tokyo, Japan, 2008), 1. The issue also contains an essay by Tomonobu Imamichi, "Eco-Ethica in the Twenty-first Century," 1–9.

22. See Denis Edwards, *Ecology at the Heart of Faith* (Maryknoll, N.Y.: Orbis Books, 2006); Merchant, *Radical Ecology;* Barnhill and Gottlieb, *Deep Ecology and the World's Religions;* Tucker, *Worldly Wonder;* Kearns and Keller, *Ecospirit.*

23. See John B. Cobb Jr., preface to Berry, *Christian Future,* x–xi.

Appendix B

This paper was first presented at World Philosophy Day 2009, held in Moscow, Russia, Nov. 17–18, 2009.

1. Regarding the original meaning of philosophical anthropology, I still find Jürgen Habermas on target when he writes that it "integrates and digests the findings of all those sciences which—like psychology, sociology, archeology or linguistics—deal with 'man' and his works" while it is "not in turn a specialized discipline." Perched "between empiricism and theory," its task is "to interpret scientific findings in a philosophical manner." See his article "Anthropologie," in *Fischer-Lexikon: Philosophie,* ed. Alwin Diemer and Ivo Frenzel (Frankfurt-Main: Fischer Verlag, 1958), 18, 20.

2. See Max Scheler, *Die Stellung des Menschen im Kosmos* (Bern: Francke Verlag, 1927), translated by Manfred S. Frings as *The Human Place in the Cosmos* (Evanston, Ill.: Northwestern University Press, 2009); and his *Die Wissensformen und die Gesellschaft* (Bern: Francke Verlag, 1926). Cf. also Manfred S. Frings, *Max Scheler* (Pittsburgh: Duquesne University Press, 1965); and Wilfrid Hartmann, "Max Scheler's Theory of Person," *Philosophy Today* 12 (1969): 246–261. In a way, the present paper is also meant as a tribute to Manfred Frings, who passed away in 2009.

3. Other important figures were Jakob von Uexküll and Adolf Portmann. Uexküll's contribution resided especially in the demonstration of the closed ecological milieu of animals and the fixed linkage between their instincts and external stimuli, while Portmann's research documented the "premature birth" of human beings and their initial developmental retardation. Both writers left their imprint on the enterprise of philosophical anthropology. Cf., e.g., Adolf Portmann, *Animals as Social Beings* (New York: Viking Press, 1961); Portmann, *A Zoologist Looks at Mankind,* trans. Judith Schaefer (New York: Columbia University Press, 1990); Jakob von Uexküll, *Theoretical Biology* (New York: Harcourt, Brace, 1926); Uexküll, *Die Lebenslehre* (Postdam: Müller and Kiepenheuer, 1930).

4. For some of Gehlen's major writings, see *Der Mensch: Seine Natur und seine Stellung in der Welt* (1940), 8th ed. (Bonn: Athenäum Verlag, 1966); *Die Seele im technischen Zeitalter* (1949), rev. ed. (Hamburg: Ro-

wohlt, 1957); *Urmensch und Spätkultur* (Bonn: Athenäum Verlag, 1956); and *Moral und Hypermoral* (Frankfurt-Main: Metzner, 1969). For some of Plessner's major writings, see *Vom Anfang als Prinzip transzendentaler Wahrheit* (Heidelberg: Winter, 1917); *Die Einheit der Sinne: Grundlinien einer Ästhesiologie des Geistes* (Bonn: Bouvier, 1923); *Die Stufen des Organischen und der Mensch* (1928), 2nd ed. (Berlin: Walter de Gruyter, 1965); *Lachen und Weinen* (Bern: Francke, 1941); *Conditio Humana* (1961), reprint (Pfullingen: Neske, 1964); and *Philosophische Anthropologie* (Frankfurt-Main: Fischer, 1970). For a critique of Gehlen, mainly from Plessner's perspective, see Habermas, "Arnold Gehlen: Nachgeahmte Substantialität," in his *Philosophisch-politische Profile* (Frankfurt-Main: Suhrkamp, 1971), 200–221. Regarding Heidegger, cf. Helmut Fahrenbach, "Heidegger und das Problem einer 'philosophischen Anthropologie,'" in *Durchblicke: Martin Heidegger zum 80. Geburtstag* (Frankfurt-Main: Klostermann, 1970), 97–131.

5. Fred Dallmayr, "Social Role and 'Human Nature': Plessner's Philosophical Anthropology," in *Beyond Dogma and Despair: Toward a Critical Phenomenology of Politics* (Notre Dame: University of Notre Dame Press, 1981), 69–93, at 73. My statement would need to be corrected for gender bias.

6. Jacques Derrida, "The Ends of Man," in *Margins of Philosophy*, trans. Alan Bass (Chicago: University of Chicago Press, 1982), 136.

7. Ibid., 116–119. As one should add, Derrida did not entirely absolve the work of the mentioned thinkers from harboring humanist leanings and thus encouraging the "anthropologistic misinterpretation."

8. On "globalization from below," see especially Richard Falk, "Resisting 'Globalization-from-Above' through 'Globalization-from-Below,'" in his *Predatory Globalization* (Cambridge: Polity Press, 1999), 127–136.

9. Jürgen Habermas, *The Future of Human Nature*, trans. William Rehg, Max Pensky, and Hella Beister (Cambridge: MIT Press, 2002), 15, 39–40. See also Nikolas Kompridis, *Critique and Disclosure: Critical Theory between Past and Future* (Cambridge: MIT Press, 2006), 166.

10. William E. Connolly, *Neuropolitics: Thinking, Culture, Speed* (Minneapolis: University of Minnesota Press, 2002). Cf. in this context Damasio, *Looking for Spinoza;* Antonio Damasio et al., eds., *Unity of Knowledge: The Convergence of Natural and Human Science* (New York: New York Academy of Sciences, 2001); Joseph LeDoux, *The Emotional Brain* (New York: Simon and Schuster, 1996); Le Doux et al., eds., *The Self: From Soul to Brain* (New York: New York Academy of Sciences, 2003); and V. S. Ramachandran and Sandra Blakeslee, *Phantoms of the Brain: Probing the Mysteries of the Human Mind* (New York: William Morrow, 1996).

11. See in this respect Diana Coole, *Merleau-Ponty and Modern Politics after Anti-Humanism* (Lanham, Md.: Rowman and Littlefield, 2007); also

my "Return of the Repressed: Merleau-Ponty *Redivivus*," *Political Theory* 37 (2009): 713–719.

12. Dallmayr, "Who Are We Now? For an 'Other' Humanism," in *The Promise of Democracy: Political Agency and Transformation* (Albany: State University of New York Press, 2010), 211–236. Cf. also Heidegger, "Letter on Humanism," in *Martin Heidegger: Basic Writings,* 193–242.

Index